The Executive MBA

The Executive MBA

Insider's Guide to the Executive MBA

Jason A. Price, M.S., M.B.A.

To order additional copies of this book, contact:
Xlibris Corporation
1-888-795-4274
www.Xlibris.com
Orders@Xlibris.com
82766

Acknowledgements

I begin by thanking the EMBA World board of advisors for their tireless support and ongoing input. The many updates to include, tough questions to answer, latest trends and challenges to address are a reflection of their invaluable input. I want to thank my staff and the entire www.EMBAWorld.com team, my business writing editor Richard Gottlieb, to my mom Judit Price, principal of Berke and Price and www.CareerCampaign.com for answering tough yet important career-minded questions, and the words and wisdom from countless professionals who helped make this book possible. Of course my mom and dad, Richard and Judit Price. The input from many contributors came from Fortune 100 to 1000 companies to family-run businesses, and not for profits. They offered their own experiences and came from distinguished programs at Baylor University, Claremont Graduate University, Wharton School of Business, Columbia University, Cornell University, Duke University, Fairleigh Dickinson University, Fordham University, Georgetown University, George Washington University, Kellogg Graduate School of Management, University of Baltimore, New York University, Temple University, University of Illinois, and Wharton School of Business. Also noted are executives and hiring managers of JP Morgan Chase, Morgan Stanley Smith Barney, and Medco Health. All of these fine people have names: RP Singh, Mary J. Kucharz, Esq., Shelly Boyce, D. Cooper, Kathryn Beatty, M.D., Synthia Laura Molina, Matt Brooks, Howard Birenbaum, M.D., Francis Petit, Audra Montefusco, Merle E. Giles, Phil Sanchez, James Cecere, Kevin McNally, Brett Tarleton, and Darcy Sementi. Thanks to the research staff at the Executive MBA Council and the Graduate Management Admission Council in Virginia. Finally, thanks to my entire Executive MBA Class of 2000 at Fordham University in New York City.

CONTENTS

Book Reviews and Reader Testimony

"Appreciate all the expert guidance!"

I really appreciate all the expert guidance. Due to your insight, I was able to carefully craft my essays to give the schools the specifics of my career and academic past. You are really good at what you do since after only 3 weeks time from submitting my application to Rutgers, I received an admissions acceptance packet in the mail two days ago. Bravo Jason!

Michael K. USMC Lance Corporal

"This Book Opened Options"

I am an IT manager currently employed but seeking career alternatives, because growth opportunities are limited with my background. My position is considered middle management, yet I can't leave my job to expand my horizons. I had no idea EMBA programs even existed. This book gave me a whole new perspective on working and learning.

Ken Johnson, IT manager, a reader on Amazon

Raising The Bar On Managing An Organization's Talent

Having managed the MBA recruiting and development programs in dynamic, global business environments, I could have benefited greatly from the practical advice and guidelines offered in The Executive

MBA—An Insiders Guide. This book provides a great overview of both the employee and employer perspectives and offers valuable guidelines for organizations' to address a myriad of important issues: From linking the graduate business education initiatives to the organizations' mission, to selecting program participants, formulating appraisal and financial sponsorship arrangements, to addressing post program issues—the author addresses it all.

This book is a great resource for any organization seeking to develop and retain outstanding managers. Senior leadership can gain insight into setting up and managing EMBA programs and the talented professionals who are attracted to these programs. The author's logical, focused, and strategic approach to create a managed program that can maximize results by synergizing graduate education and organizational mission is clearly outlined.

Gary Wallrapp (Boston, MA, USA
—Former Employment Manager, Reebok International, Ltd.)

"Recommended for Anyone Considering an MBA, Especially Women!"

I work for an inner-city bank and as a working mother my options in getting ahead are limited in my company. Certainly an MBA can help and the executive MBA route seems viable. I don't see myself CEO of the bank, I am not that type, but the delivery of the education and types of projects plus accommodating work and family seems appealing.

After reading this book, "executive" is just the name of the style of the delivery of the education and most who attend the EMBA are simply aspiring professionals looking to get ahead like me with around 10 years or more work experience. The section for working mothers was excellent and the sample schedule and testimony from actual women was great. I strongly recommend this book for anyone interested in getting an MBA. Helpful and practical advice.

Kathy Clance, Banker, a reader on Amazon

Amazon Rating
Average Customer Review
4.6 out of 5 stars

Barnes & Noble Rating
Average Customer Review
4 out of 5 stars

FOREWORD

EMBA: Every Man's Business Advantage

By Ken Shelton

When Jason Price asked me to write a Foreword to his book on the EMBA movement, I had many reasons to say no: In my 26th year as editor/publisher of *Leadership Excellence* magazine, I face many challenges in my day job and have no time for extracurricular writing assignments.

But then I realized: My dilemma is that of every EMBA candidate (someone with a day job, life, and business challenges, and little time for extracurricular study).

For example, when my son, Andrew, started his rigorous and highly-rated EMBA program at the University of Chicago three years ago (on top of his full time job), his wife had just delivered their first child, had recently graduated from medical school, and was about to start her demanding three-year, 80-hours-per-week residency.

Needless to say, I had my concerns. I questioned the timing, the work load, the debt load, the stress load, and possible neglect of their newborn, my first granddaughter.

Today, three years later, I am truly amazed by what I see: His wife is finishing her residency with high praise from the hospital; he is graduated with greater confidence and more career options; and my granddaughter is healthy and happy.

On paper it didn't add up—nothing about his pursuit of an EMBA degree made sense to me. Paradoxically, it made all the difference to him. "The EMBA program kept me sane," he said. "I enjoyed every minute of it—the classes, homework, team assignments, professors, peers, and the challenge." And he didn't throw the baby out with all the EMBA bathwater: "The key to juggling the baby with the EMBA was to attend to her needs first—whatever it took. I never started my homework until I had her bathed, fed, and in bed for the night." And he never shortchanged his current employer either. In fact, they value him all the more and hope to keep him—even as some prospective employees are offering two to three times more money!

I am not trying to make my son the poster child of the EMBA movement. I'm only suggesting that what Jason Price has done in creating the EMBA community and directory is a great service to all concerned with EMBAs: students, schools, employers, and the extended family of stakeholders.

For example, on a very personal note, I know my professional life would have been much different had I met Jason Price 36 years ago and attained a MBA or EMBA education and degree. I once knocked on the door of the MBA admissions office at Brigham Young University, circa 1974, and was rebuffed by the secretary. While I then went on to get a Master's degree in Communications, I was locked out of the C-suite and doomed to making a living as talent.

What impresses me about EMBAs, including my son, is that they combine talent with management (and leadership). This not only boosts their market value and options, but it also makes them more valuable in their current roles.

I cite two other EMBA cases in my immediate neighborhood. One is a Dean of the College of Engineering who recognized the need to gain more people, project, and program management skills. I see that his EMBA program and degree has enabled him to excel in his position and gain and keep the respect and confidence of the administration, faculty, and alumni of the college and university.

The other case is an entrepreneur who literally started his company in his basement. But after growing the business and his family of five children, he had to move out and move up. He recognized the need to broaden his base of management skills in order to take the company to the next level.

Jason Price is the pied piper of the EMBA world. I've seen him out and about for a decade, tooting his flute and attracting this growing crowd of EMBA schools, programs, students, and employers. And unlike Harold Hill, aka the Music Man, Jason is the real deal—the Price in this case is always right. The EMBA has an important role and place in the world, and its graduate degree holders are its ambassadors.

So, I highly recommend this man, this book, this movement. The EMBA is akin to Aladdin's magic carpet—it takes you on the ride of your life. And, thanks to Jason Price, you have a place to go for direction.

Ken Shelton is editor and publisher of Leadership Excellence *magazine since 1984. Visit www.LeaderExcel.com*

INTRODUCTION

The Insider's Guide to The Executive MBA

You are thinking about getting your MBA. You have too many questions and not enough answers. How much will it cost? What is the return? Is it worth it? How long will it take? Do I need a top ranked school? The questions keep coming. I have heard them all.

If you are considering the idea of graduating through an Executive MBA program then the decision becomes even more complex. What is the difference between an MBA and an Executive MBA? Are these programs accredited? How do I manage work with school? How long will it take? What are the costs? What do I need to do? WHERE DO I BEGIN???

Ok, settle down. The decision to attend business school should not be taken lightly, yet more than 100,000 graduates each year earn their MBA. But there are answers to all the important questions.

You owe it to yourself to know the different types of programs and various learning formats offered through the MBA. Over the past several years many schools have adapted to the realities of the working world and professional lifestyles, and have modified the delivery of their education. The Executive MBA provides the best approach for innovative learning and teaching formats. The classroom setting may be over a weekend or weeklong period and your classroom may be held in the boardroom of a Fortune 500 company or in a completely different country. The Executive MBA is hands-on and highly practical. It is not designed for everyone and the reasons for pursing this path should be fully explored.

How does one makes sense of all this?

How does one piece together various elements of society, the impact of financial markets, government policy, and the perspective of market behavior to fully appreciate how complicated the system called our global economy has become? These topics are not easy to comprehend; and, while financial talk shows and a subscription to the *Wall Street Journal* may help, you either have to live it, study it, or do both. You may find business school a perfect fit or not a good fit at all. Better to discover this now than at 1 am in the dead of winter cramming for an Accounting final.

When is the right time to pursue an MBA? Can an MBA truly enhance my career? Does such an investment justify the expected return? What value does an MBA bring to the company? How do I get my employer to help pay for the investment? What role should employers play in the education of its employees?

Separate from the full—and part-time MBA programs is the Executive MBA (EMBA). Of the more than 500 graduate business schools worldwide, approximately 200 schools in the U.S. and another 50 in Europe, South America, Asia, and the Middle East, with various campuses, offer EMBA programs. While Wharton, Kellogg and other prestigious schools provide EMBA programs, other do not. Harvard University and its world-class Harvard Business School (HBS) and Stanford University's Sloan Business School do not host EMBA students. Why do these schools among others with traditional programs opt out of the EMBA? Universities are businesses with limited resources and a lot of resources are necessary to get EMBA programs going. Both Harvard and Stanford can afford the EMBA venture but choose not too due to their have strong executive education programs and perhaps feel an EMBA will cannibalize their traditional programs.

During recessions when corporations downsize and new jobs are scarce, pursuing an MBA seems like a viable option. When the economy is robust and jobs are plentiful, people confident in their economic health and already interested in the MBA may be more inclined to make the move and apply to a part-time or full-time graduate business program. No matter what the economic environment, it seems that business schools can always count on a steady stream of applicants year in and year out.

Important Distinctions of MBA Programs

Most people are familiar with what we will call the traditional MBA. This MBA is a two-year, full-time program, typically attended by very bright and highly motivated young men and women in their early to late twenties. Although a high percentage of students are recent undergraduates, a significant number are young adults returning to school after only a few years working with a company in an entry or mid-level position. They have consciously made the decision to withdraw from the workforce to pursue an MBA to then either enhance their current company standing when they return, join a new firm, or change careers.

The traditional MBA includes the part-time program which usually requires completion within five years. Part-time students tend to be slightly older (late twenties to early thirties) with, on average, three to five years' work experience. They are equally as bright and ambitious as students attending the full-time program but prefer to stay employed to earn salary, maintain position on the corporate ladder, or perhaps change careers. Both the full—and part-time programs hold the same accreditation, require the same number of credits for graduation, and are equally rigorous academically.

The Executive MBA is designed for working professionals with practical business experience seeking an MBA on an accelerated schedule while maintaining full-time employment. The average age of the EMBA student is 33 years, with a range of 28 to 55 years old. These students have a minimum of seven years' work experience and preferably (though this is not a requirement in some schools) at least three to five years working in middle to upper management. On average students have approximately 13 years of work experience overall. EMBA students represent their companies and are expected to remain with the company long after graduation. Students on a fast track to executive status are not attending the EMBA to change employers or careers, although both of these situations do happen on occasion.

Approximately 6,000 working men and women graduate through Executive MBA programs each year. EMBA students are expected to enhance their existing positions at their companies. According to the former executive director of the Executive MBA Council, "The EMBA offers an exceptional learning experience for highly motivated professionals in the form of a relevant, focused, and graduate business education that complements personal and professional life. Attendees graduate within two years and work full-time without missing a beat." The Executive MBA is a fully accredited MBA. Upon graduation, the diploma will state *Master of Business Administration*.

An EMBA class consists of managers, vice presidents, directors, business owners, founders, and mid-to senior-level business professionals, even CEOs. They work in corporate, non-profit, and family-run businesses. They bring to the classroom examples of their successes and failures after working full-time for many years. Some are lawyers, some are doctors, others are working parents; but they all have in common a rich understanding of the business world, the maturity to explore business concepts beyond the theoretical, and an intense desire to improve their skills and apply newly-acquired knowledge to their organizations in real-time. Some attendees may not be in pursuit of a larger paycheck, greater prestige, or career advancement but rather the satisfaction for intellectual growth.

The Executive MBA curriculum is equally as rigorous as the traditional MBA. Practically the same textbooks and business cases are used in such core classes as accounting, finance, marketing, operations, and statistics. The curriculum differs by introducing executive level topics on management and leadership, perhaps requiring international travel, and addressing certain thematic topics that may constitute the overall character of the program. Woven into the curriculum is an education that uniquely capitalizes on the collective experience and knowledge of the classroom—a key differentiator from a traditional MBA. Look in the Appendix for sample curriculum from various schools.

The Executive MBA course work bridges a gap between the business school and the corporate world. Companies may sponsor employees to attend the EMBA and can play an active role in the delivery of the education. Corporate participation in the form of sponsoring consulting projects, offering corporate facilities as classrooms, and involving corporate management in course study are only a few examples where sponsoring employers get involved in academia.

EMBA classes are typically held in executive training centers, in corporate boardrooms, and even on machine shop floors in foreign countries. Rather than in an academic environment on a school campus, many programs prefer the corporate atmosphere. The state-of-the-art facilities and enriching executive study environment are ideal for concentrated, focused learning and team building. Housing, meals, and recreation are provided. In recent years cut backs have forced more schools to utilize the university campus but the emphasis to learn onsite and away from campus grounds is still common and encouraged.

Choosing the educational endeavor and then selecting the right business school to attend is only one side of the equation. The other side is deciding the right time to attend business school. Is your career due for a 3,000-mile tune-up or a 100,000-mile tune-up? Will a few more years of work experience matter or make all the difference in your education and career? Do you prefer an applicable and practical education or one without the work experience—a more theoretical education. By understanding all your options regarding business school, you can at least make the best decision possible, no matter what decision that may be: Executive MBA, traditional MBA, part-time MBA, or no MBA.

In your possession is *Insider's Guide to the Executive MBA*, a comprehensive book to help you better understand the Executive MBA no matter whether you are just starting out in your business school search, have worked for several years and are now interested in the EMBA model, or are an employer yearning to learn more about the EMBA in order to set up an employer sponsorship program.

Insider's Guide describes various programs, illustrates in-depth classroom environments, and demonstrates the integration of technology and the global campus into the Executive MBA learning model. *Insider's Guide* provides real-life testimony about the Executive MBA from graduates, hiring managers, university administrators, and senior corporate officers actively seeking employees with such credentials.

Insider's Guide also provides corporate managers, human resource officers, and career experts with step-by-step guidelines on how to identify and evaluate prospective employees for the EMBA and how to create and formalize an institutional corporate sponsorship program. From recruitment to retention to immediate return on investment to protecting the investment, read why many employers encourage attendance by sponsoring employees to attend an Executive MBA program.

Prospective students should ask themselves:
- When is the right time to attend business school?
- Am I prepared for the rigors of an MBA?
- Can a few more years of work experience add significantly more value to the class work and overall degree?

Employers should ask:
- How can the company use the Executive MBA as a competitive advantage?
- How do I create a selection process and choose candidates fairly and equitably?
- How can I protect the financial interest of the company and still offer financial sponsorship?
- What are my competitors doing in terms of professional development?

As with any journey, learn all the options and include the EMBA in your mix. Prospective students should start the journey by taking the learning-style EMBA self-assessment evaluation found in the Appendix. Use this evaluation to determine whether the Executive MBA is right for you. If you are an employer interested in learning more about the Executive MBA and possibly creating a sponsorship program, go directly to Chapter 6: The Corporate Perspective.

A brief note about the many voices you'll see quoted in the text that follows: The job titles listed after the speakers' names were current at the time each person was interviewed. They do not necessarily reflect the person's current position or job situation.

CHAPTER 1

A Career in Flux

1.1. Hitting the wall

Seasoned professionals are savvy businesspeople, but their past education and experience cannot prepare them for our dynamic global economy. To be an effective manager requires a broad and deep understanding of certain traditional business principles while internalizing the rapidly changing marketplace from the use of technology to the application of new business rules, government policies, and international trade practices. If this understanding is not acquired on the job it must be learned in the classroom.

The following are typical statements overheard from people entering the Executive MBA:

> *"I've got a strong quantitative background but wanted to round out my management skills."*

> *"My family business needs new thinking to stay competitive and I know a smarter competitor is a savvier competitor."*

> *"I am at a point in my life where certain goals have been achieved and certain needs satisfied. Now it's time to make new challenges."*

> *"My knowledge in banking is narrow and deep, just what is needed to get my job done. I need to round out my*

skills for the long term not just what awaits me around the corner."

"As a consultant, I need to learn how to better leverage knowledge as an asset to reach new markets."

"It's simple—you hit that wall, the feeling you get when reached a plateau. I surpassed my boss long ago. I have all this experience. I need to take myself to the next level."

"If you are not swimming you are sinking especially at my age. I love to learn and am glad to be surrounded by distinguished and highly motivated professionals."

"No one reads their financial performance reviews at my medical practice. Anything with spreadsheets scares my partners. Someone has to start addressing these cost management issues or we'll sink."

"I am looking for a new career outside of accounting. I don't want to transition over to the client but shake up my career by getting exposed to a diversity of business issues."

What cannot be achieved on the job may be possible at school and vice versa. When the two are intertwined, as they are in the Executive MBA, the educational experience comes alive: Write a business plan, conduct a strategic analysis, dissect income statements, study on location at the corporation, brainstorm with a group of senior managers, and present to a board or CEO of a Fortune 500 company. These exercises become lively activities and will open new doors at your own place of employment.

The Middle Manager Squeeze

Today white collar workers account for almost 50% of the entire labor force, outnumbering blue-collar workers by approximately 11 million. If you're typical of the group, you find yourself working harder, faster, and smarter for a relatively flat financial reward in a world where the cost of many things rises at double-digit rates. In the past ten years when wages held steady (with only a two percent increase adjusted for inflation), healthcare premiums rose 64% and college tuition 23%. What can you do to escape this squeeze?

A proven solution, not surprisingly, is professional development. Advanced education is an option that has always been open and, surprisingly, growing in demand with white-collar workers. Education opens new doors, increases career marketability and offers mobility. If you're reading this book, this is an idea you're already considering and one well worth greater thought.

Axiomatically, an employee with greater education can command higher salary. In the business world the most familiar degree is the MBA. A survey of corporate recruiters who tracked clients over a ten-year period found that workers with MBAs commanded a 27% pay jump. That's unquestionably attractive. However, not everyone already in the workforce can take two years off to pursue the degree full-time or spend three to five years getting an MBA part-time in an evening program. These hard facts have led an increasing number of working professionals to turn to the Executive MBA. The EMBA field has seen accelerating growth in the last decade, and an increasing number of middle managers are turning to this highly practical form of education.

While EMBA programs often include CEOs and other executives in their classes, this is not a degree reserved or even designed for only the upper ranks of management. If you're a middle manager looking for a way to move your career up to the next level and beyond, an EMBA may be just the spark you're looking for to get out of the middle manager squeeze.

1.2. Evaluating the EMBA decision

I had entered my first master's program immediately after undergraduate school and sat in a classroom full of doctors, nurses, and medical administrators who were representative of my field, as I formerly pursued a career in health services. Having no practical experience of my own beyond a few hospital internships, I realized how little contribution I could make to classroom discussions, class papers, and school projects. I had no credible reference points and no material to work with. I never felt so helpless. I had to rely on my classmates to give me real-life workplace perspectives. My exceptional undergraduate grades and GRE scores were sufficient to get into graduate school, but I do not thank the program for accepting me at so early a stage in my career path.

When considering returning to school for my MBA, I had seven years of work experience, an MBA in its own right! I was earning a competitive salary at a top-ten marketing firm on Madison Avenue as a creative team manager for several large pharmaceutical accounts. Each workday I interacted with senior staff, managed a team of copywriters and art directors, and built a solid rapport with my Fortune 100 clients. Everything should have seemed right, but I was greatly troubled. I frankly yearned for a change of pace and had a desire for more and not necessarily at my company either. I wanted to understand business issues from more than just a marketing standpoint. I yearned to learn strategy, leadership, analysis, and finance. I began to fear that I would be type-cast and put in a corner with a set of specific yet narrow skills that would ultimately be the death of me. I felt I needed a broader perspective on business and to expand my skill set to include a higher class of business issues than just ad copy and branding. I began to feel that an MBA would expand my own horizons and give me the credibility to lead. I felt that an MBA fit appropriately into my five-year outlook. Once I became accepted, I knew I was right.

While working at the ad agency, I felt I practically wrote some of the chapters in the great unpublished book on pharmaceutical marketing. But I also knew the world was much bigger than that and that technology, operations, finance, and governance were issues worth deeper exploration. My desire to achieve a senior position with my employer would require broader expertise that I simply did not have.

Returning to school had to meet certain conditions: 1) I wanted to be surrounded by people more knowledgeable than myself from a diversity of industries; 2) I wanted to use my years of work experience as a source to draw from for school; and 3) I needed to maintain full-time employment until I was ready to make a shift within or outside my company.

A friend attending the Executive MBA program at Stern School of Business at New York University invited me to the school's open house. I heard firsthand from a highly regarded faculty about the rigors of an Executive MBA, the coursework, study tours, and student projects. I met an impressive group of EMBA applicants, representing a wide range of business skills and job titles that ultimately led to some excellent networking opportunities. In addition, being among these students gave me a renewed sense of ambition for school and rekindled my passion for learning. It also inspired me and reinforced my aspirations to elevate my career to the next level.

While at the NYU reception, I took a close look at the current class. Their ages ranged from late twenties to early fifties. Many were married, and some had children. There were even a few doctors, a lawyer, a CEO, and several owners of small and family-owned businesses. A few worked at non-profits. There were a significant number of women, and all who were present, including visitors like myself, were experienced business professionals. Their presence suggested that studying with a group of proven working professionals would be an ideal way to learn. I left that evening with a much stronger perception of the Executive MBA and its potential for me and my future.

> *It is important to set your personal goals—what you want out of the endeavor—before you enter the program. To achieve those goals, you will undoubtedly make life sacrifices, but don't sacrifice your life entirely. Enjoy the journey and have some fun. It is a life-changing experience.*

—Overheard by an EMBA student at the NYU reception

While my interest in the Executive MBA grew, I still knew little about class size, curriculum, program concentrations, teaching styles, school resources, study tours, and most importantly how all this would prepare me for what I knew I wanted and needed to enhance my career. I wanted to hear from students about their weekly time commitment for schoolwork and get an understanding of how they managed personal and professional challenges while in school. What tricks or rituals did they use to juggle work, school, and family? Why would doctors and lawyers bother with an MBA? How do programs differ from one another? What kinds of real-world experiences were students exposed to during their course studies? How could I use my years of work experience to add value to the education? And how could I transfer my classroom knowledge immediately to the workplace.

1.3. Seeking Corporate Sponsorship

When I finally made the decision to apply and sought corporate sponsorship, I quickly realized that my employer had never heard of the Executive MBA. I found myself explaining, re-explaining, and even educating the head of human resources about the EMBA curriculum and class schedule. EMBA program administrators from various schools offered to make presentations to my employer on my behalf. However, internally there was no real interest in providing me support or creating a company sponsorship policy. I believe that a lack of familiarity with this type of training in addition to other budgetary considerations played a role, because the program does require a substantial financial commitment. In the end my employer did support me by accommodating the monthly schedule, which required me to be out of the office for one Friday each month.

I found a perfect fit. I attended the Fordham University Executive MBA program because of its concentrated global management focus. I fulfilled my academic aspirations; met a group of fantastic professors; studied with a group of talented businessmen and women; and traveled across the globe working on real-world, practical, yet academic projects in Ireland and China.

Schoolwork accommodated my hectic work schedule. While attending school, I helped create a technology company, managed offices in the U.S. and Europe, won a prestigious technology and business award from Microsoft Corporation, and even made some money. Could I have achieved all this without attending business school? Perhaps, but the contacts and skills I developed—the discipline to solve complicated problems, an ability to negotiate and manage work groups across geographic borders, and a general understanding of important business topics—all significantly enhanced my two years of attending the Executive MBA.

CHAPTER 2

Is an MBA Necessary?

2.1. Do I Need an MBA?

It is clear that a degree from Wharton or Harvard or any of the other world-class business schools can add an entirely new dimension to your career. However, not everyone can get accepted and attend these schools. It is also clear that graduates of other schools can and do lead successful careers. At the same time, graduating from a prestigious school is no guarantee of success. Much still depends on insight, motivation, character, fortitude, and experience. After all, people such as Michael Dell and Bill Gates do not have graduate business degrees and seem to be doing quite well. In addition, recent corporate scandals and the financial meltdown may bring the skeptic to believe the suggestions that an MBA is not worth the time or expense. So it is understandable that, given the time and financial commitment, it is reasonable to ask whether pursuing an MBA is really worth it.

The key question is how valuable is the MBA in helping advance a career? Studies have shown that an MBA does add value to your career prospects regardless of the school. In fact, in corporate life a large proportion of middle and upper management personnel have some form of graduate or executive level training. It is also clear that valuable theoretical and practical skills can best be taught in a formal classroom setting. Corporations are growing increasingly reluctant to pay for training and education; therefore, entering the work force with an MBA may give you an advantage over your nearest competitor. The long-term value of an MBA is well established.

2.2. Measuring the value of an EMBA

The most obvious way to measure the worth of an EMBA is salary growth. A first-of-its-kind 2010 survey of EMBA graduates dealt with those who had finished their studies an average of 9.5 years earlier. The survey showed substantial increases in participants' salaries over the decade that elapsed from the time of their graduation to the time of the survey. The increase in salary averaged out to 131% from $92,000 at the time they entered the program to $213,000 ten years later and many with the same employer. Thus, the survey—which is only one study and not conclusive—suggests that an EMBA makes sense from an economic perspective for both the employer and employee. However, the study went further and measured less tangible factors. When asked whether the experience was worth the investment, 91% replied in the affirmative, and 99% reported that they would recommend the education they got to others.

EMBA Survey Results Summary:

- Salary increase of 131% over ten years;
- Employee Retention: 40% of respondents are still with same employer;
- Worth the investment: 91% reported yes;
- Recommend the education: 99% reported yes;
- More or less optimistic of the future: 60% more optimistic; 25% much more optimistic; 15% no difference.

Another consideration of the EMBA from an employer standpoint is employee loyalty or employment retention. Forty per cent of respondents reported they are still with the same employer from when they entered business school. Retention suggests the following: job growth and job satisfaction is possible in the near future after graduation; a moral devotion to stick with the same employer; an obligation by employee for employer support legally or voluntarily, and the education is respected and valued at the firm.

Of course, an MBA of any type does not make its holder immune to the realities of the workplace and global economic trends. Conducted at the time of the current severe recession, the study showed that 7 percent of the respondents were unemployed or in career transition, and some commented that the current stagnant job market made it difficult for them to make moves they wanted to make. That said, Arelia Jones of Washington University's Olin Business School noted "the school has had six current EMBA students lose their jobs through down-sizing. Four found jobs after looking less than two months." Of Vanderbilt's class of 2009, 22 percent received a promotion after the first year of the program, 52 percent reported salary increases, and 74 percent gained greater managerial responsibility.

The survey also identified that graduates of the EMBA, the products of the education, overwhelmingly valued the experience and were practically unanimous in recommending the education to others. Graduates reported being satisfied both during and after completing the education.

Finder's Fees: Schools are known to reward alum for student referrals ranging from gift cards to monogrammed leather bound folders to exclusive seating at university events.

2.3. MBA and Still No Career

For many recent undergraduates getting an MBA allows them to buy time to find the next great career. We often hear recent undergraduates express uncertainty about what they want to do after graduation. After spending four years in college and $60,000 to $120,000 or more in tuition, many consider working for a year and then taking the LSAT or GMAT. A significant proportion of newly-minted MBAs speak with the same career uncertainty. The soaring cost of higher education makes business school an expensive proposition, especially if there is no solid career path in sight after graduation. Today we are all independent contractors in one way or another, responsible for managing our own careers. We must take charge, develop our own job skills, and manage our own destiny.

Can b-schools stymie growth? Ray Kroc of McDonalds, Sam Walton of Wal-Mart, Bill Gates of Microsoft, Richard Branson of Virgin, and Anita Roddick of the Body Shop do not have any advanced degrees.

What is your reason for an MBA?

- A desire for the credentials,
- A desire to make more money,
- A yearning to change careers,
- An opportunity to advance in job status,
- An opportunity to buy a productive time-out to search for career alternatives,
- Shelter from a recession,
- One or more of the above.

2.4. Alternatives to an MBA

Answering "yes" to any of the above is certainly acceptable but not necessarily the right reason to get an MBA. You can meet most of those goals without an MBA. Consider the following:

- Take a few classes on a specific subject,
- Attend a business school certificate program,
- Visit a career counselor to identify interests and ambitions,
- Work with HR to address on-the-job shortfalls or reassignment,
- Take the plunge and change careers voluntarily.

These suggestions can be accomplished more quickly and inexpensively without assuming the significant responsibility of a two-year full-time or five-year part-time MBA program. You must be completely clear and confident that attending business school is the correct next step. This very personal decision requires doing some homework; otherwise, you will set your career and bank account back considerably.

Certificate cum MBA: Claremont Graduate University's Drucker School of Business offers graduate business certificates to those who complete certain program modules. The certificates are part of the Executive Management Program. The certificates can then be combined along with the fulfillment of 20 additional units to complete the EMBA.

In addition, attending the right business school does not guarantee that you will secure your dream job. Some companies only recruit from certain schools. Some companies only recruit from specific types of programs and are particular about a school's accreditation. Some companies recruit candidates only after they fulfill a specific internship. In sum, even with an MBA, your career remains largely independent of the school you attended and the type of diploma hanging on your wall.

Whatever the reasons for doing it or the circumstances under which it is done, pursuing an MBA is a big decision and an expensive one, with most graduate business school tuitions costing in excess of $60,000. You need to decide why you want an MBA. Then, as you learn about the EMBA, determine if it is right for you. The following sources can help you in this important career decision:

- Consult with colleagues,
- Talk with your spouse or partner,
- Explore a few executive education programs,
- Contract with a career counselor,
- Meet with an executive recruiter,
- Talk with MBA and EMBA graduates.

2.5. Who Attends the Executive MBA?

As noted in the introduction, each year an estimated 6,000 students graduated from the more than 300 EMBA programs worldwide. Attendees were divided equally between employees from Fortune 500 companies and small and medium-sized businesses. Some students were CEOs and private business owners, while others were managers at non-profit organizations.

A typical EMBA class will consist of a broad range of job classes and titles including doctors, lawyers, bankers, marketers, accountants, and those from non-profit organizations. Forty percent or more are women, and many students will be married and have families. All will be highly motivated and posses an intense desire to learn. A number of them will have driven or flown great distances to attend class. One thing for certain is that all of them maintain full-time employment, many in high-pressure positions.

As much as two-thirds of the students either self-finance or are partially reimbursed for the school expense by their employer. Up to a half will be fully self-sponsored—they paid their own way, receiving no corporate financial sponsorship.

The ideal candidate for an EMBA program has on average seven years of work experience and is between the ages of twenty-eight and fifty-five with at least some work years in management. A recent EMBA Council survey found that on average these students were 36 years old and had 13 years of work experience.

The typical candidate has not only many success stories to share with fellow classmates but also a few job failures and other professional disappointments. This candidate demonstrates leadership on the job as well as in the classroom and balances work life with personal, civic, political, or religious activities. The ideal candidate also looks for new challenges and has a passion for learning. Such passion is important. You'll be learning a lot very quickly, and you'll be challenged to do so at every turn.

At this juncture in life, the candidate understands the short and long-term benefits of an MBA. Realistically, the right time to attend business school comes after a period of personal growth and professional work experience, not early when a career is just beginning to take shape. Graduates of the Executive MBA agree that an MBA is a career tune-up at 100,000 miles, not at 3,000 miles.

Some people worry that their age makes them poor candidates for an EMBA. It bears repeating that 40 (or older) is not too old for a business school education. Too many people convince themselves that going back to school is simply not an option for established professionals. However, Marie Field of QS Network (an educational and career specialist network) and TopMBA (a partner of EMBA World and a resource for MBA applicants and executives) notes that such an attitude may cause people to miss out on the one thing that can bring back their enthusiasm for their work. When it comes to business education, age can be an advantage rather than the disadvantage that many assume it to be. The EMBA equips experienced managers with sophisticated, diverse skills, and strategic thinking that they can apply to their job immediately.

> *The average age of my class was thirty-three years old. You got to a certain level in your career and now you want to take the next step. You are not so much interested in switching careers as you are at advancing your career. For others in my class, they do wish to switch careers. There are several doctors, and the EMBA allows them to earn a salary while at the same time be surrounded with people their own age group and experience level, not necessarily the post-college crowd.*

> *From New York, the longest commuters we have, I believe, are from Boston and Washington DC. We are diverse culturally and professionally. Represented in the classroom we have law, medicine, advertising, entrepreneurs, and nonprofits. B-school offers a unique opportunity to connect with people and build strong dialogue and bonds with people you would not necessarily connect with. The EMBA creates*

an opportunity to make these connections and I have created life-long relationships.

—RP Singh, New York University EMBA student, Director of Business Development, Reuters News Service

The average age was between 30 to 35, the youngest being 26 or 27 and the most senior was a physician in his early 50s who flew in from Atlanta and another physician from Phoenix. Most were married and about half had children. The profile was 60:40 male to female, and there were 100 students. Geographically we were primarily from the East Coast. About 30% were from Philadelphia, 30% from DC, and 30% from NYC. The balance was from Rochester, Atlanta and Phoenix—no one from outside the country.

—Shelley Boyce, Wharton EMBA graduate, CEO of Med Risk

The EMBA has helped my career in a way no other program can. Unlike a full-time program, I was able to continue to advance my career while in school. Rather than putting my advancement on hold for two years, I was able to maintain my status and achieve economic and title increases while attending business school. Perhaps more importantly, I was able to apply what I was learning as I learned it. This increased my retention and lifted my abilities on the job.

—Kevin McNally, New York University EMBA graduate, Director, Morgan Stanley Smith Barney

Taking the time to explore all your options is the first step toward a more satisfying learning experience. Taking the time to learn about the Executive MBA is well worth the payoff in advancing your career. As the 2010 EMBA graduate survey notes, not only were they satisfied with the education but would recommend it to others.

CHAPTER 3

Choosing the Executive MBA

I spent a lot of time examining the EMBA. I felt that at my stage of professional development, I was taking on expanding managerial responsibilities at the organization. I was at a point where I had to deal with complicated staffing, budgeting, and operational issues. How were we going to build ourselves strategically and how were we going to build for the future? I felt that for my total professional development, the skill set and the tools of the EMBA were exactly what I needed to enhance and augment my professional career. With the passion toward my job and my role at RJC, plus my financial and family aspects, I was not prepared to leave my job and attend a traditional two-year MBA program.

—Matt Brooks, Georgetown University EMBA graduate, Director of the Republican Jewish Congress

I evaluated both the part-time and full-time programs as well as different Executive MBA programs. Overall, the EMBA presented the most advantageous opportunity in that I could augment my work with what I knew I needed to further my career. I began questioning business practices, principles, and desired to return to school. I eventually attended Duke's Global Executive MBA, which involved schoolwork on campus for two weeks at a time, an extended period of time via computers, and five residencies, three away from the Duke campus outside the country. These past two years have been an incredible learning experience that I would recommend to anyone going back for the MBA to consider the Executive MBA.

—James Cecere, Duke University EMBA graduate, VP of JP Morgan Chase

3.1. The Overwhelming Pros for Attending an EMBA

1. Prestigious faculty,
2. Student-driven classroom discussions,
3. Great networking opportunities,
4. Exposure to real-life business issues,
5. Study on location—residencies,
6. Global consulting projects,
7. Accomplished within two years,
8. Immediate payback by applying lessons at work,
9. Focused curriculum,
10. Corporate sponsorship,
11. Maintain employment,
12. Supportive administration and faculty.

There is no one reason to attend an Executive MBA program—there are least twelve. The EMBA offers hands-on experience in starting, building, expanding, and managing a business. Typically accomplished in two years, the program draws many of the best and the brightest both in faculty and in student body. I feel the EMBA is an incredibly valuable degree. It means that the candidate is someone with tremendous practical experience, the kind of experience I evaluate to hire. I also feel that the EMBA offers the company, along with the individual a richer, more thorough perspective of the issues facing a competitive environment . . . I got my MBA early in life between the ages of 22 and 24 years of old. Now looking back, I earned this degree early in life, possibly too early, without first getting my feet really wet with experience. I am actually evaluating the decision to get a Ph.D. or an EMBA. Getting an EMBA is not just about getting a degree, but it is about getting educated.

—Synthia Molina, Former admissions officer for Claremont Graduate University, the Drucker School; CEO of Mission Accomplished/ Intelliworks

I believe the value of professional training is not what you learn from a book but what you learn from people around you and the application of that learning: Living it, being it. That's why you need to have five or ten years of work experience to truly grasp the value of the MBA. You need that maturity level. Obviously, attending the EMBA allowed me to continue to work, but it also allowed me to apply what was happening in my career. Whatever I was studying in school, the application of it was close by and reinforced the instruction.

—Shelley Boyce, Wharton EMBA graduate, CEO MedRisk

While theory is part of the academic experience, classroom discussions are intense and provocative, interspersed with real-life cases. A business class case study on the launch of a new pharmaceutical treatment may be theoretical for one student but a real-life application for another. Apply what you have learned and learn what you've applied—that's the EMBA experience!

The learning environment varies from executive training center to corporate boardroom. Some programs rarely utilize their own campus, instead they hold classes at company headquarters or executive training centers, although cut backs have pushed more programs back onto campus. Students study practical business issues, and many evaluate these issues firsthand at the company and on foreign soil. Students meet with corporate leaders across the globe and participate in global, joint-consulting projects. NYU students consulted on media and technology for the Walt Disney Corporation while visiting Silicon

Valley. Fordham University students consulted on a market entry strategy for a fast-growing computer company while studying in Beijing, China. While visiting Hong Kong, Wharton students studied go-to market strategies for mobile phone applications and their usage in day-to-day life. Georgetown students consulted on the privatization of air traffic control services for the British and Scottish governments. These are just a handful of the many dynamic and highly practical business school projects that have been part of Executive MBA curriculums. Most programs you consider will offer similar experiences.

See who is on the EMBA advisory board: The school's EMBA advisory board contains CEOs, alumni, corporate sponsors, and other executives who work to ensure the EMBA maintains its high level of quality and relevancy to ensure that students succeed. The advisory board reviews upcoming programs, recommends field projects, and may even guest lecture.

Attending the Executive MBA also affords a certain level of convenience not open to the traditional MBA program. For example, the university assigns a program administrator to handle most administrative responsibilities such as scheduling classes, picking up books and coursework, and arranging study tours. Some schools even provide students with customized laptop computers for a fee. Whenever necessary, administrators provide students with the resources to remain connected with the office while sitting in class.

3.2. The Traditional Cons Against Attending an EMBA

1. Not for everyone,
2. Unorthodox learning style and teaching format,
3. Requires predefined years of work experience,
4. Lack of corporate support: time away from office and/or tuition reimbursement,

5. Applicant may seek a broader, more generalist business degree,
6. Too demanding a commitment for student, family, and employer,
7. May turn a 50-hour workweek into an 80—to 100-hour workweek,
8. Limited class meeting schedule makes absences from class not tolerated,
9. Limited or no participation in career services,
10. Cost prohibitive.

An MBA is a terrific learning experience, whether part-time or full-time. But the Executive MBA is not an experience for everyone, especially if you prefer to work alone rather than in groups. The EMBA is heavily focused on group projects and student collaboration. Groups are usually permanent throughout the two years, and, if certain personalities within the group do not mix, the potential for conflict can drag down the entire business school experience.

The course work and class discussions are intense and rigorous and participation is mandatory. Members of the group hold each other in check with high expectations, even though you may prefer more private time and project independence. Some schools may require corporate financial sponsorship. The EMBA is considerably more expensive than a traditional MBA or five-year, part-time MBA. Additionally, employers may not accommodate the hectic and potentially erratic work absences vital for fulfilling the EMBA.

> *The EMBA is not to be taken lightly; it is a true MBA experience. We had a combination of exams and papers. You have to stay on top of the work, stay disciplined, and communicate with your group and professors often . . . Time management is critical and the potential for conflict was always present. Client needs drive my business and I can't leave work unfinished, especially without sufficient backup. Neither my management nor the client would stand for a reduction in service levels. Therefore, it's key to have backup in the office. There may have been some difficulty at times back in the*

office when I traveled for school and a big project was pending completion, but by and large, it was handled. Effective personal time management, coordination with the team, and support from your superiors were the necessary ingredients.

—James Cecere, Duke University EMBA graduate, VP JP Morgan Chase

The timing may be right to pursue a full—or part-time MBA. Only you can decide this. You may have less than the preferred number of professional or managerial years considered desirable for an EMBA. You may prefer a generalist focus in management or marketing and have no use for or interest in such specific exercises as Asian or Latin American business practices. You may desire greater academic freedom such as the ability to select your classes, set your schedule, and attend a broader mix of electives typically unavailable to the EMBA student.

When evaluating any MBA program, consider the following:

- Is the program accredited?
- When is the accreditation up for renewal, and will it be renewed?
- How many electives will be accessible, and what are the choices?
- Is there a program concentration or focus?
- Will I be away from work too often and irregularly?

3.3. Trends in the Executive MBA

The first Executive MBA launched in Chicago in 1943. By the 1960s a majority of schools offered their own form of executive-type MBA to help train future business leaders in conjunction with fulltime employment. Now there are nearly 300 programs worldwide. In 1981, the non-profit EMBA Council organized schools to share knowledge and adopt trends that would further excel EMBA education. The Council is credited in supporting schools to define their own unique path while ensuring the delivery of a high quality business education in accordance to the accrediting body AACSB.

Innovations in technology, communication, the interconnectivity of the global economy, even the influence of an international English language generally used in business around the world, and international travel, which we take for granted but was not even thinkable in 1943, enables EMBA programs to innovate and experiment in many ways not possible in a traditional MBA.

Most schools originally followed the Chicago style where schools offered a fast-track or accelerated program that employees could take while on sabbatical or over vacations, compliments of the boss. Most corporations rewarded star employees with this opportunity for further advancement. The course work was flexible and accommodating enough for students to attend and continue working up the corporate ladder.

Much continues to change from those formative years when EMBAs first launched. Cross continental innovations, information technological implications, even course work addressing business ethics are in greater demand in the EMBA. A recent court case addressing the tax implications of the EMBA is opening opportunities to student shouldering the expense. Combined, all of these represent a handful of the new dynamics that the EMBA is experiencing in the twenty-first century and represent important trends in the industry of graduate business education.

Three P's In a Class: Eco-friendly classes are increasingly popular. People, Product and Profit—
a look at green-friendly companies that emphasis sustainability in the entire business cycle.

Global Campuses and Collaborations

EMBAs are rapidly gaining credibility and the number of programs around the world is growing. It is not uncommon for students to cross continents to attend classes. As many as 30% of Duke's Global Executive MBA students are from outside the US. The London Business School reports as many as 10% of its students come from outside the UK and up to 50% are non-British by nationality.

Temple University's Fox School proudly boasts of a campus in Tokyo, a partnership with the ENPC School of International Management in Paris, and regular classes in India. Furthermore, it claims to have the oldest U.S. business campus of any school in Rome.

Many programs follow suit. Columbia University offers a joint program with UC Berkeley and the London Business School. The Washington University-Fudan University Executive MBA program in Shanghai began courses in April of 2002 after receiving approval to offer the EMBA by the Chinese Ministry of Education. There is the self-declared "most international EMBA", a joint venture of four top programs: Purdue University's Krannert School, CEU Business School in Budapest, TiasNimbas University in the Netherlands, and GISMA in Germany's Hanover. Graduates receive an MBA from Purdue and a second MBA from one of the European schools in the partnership.

The TRIUM Executive MBA Program, a tri-alliance of the NYU Stern School of Business, the London School of Economics and Political Science, and the HEC School of Management in Paris is a thriving program ten years old and going strong. Fordham University holds exchange programs with Beijing University. Going in to the second decade of this century, we see the launch of IE Brown Executive MBA. Brown is one of the few Ivy League schools without an MBA but provides strong liberal arts, engineering, and medicine programs. The unique marriage of IE and Brown University launched in 2011.

Concentrated Teaching Format

The EMBA learning format varies from school to school. Weekends, bi-monthly, or even week- long sessions present opportunities in school delivery. With seasonal industries like accounting where January through April are the busy months, schools introduced industry-specific EMBA program over summer sessions.

Another big trend that continues unfolding is the increased intensity of the delivery of the education. Driven by increasing demands made on students at their places of employment, programs aim to maximize the value students get while in the classroom. Many schools now offer longer, more intensive training sessions that meet less frequently—a *once you have them, teach them* approach. Many business school applicants who would have opted for traditional offerings are attracted to the concentrated EMBA programming.

Innovative Uses of Technology in the Classroom

Technology has clearly affected the Executive MBA program and business at large. Many schools are adapting e-Learning models that incorporate web-based applications into their curricula. Schools are demonstrating novel uses with technology to connect, deliver, and archive the delivery of course work. For example, IMD and the Hass School of Business at Berkeley make class lectures available via podcast. The University of Illinois bridges multiple campuses throughout Greater Chicago using real-time digital conferencing. Most EMBA programs subscribe to group-ware platforms to link students, faculty, and administrators in virtual private networks. Innovations of this kind are available in most EMBA programs. Podcasts, mobile connectivity, and even academic social media networks are in place.

However, the efficacy of technology as a tool to deliver and augment graduate business education is open for discussion. A few EMBA programs use technology in place of the classroom. Some programs are building the entire learning model around computer applications. Others have taken a completely opposite approach and minimize the use of technology, using it only for research and assignments. Most EMBA programs fall between the extremes.

Ethics and Morality Coursework

A discussion about business school in the second decade of the twenty-first century is not complete without an examination that schools are taking toward ethics and morality in the workplace. The scandal-driven 2008 economic meltdown will continue to resonate for a long time in textbooks but may escape immediate memory the further we move away from 2008.

How you conduct yourself morally and ethically in the business world is based on character not education so those who pointed at business schools at fault were unfortunate and baseless. But, business schools are well suited to address the topic and many have built business ethics classes into the curriculum. Classes include case studies and simulations and it is worth inquiring with interested schools on what they are doing to address the issues. Additionally, in the after math of 2008 came schools with oaths of conduct required by all graduates upon graduation. The oath is further discussed in chapter 5 under the leadership section but to summarize below is what two students of Harvard University have done to address this issue:

> Take the MBA Oath: Max Anderson and Peter Escher of Harvard are trying to install an ethos back into the profession while schools are creatively trying to address the backlash from the 2008 financial crisis. They have launched a universal MBA oath that all graduates can pledge to upon graduation.

Adoption of the Executive MBA in Other Fields

As a concept, the executive learning model is so successful in helping professionals obtain a graduate business education that the executive-model has surfaced in other degreed programs.

The Mailman School of Public Health at Columbia University offers an Executive MPH. Hospital and health care administrators, doctors and nurses, social workers, and government and foundation researchers can graduate through a two-year course of concentrated study with classes held over one extended weekend per month while maintaining full-time employment. UCLA, Drexel University, and the University of North Carolina among others offer similar programs, and USC offers a Master of Medical Management.

The relatively new Geneva School of Diplomacy and International Relations, located in Switzerland offers an EMIR—Executive Masters in International Relations--that can be completed in as little as 18 months. Lawyers who want a master's degree can attend St. Louis's Washington University Executive LLM (Master of Law) degree, which the school offers in collaboration with Korea University. Indiana University-Purdue University offers an Executive MA in Philanthropic studies. USC Master of Medical Management (MMM) degree provides the formal business education physicians seek in order to realize their professional goals.

The curricula of all these programs are modeled after the Executive MBA and are taught by distinguished faculty. Like the EMBA, all of these programs cater to busy professionals with a number of years of experience in their respective fields.

We see a number of trends taking place in the EMBA world. For example, in the last few years our EMBA students have come from a slightly younger group. In our case that means 32 or 33. While our evening and part-time programs of the regular MBA programs have seen enrollment drop, the EMBA seems to be what students want. It's more efficient.

We also find that students are more price sensitive to the cost of tuition than they used to be. Just as companies have experienced drop-offs in their business during the current recession, we face a softer market for our product—education.

Some schools charge upwards of $100,000, and I think they may face setbacks or even a bust if expenses do not slow down or retract. If the real estate and stock markets can have their bubble burst, why not academia?

Another movement that we've noticed is in the admissions process. More and more schools are dropping the GMAT requirement. However, we think that those schools are doing so for competitive reasons, and at Fordham we'll continue to require the test for admission.

Perhaps the most interesting trend over these past few years has been the growing collegiality among business schools. By sharing classrooms, schools expose students to a wider pool of professors and subjects. The deans of the various Jesuit Institutions—such as Fordham—are working on closing gaps in current curriculums through cooperation, and similar alliances are happening with the Ivy League schools and others in geographically common locations and with similar reputations.

—Dr. Francis Petit, Associate Dean, Fordham University

Tax Implications in Education

A final trend worth noting is a recent court ruling with tax implications. The courts overruled the IRS in a tax claim by a graduate business student who claimed the education as a necessity for her career. Such implications open the possibilities for many more students to claim a tax deduction on the educational expense. A detailed review of the deduction is explained in Chapter 9 of the Insider's Guide to the Executive MBA and here is a summary of some of the findings:

- Deductibility for an education expense comes down to the reasons for the need for the education and who is requesting the need.
- The cost of an education can be deducted if:

  o The education maintains or improves skills you require in order for your employment or trade *or*
  o The education is an expressed requirement from your current employer as a condition for your retention or maintaining or improving your status at your current place of employment.

Of course like with all tax questions, one must consult with a tax specialist to fully appreciate the new law. The recent ruling does enable more students to finance the education given that most students of EMBA self-finance most if not all of the education.

CHAPTER 4

Describing the Executive MBA

4.1. Defining the EMBA

An accredited Executive MBA program combines a professional education with concurrent work experience, delivering a unique opportunity to build a foundation for professional growth and a future role in senior management. Small classes comprised of an exceptional group of students provide a distinctive form of learning described as "a path open to only a few" according to one university administrator. The collective professional knowledge from class members enriches learning through the sharing of diverse perspectives acquired through real-world experience. This sharing generates a challenging, stimulating and enriching learning experience virtually unique to EMBA programs.

In addition, students enhance their skills through the immediate application of learning to their day-to-day work experience. EMBA programs meet the needs and the demands of their constituency through a well-planned and rigorous curriculum, organized over a two-year period in ways that accommodate the schedules of busy professionals. The Executive MBA Council supports EMBA programs designed to offer working professionals this educational opportunity with minimal disruption to both personal and professional lives.

4.2. Major Characteristics of the EMBA Program Focus (Concentration)

Whether it is through the executive or traditional program, you will graduate with an MBA, a general management degree. The difference is that a number of EMBA programs offer built-in concentrations that focus on certain aspects of business practice. These programs include core management and finance classes, typical of a traditional MBA, but at the same time they offer specialized study under the general heading of, for example, information technology, finance, health care, pharmaceuticals, or global management theory. There can also be a geographic focus such as a concentration on particular markets (e.g., Asia, Europe, or Latin America) or management theory (transnational, international, multinational, or global).

As it states on the Colorado University website:
Unlike more traditional MBA programs, Colorado University's Executive MBA course emphasizes global decision-making skills over day-to-day operations.

The Executive MBA course is structured so that its concentration is woven throughout the curriculum during the two years of course work. Special attention is paid to the program's focus, but the overall quality of the education must remain rigorous and as competitive, if not more so, as a traditional MBA.

Program concentrations have their advantages. For example, the focus may open new doors, exposing the student to an array of business issues relating to a specific industry, particular geography, or even some general global market issue that would be entirely new. It may complement an existing career significantly by delivering a set of concentrated classes relevant to the profession. At a minimum, no matter which EMBA program you attend, you will be able to apply general business theory to your day-to-day work activities as if you were completing a traditional MBA with the added expertise in a particular concentration.

University Program Focus

Here's a sample of some of the different focuses of different schools. Do note that some universities offer more than one type of EMBA.

- University of California, Irvine, Health Care Executive MBA
- New York University, Finance or Management EMBA
- George Washington University, Global Technology Management
- Tulane University New Orleans, EMBA, Asia EMBA, Chile EMBA
- University of Colorado, EMBA in Health Care
- Columbia University, EMBA-Global
- Duke University, The Duke MBA-Global Executive
- Georgetown University, International Executive EMBA
- University of Minnesota, Vienna EMBA, Warsaw EMBA
- Pepperdine University, EMBA in Science and Technology
- University of Tennessee, Physician's EMBA
- La Salle University, EMBA in Science and Technology
- Auburn University, EMBA for Scientist, Engineers, and Physicians

Preset Curriculum

The EMBA curriculum requires fulfilling the same set of core classes as the traditional full—and part-time MBAs. The EMBA curriculum also offers a set of specialized classes focused for the executive. Core classes include business statistics, managerial accounting, marketing, organizational behavior, finance, economics, and technology. Many of these classes will be taught by professors using the same textbooks as the traditional MBA. EMBA students may review similar case studies, complete similar assignments, and examine the same works by business management theoreticians such as Porter and Drucker. Additionally, in order to maintain accreditation, business schools must adhere to and students must fulfill a core set of class hours. Remember, when you graduate from the Executive MBA program, the diploma will read Master of Business Administration.

As you progress through the program, the curriculum intensifies with managerial level classes that offer less theoretical and more practical application—particularly in the second year. These classes address the program concentration and may include class work and simulations in negotiations, global communications, and leadership. A deeper review of the EMBA curriculum can be found in section 5.3 and the Appendix.

4.3. Inside the Classroom

The structured, pre-set EMBA curriculum, limits the number of electives a student can take and special arrangements are usually required to make exceptions for classes outside the program. There is less flexibility toward electives than allowed by the traditional MBA, which offers students a greater choice of electives. There is consensus among EMBA administrators that more should be done to offer a wider breadth of electives as the traditional MBA does, and some schools have already begun addressing the issue.

Columbia University offers students the opportunity to choose from over 20 different class electives. With approval, some b-schools will allow you to substitute a business class elective with another graduate course offered through the university.

Managed Course Load

Recognizing the demands of student and work life, administrators work with professors to assure that course load per semester is manageable. For example, a semester heavy in more than one quantitative class is usually balanced with an elective or a qualitative class. The preset curriculum typically keeps to four classes at a time, and exams are staggered to avoid conflict with other exams on the same day, or, if it is possible, they are scheduled during the weekend session.

> Staggered course load: NYU students carry no more than two courses at any one time, but may work through four to seven courses per semester. Columbia University schedules four courses each semester with five semesters required for graduation.

Lockstep Class Progression

Students progress toward graduation as a unit, in "lockstep" formation, a phrase coined by the Executive MBA Council. Students are locked together as a single unit or cohort and move together at the same pace throughout the entire program. As a cohort, students attend the same lectures each semester, one semester at a time, travel together, and graduate together. Most Executive MBA programs function in a lockstep progression and over two years promote phenomenal networking and student bonding.

Stepwise Curriculum

Many programs design their curriculum in a stepwise format, building upon a foundation of knowledge as the program progresses from semester to semester and from year to year. Usually core classes in statistics and accounting are taught in the first year, which establishes a framework of fundamental business considerations that pave the way for strategic management, competitive analysis, and global communications courses in the second year.

The stepwise format adds to a student's knowledge base as retention increases and depth is added to an increasing level of sophistication on future subjects. The delivery of the curriculum is staggered in a stepwise manner and adjusted to accommodate the demands of a full-time employee. In its program brochure Boston University illustrates the two-year curriculum with dates and arrows pointing from one course to the next building upon the course work from prior sessions. Witnessing the value of this format, other universities have devoted similar attention to building their own stepwise format.

Interwoven course work: According to Boston University administrators, the curriculum follows a stepwise format that weaves three clusters of courses or learning modules with four, one-week intensive residential modules, often in a foreign country. The BU program offers an integrated model of learning and doing, concluding with a year-end final or Capstone project. See FAQ for a definition of Capstone.

Meeting Schedule

For a school to maintain its accreditation, students must receive a specified number of classroom hours per semester. How these hours are delivered is left to the discretion of the school. The intent of an EMBA is to make attendance feasible "without interrupting the work schedule of a full-time employee." Classes meet on weekends or evenings over the course of fourteen to just over twenty-four months. The EMBA is designed to provide the rigors of a traditional MBA but accommodate full-time work. EMBA classes are typically held on weekends, monthly or bimonthly, or as several intensive one-week studies, known as one-weekers, across the globe over the course of two years. How practical it is to fly across country or the globe to attend classes on a bi-monthly schedule is a question worth asking. Not only is this taxing on the body and costly, and the romance of global travel has waned since the attacks of 9-11. Program administrators and EMBA program brochures do tout the global classroom concept, yet much of this is through closed-circuit television and via the use of the Internet rather than—beyond a few study tours—students' traveling physically across continents.

Fordham University students meet Friday through Sunday, one intensive weekend per month for 22 months; Baylor University meets Monday and Thursday two weekends per month for 21 months. Boston University meets Friday and Saturday every other week for 18 months.

Corporate Sponsorship

There are two forms of corporate sponsorship: time away from work and financial support. Both are essential characteristics of the Executive MBA. The employer must agree to release the employee from work duties in order to attend classes and study tours, which may be as long as one week. The application process requires employer signature that pledges to minimize work related travel and recognize the employee's educational endeavor.

Financial sponsorship is ideal but not an absolute for acceptance. Indeed, financial sponsorship as a requirement for acceptance is a myth. Strong candidates will not be refused acceptance based on lack of employer sponsorship. Indeed financial sponsorship is growing increasingly more difficult to come by, and schools need to fill their classrooms.

Back in 2001 EMBA World looked at who pays for the education. Based on a study by Cambria Consulting and reported by *Business Week*, approximately 80% of EMBA students received some level of employer support and as much as 50% of all students received full support. Over time these rates have diminished considerably. As the table demonstrates from 2001 to 2010 the trend has been to rely less on corporate support, and these reasons primarily have to do with the economy. Where once corporate sponsorship was a near guarantee for a steady stream of students, this is no longer the case. Despite the drop in sponsorship there was a rise in EMBA applicants from 2004 to 2006 reported by the schools with the simple reality that an increasing number of students are willing to finance their own way.

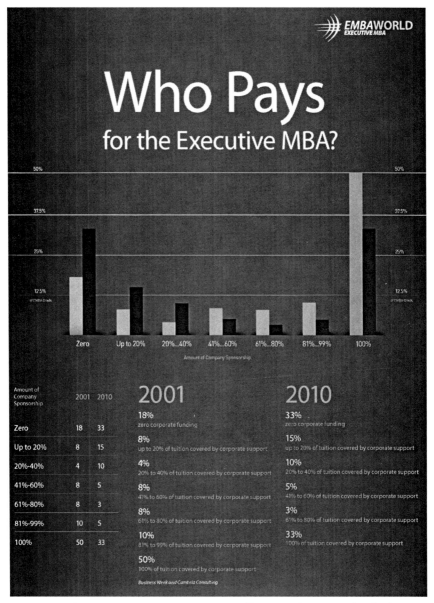

At Washington University in St. Louis, for example, upwards of 34% of recent classes had no financial support at all. In past years those students depending solely on their own finances and loans had been only a little more than half that.

Georgetown's McDonagh School of Business similarly reports that one-third of its EMBA students are self financed, while one-third enjoy partial employer financing and the other third full employer support. Many programs report that companies are cutting back, either not sending people at all, not covering full expense of those they do send, or sending fewer employees to the EMBA programs. Georgetown University suggests that prospective students should start a conversation about company sponsorship early in the process. Speaking to alumni or current students who persuaded employers to contribute to their education can provide some useful tips on the process and what has worked and not worked for others.

Hard cachet: Corporate education is a lucrative business. Corporate sponsorship offers the school lots of corporate dollars as well as the cachet of associating the corporate name with the university and vice versa.

No program will turn away qualified candidates who rely on self-financing, partially or completely, to pay for the EMBA. In fact, more weight is given to student attendance than to financial sponsorship. Without permission to leave work for school and attend study tours, an applicant will have a difficult time getting accepted; or, if they do gain entrance, students without such permission will find it hard to complete the program, as class attendance is vital. Most programs will require a letter from the employer mandating that a leave of absence will be granted.

Program administrators are only too willing to meet with employers to discuss classroom demands and corporate sponsorship. For employers in need of guidance in forming an EMBA sponsorship program, refer to Chapter 6.

The sponsorship letter and release form: Whether you receive full or partial financial sponsorship or are self-sponsored, your employer may be asked to sign a sponsorship letter or release form; either can be found in the business school application.

Residency (Study Tour)

Residencies are class sessions held away from the regular campus setting and conducted at an educational training center. A residency may last a week or more and may be the culmination of an entire semester's worth of work, usually delivered in the form of a group presentation to the corporate board. Regardless of the setting, the residency is meant to place students in a hermetic study environment with class lectures, professors, and classmates—away from work and family distractions. The residency encourages a rich student-to-student bond and powerful student-to-professor interaction. Students will dine, study, work out, and sleep within the confines of the training center.

The study tour creates an opportunity to learn on location, firsthand, and in real time in such settings as the Boeing plant in Seattle, the Intel manufacturing plant in Ireland, or with the EU trade counsel in Maastricht. The residency exemplifies the unique learning experience of the EMBA. The residency is an entire exercise in leadership, teamwork, and real-world problem solving. Tackling business issues using the world as your global classroom offers an intensely rich educational experience that simply cannot be replicated in any other form of professional education.

Going beyond the expected:
Wine tasting, golf lessons, and jazz

At least one program has begun to innovate beyond its available electives and broaden students' experience even further. In an interview in the Spring 2010 issue of *CEO Magazine*, Francis Petit and Mary Kate Donato from Fordham University's EMBA program flagged their institution's variety of non-academic initiatives which, they believe, help to round out each individual's personal portfolio of skills. These parts of the program involve some surprising activities including a wine tasting seminar, a golf clinic, a management jazz simulation, and an international basketball game.

When exploring programs, ask the following questions:

- Is there a program concentration?
- Does the curriculum follow a step-wise approach or other learning format?
- How many electives will be offered and what are the choices?
- What will the class schedule be?
- Where will the residencies take place, and have the assignments been established?

CHAPTER 5

The Executive MBA Learning Model

From lectures to webinars, from independent study to group study, from the university campus to the corporate campus, whether taught locally or globally, the Executive MBA curriculum offers a unique learning experience. The education delivered draws upon a variety of teaching methods and settings to address complex and critical business issues. Professors combine classic managerial theory with cutting-edge technology, while students incorporate business principles with a diversity of real-life professional experiences.

5.1. The Participants

The Student Body

The hallmark of an Executive MBA is the unique learning experience shared by highly motivated students and seasoned faculty. As mentioned previously, the average age and years of work experience is generally seven years greater than the averages of students in most full-time, traditional programs. Executive MBA students garner a richer learning experience while remaining employed, as they are able to apply complex business concepts that can make an immediate impact on the job and in the classroom.

Indeed, students frequently lead the class, as they analyze real world experiences about the subject at hand. Students share a plethora of enriching stories about professional successes and failures. They learn as much from each other as they do from their professors. A typical class will consist of VPs and senior VPs, regional managers, senior engineers, chiefs of staff, and well-established medical and legal professionals. They will come from banking, finance, manufacturing, insurance, hospitals, government, non-profit, and consulting.

The friendships built through an intense environment will last forever, and have led to an invaluable network throughout the industry. Our trip to South Africa was something special—especially seeing my classmates in action, many of whom work on Wall Street. We met with the Central Bank and business leaders in Pretoria, Johannesburg, and Cape Town. The experience is something most professionals and full-time MBA students will never appreciate.

—Kevin McNally, New York University EMBA graduate, Director, Morgan Stanley Smith Barney

I was blown away by the talent and the absolute raw intellectual depth of my classmates. We had a cardiologist, a former Navy Seal, and a senior manager of a Fortune 500. At a relatively young age, we were all accomplished in varying ways. Ages ranged from 29 years old to as high as 55 years old. We were competitive but not cut-throat. We still stay in touch, have mini reunions and many of us continued to work together in corporate and entrepreneurial settings. Throughout my experience, I learned as much from my fellow classmates as I did from professors—no doubt about it.

—Matt Brooks, Georgetown University EMBA graduate, Director of the Republican Jewish Committee

What were so unique to the EMBA were the types of students the learning model attracts. I had classmates from all over the world and from all types of backgrounds. They come from all

over the world and bring to the table various perspectives that
you would otherwise not receive if you were taking classes in
a traditional program.

—James Cecere, Duke University EMBA graduate, VP
of JP Morgan Chase

Intimate class size: The graduating class of the
Executive MBA averages thirty-five candidates.
Programs are purposely small due to rigorous
selectivity of candidates and the maintenance
of a concise ratio of students to professors.

The Faculty

Senior faculty, which includes department chairs, industry leaders
as adjunct faculty, and guest lecturers who have published or have
excellent credentials in a specific field of expertise often find the
teaching opportunity intellectually rewarding and professionally
challenging. They come with high academic achievement and with
diverse personal experiences working with national and international
companies. In fact, professors frequently compete for teaching positions
and often consider teaching in the Executive MBA an honor.

Exceptional faculty, combined with a highly motivated and professional
student body, represent an impressive collection of brainpower and
real world expertise that generates stimulating class discussions and
group projects. Often the dean and other visiting faculty will sit in
the back of a class as guests, quietly, intently absorbing the content
of various compelling discussions. In addition, the faculty—many of
whom are working on a research project, serving as a consultant, or
pursuing some other objective—see the classroom as a learning center
for themselves not just for their students. They recognize the great
networking opportunities that the class offers to them, too.

We were really impressed with the quality of the faculty. There is a higher level of understanding, higher level of enthusiasm, and higher level of communication skills coming from the faculty than I ever could have realized. When you have a professor like Aswath Damodaran, who can communicate complex subjects like discounted cash flows in such a manner, this makes all the difference.

—RP Singh, New York University EMBA graduate, Director of Business Development, Reuters News Service

My favorite classes were Entrepreneurial Law with Dr. Shell, and Negotiations with Stewart Diamond, who put us in groups and made us negotiate, and management courses with Michael Useem, a nationally known professor, speaker, and leader.

—Shelley Boyce, Wharton School EMBA graduate, CEO of Med Risk

I found professors to be extremely accessible despite their rigorous teaching and consulting schedules. I always found professors were willing to meet before or after class if necessary.

—Mary Kucharz, JD, University of Illinois EMBA graduate, Assistant Corporation Counsel City of Joliet

---

Tenured vs. non-tenured: Some administrators promote their program as taught only by handpicked, tenured professors. The issue of tenure is somewhat contentious as the notion of guaranteed lifetime employment may raise eyebrows among a classroom full of managers. However, programs with adjunct professors definitely add value to the mix, particularly when their own enterprising work is entered into the class lectures before reaching the Wall Street Journal, other business publications, or a TV report.

The Administrators

Exercises mind and body: The greatest exercise
you get is the first day of class when the books
are handed out. Columbia University Program
Administrator

Being a student requires managing an already hectic sixty—to eighty-hour work week, if the week is not even longer, along with meeting family obligations and now school demands. Most EMBA programs assign administrative staff exclusively to serve EMBA students to help manage the program's administrative issues. Simply stated, you will not stand in line to register for class.

The administrative staff will handle tuition processing, course registrations, textbook dissemination, and scheduling study tours. Administrators offer secretarial support and serve as an extension of the student's the office while he or she is in class, and they also serve as advocates for student concerns to the dean and faculty.

> *I almost had to miss an entire weekend of finals and class presentations. An FDA inspection was coming due. I had prepared for the exams, and missing finals would really have set me back. Fortunately, my program offered secretarial assistance. I was only a phone and fax away from my staff before and after classes. Fortunately, we passed inspection, and I passed all my exams.*

—D. Cooper, Fairleigh Dickenson EMBA graduate, Vice President, Merck-Medco

> *Our administrators could not have been better. They were approachable; they were people always present and willing to help—and this was a huge plus. They named an administrative support person who was always there*

for us. This person got our books and was always extremely well organized.

—Kathryn Beatty, M.D., Columbia University
EMBA graduate

Grade point for tender loving care:
Northwestern's Kellogg Graduate School of
Management tops the list for TLC with Wharton,
University of Chicago, Michigan University, and
University of North Carolina, near the top in
student satisfaction. Source: Business Week.

Questions to Ask and Consider:

- What is the background of the faculty, and how many are tenured, adjunct, or visiting?
- Can you describe the profile of the incoming class?
- How many years of work experience does the program generally expect of each student?
- What is the breakdown of full-time vs. adjunct faculty teaching in the program?
- What level of support can one expect from program administrators? (Ask a recent graduate.)
- What other sorts of services do the administrators provide to help students?
- Does the program offer students with secretarial support during work-related emergencies?

5.2. Academic Settings

Welcome back to school! It has been awhile since you've set foot inside a classroom. Remember the old dusty chalkboard with pull-down map, doors that creak, and burnt-out light bulbs still left unchanged? What fond memories. In the Executive MBA program, chances are that less than half of your class time will even be spent inside a classroom or grand lecture hall. Typically, classes are held in modern electronic classrooms, executive training centers, or even in corporate boardrooms of Fortune 500 companies either in the U.S. or abroad. The world becomes a global classroom.

Residentials

Residentials are classes held at a professional training center or other corporate setting away from campus where traditional MBA classes are taught. The venue may represent the setting for the entire two years of the program. Typically a residential is a weekend or weeklong learning session. If the residential is held on campus, as it is in some programs, university housing and executive dining are provided.

When located away from campus, the setting is an executive training center geared for twenty-first century connectivity: state-of-the art audio/visual equipment, dedicated T1 lines, and tools for global teleconferencing. These settings may also include access to the sports complex, corporate dining facilities, and four-star accommodations.

Since lectures go late into the evening and start early the following morning, residencies include housing and meals. The hermetic study environment ideally suits the EMBA, as it shelters students from outside distractions during the intensive weekend and the weeklong learning sessions.

Hide and seek: Cornell University holds classes on alternate weekends at locations that include the IBM Palisades Executive Conference Center. IBM Palisades is a hundred-acre corporate campus fifteen miles north of Manhattan and within thirty miles of all New York City area airports. It serves as an ideal setting for classes to meet in state-of-the-art classrooms, and each of the two hundred guest rooms is equipped with an IBM computer featuring Internet connection and desktop applications.

The center includes restaurants, world-class fitness
facilities—with an indoor lap pool and outdoor
running trails, lounge and recreation areas, and full
hotel services. A touch of class: Washington University
in St. Louis holds classes on-campus at the modern,
five-story, 135,000-square-foot facility. The Center
offers EMBA students elegant accommodations,
dining, lounge, a fitness center, a pub, and a business
center under one roof. Similarly, Fordham University
hosts classes in Manhattan at the Lincoln Center
campus and three weekend residentials at a beautiful
conference center less than a half-hour drive from the
city in Tarrytown, New York.

When the residency calls for participants' presence on the actual campus of a corporation, the classroom is in the corporate boardroom and housing is at a contracted hotel nearby. When the corporate boardroom becomes the classroom, students meet with senior officers from the host company—sometimes with the CEO or CFO, tour the facility, and lunch with employees. When classes are held at a corporation, anything is possible. It is not unusual for a Larry Ellison, Eric Schmidt, or Jeffrey Immelt of GE to check in on a class and answer a few questions.

Fordham meets Bloomberg: Students received
first-rate treatment from America's most
successful financial media company, met
with founder Michael Bloomberg, and used
Bloomberg terminals for their global financial
management class.

Study Tours

With study tours the Executive MBA course work turns the world into a global campus. Study tours are part of the curriculum and a requirement for graduation. Students meet and learn from businessmen and women, government officials and politicians, and senior members of the corporate world. Courses such as cross-cultural negotiations, critical operational analysis, global communications, corporate leadership, and business strategy are taught in the boardroom of Lufthansa Airlines in Germany, a GE power processing factory in Budapest, Hungary, or the halls of British Parliament. Classes begin on the whiteboard or teaching virtually then on the blackboard platform back home, but ultimately finish on the shop floor next to a computer assembly line in Beijing, China. Intense class discussions combined with electronic case studies, case analysis, guests lecturing the group, and hands-on consulting projects are often held on-location in the territory under study.

Duke's Global Executive MBA may best exemplify how the global community serves as the classroom. Duke's GEMBA (Global) and WEMBA (Weekend) offer more study tours than any other EMBA program.

> *Special to Duke was the global emphasis. International business practices are best absorbed in an international environment. The fact that the program facilitated the visitation of local or multinational companies, and sponsored speakers from local businesses or government officials, cannot be replicated in a classroom in Durham, North Carolina. There is no traditional MBA program that can address practical business problems and then experience them in a local environment.*

> *Duke arranged study tours throughout the world. For example, we spent time at a Panasonic manufacturing plant in the Czech Republic discussing their business model and in China we toured technology companies learning various business models under communist rule and also had a day to rappel the Great Wall! For our third trip we went to Sao Paolo, Brazil, and a week later went to Santiago, Chile. Duke professors were outstanding and the bonding that*

forms among classmates and professors was fantastic. Our time is well spent, rigorous and constantly moving forward examining critical business issues many at the company floor in Hong Kong, Prague, Beijing or elsewhere.

—James Cecere Duke EMBA graduate, VP Investor Services, JP Morgan Chase

Questions to consider:

- How many residentials will be offered?
- Where will the residentials be held?
- Which courses will be taught during the residential?
- Are there additional costs associated with the residential?

5.3. Inside the Classroom

A closer review of class schedules and a sample of individual program curriculums can be found in the Appendix.

Curriculum Model

Year I Curriculum

In the first year the central focus of the EMBA is laying the groundwork of essential management knowledge. The year will be weighted toward core courses including the basics: economics, finance, managerial accounting, management science, marketing, operations, governmental and legal policy, and business statistics. The first year may conclude with a study tour.

Year II Curriculum

In the second year course workload moderates as you settle into a study pattern and work routine. By now, students will have developed stronger working relationships with classmates and have a better feel for faculty expectations with presentations, papers, and class work. Core courses in the second year may include advanced levels of finance, management, and accounting and may also introduce courses characteristic to the program concentration and executive-type subjects such as global management, executive communication, and leadership. EMBA students find the following four courses their favorite and most memorable:

Cross-Functional Foundation: Solving complicated business issues often calls for cross-functional, cross-disciplinary approaches. These classes integrate coursework and case studies across disciplines and draw upon a diversity of student perspectives.

Global Management: Students study strategy, geopolitics, and the history of corporations under various global structures including: national, multi-national, global, and transnational.

Executive and Global Communications: Communicating effectively, orally and in writing, especially for students for whom English is a second language, can be a challenge. In this course students will master the concept of "International English" and study foreign business and cultural practices. Students learn to understand and use this knowledge to their advantage when practicing business and negotiations in foreign countries. Students learn when to kiss, bow, or just shake hands.

Leadership Skills: Defines leadership and simulates critical and key decision making opportunities. (A lengthier discussion on leadership can be found later in this chapter.)

Typical Learning Schedule

Sample Class Schedule

Breakfast is served from 7 to 8 A.M. Class begins at 8:30 A.M. on business statistics, which ends at 10:30 A.M. Starting immediately at 11:00 A.M. is Operations Management, which concludes at 1 P.M.

for lunch. Class resumes at 2:30 P.M. with a guest lecture on eCommerce and a marketing class follows till 5:30 P.M., when class concludes for dinner.

Depending on the amount of material to cover, professors do have the prerogative to extend class time or simply work through dinner. Professors who deprive hungry students of eating do not win popularity contests but are committed educators. Evening lectures, although not customary, may include structured lessons with professors, review sessions with classmates, one-on-one reviews with tutors, or course films that extend late into the evening. This cycle repeats the very next day. See sample class schedules in the Appendix.

Class Lectures

Teaching managerial accounting and business statistics is best accomplished on a chalk—or whiteboard with a professor reviewing examples in front of the class. Core classes will often be taught this way. There are no shortcuts to teaching business statistics, accounting, financial analysis, or portfolio management. These courses require a lot of class time and outside preparation.

> *I found the workload with law school similar. I went to law school full-time, and I consider the EMBA full-time. Similar workload and the same demand to complete papers, prepare for exams for my quantitative classes, and always the need to come to class fully prepared in case the professor makes you his unlucky target. There were no cutting corners with this MBA.*

> —Mary Kucharz, JD, University of Illinois EMBA graduate, Assistant Corporation Counsel City of Joliet

Case Studies

Whether or not they are valued for their practicality and enlightenment, case studies published by Richard Ivey, Thunderbird School, and the

Harvard Business School are staples in graduate business education. Case studies introduce business concepts through complicated and provocative real-life business situations.

Students provide detailed analysis, evaluating the corporate decision made in the case study. Students dissect business decisions using the tools taught in class and gained through years of practical business experience. Part of the analysis may include one-on-one debate discussing the merits of the corporate decision or provide alternative choices. These case studies run the gamut from financial arbitrage in foreign currencies to marketing of new products to corporate restructuring. Since most business cases resemble actual events, don't be surprised if on occasion a classmate finds himself defending his boss's actions or if the person profiled in the case happens to make a guest appearance.

> *For practically any topic discussed in class, there are at least two people who have hands-on experience in that area. You see an immediate relevance to what is discussed in the classroom because students are often dealing with the very issues appearing in business cases. Students reach a marvelous crescendo of energy that I have not seen elsewhere outside the EMBA.*

—Phil Sanchez, Director of the Baylor EMBA

Study Group

Study groups are critical to the learning experience and serve as a trademark of business school, especially in the Executive MBA program. Study groups are held in high regard for their learning potential and emphasis on group management. A successful class is driven by the ability of students to work together much like a sports team. In fact, while interviewing applicants for the EMBA, the selection committee gauges a candidate's temperament, attitude, and experience working with others. The goal is to leverage the knowledge and expertise within the group to maximize the learning experience. The final decision for acceptance may put strong emphasis on your ability to work well with others.

Each school has its own methodology for assembling study groups. Some groups are self-selected by the students after a brief orientation, while others form groups determined by scores taken from personality tests and learning style questionnaires. Living and working in close proximity to one another may also shape the creation of each study group. To help students coordinate this exercise some schools provide introductory courses on the subject. For example, Boston University leads off the program with a study on group dynamics. This class aids incoming students in managing group decisions, group conflict, and group authority. Such classes help set the tone for study groups over the next two years.

As one business school dean was overheard saying to his incoming class: "You are all one of the following three types of people: one, bean-counters (finances and accountants); two, gear heads (engineers and analytics); or three, poets (the English and art majors). Each is important and must be represented in your study group." Assembling a cohesive group of people with a balance of skills that can work together for the life of the program can be an exciting and scary proposition.

Another perspective on the personalities you'll meet in a typical EMBA group is classifying them as

- Managers,
- Changers, and
- Drivers.

Perhaps you'll recognize yourself in one of these descriptions.

Managers (the most common personality in the EMBA classroom) are there not so much to switch careers as to advance in their existing one. For them the EMBA is an important way of propelling their careers to the executive level, as it is one of their employer's requirements. For them the experience is a rite of passage.

Changers are the second most common personality you're likely to find among your classmates. They are seeking a new direction within or outside their firm—perhaps not immediately but in the long term. Changers are typically contagiously optimistic, and they are also more likely than the other two groups to have financed their education themselves.

Drivers are typically not in school out of necessity. They attend for the love of learning. They often bring refreshing perspectives and good humor to their courses and projects and stand ready to challenge their teachers and to bring their colleagues back to earth during intense discussions.

> *We employed one very valuable ritual, which I would recommend to anyone considering an EMBA program. I participated in a study group throughout the two years, and it was especially helpful during the first year core courses. We made a pact to meet every week and to make these meetings as enjoyable as possible. We would meet every Tuesday at one of the team member's offices, usually at PWC. The secretary would call us in the morning to remind us and get our dinner orders. When we arrived that evening, we got right down to work. Whenever there was a group project or exam, we would walk through the problems. We kept the schedule to Tuesday evenings in order to give us additional preparation time before class on Friday. By making this commitment to the study group as well as to ourselves, we were able to give the program an appropriate level of priority.*

> —Shelley Boyce, Wharton EMBA graduate,
> CEO MedRisk

> *A study group becomes a family. You learn to love each member because the alternative is ugly. Students tend to recognize the*

value of working together and assisting each other to enhance the overall group and individual efforts. Overall we all worked together well. While competitive, it was never cut-throat. We were all professionals, executive level people.

—Brett Tarleton, Fordham University EMBA graduate, Elkins McSherry Hedge Fund

Some of the best education came from my classmates. While working closely with them, I learned so much, and we helped each other out while working closely through tough assignments.

—Kathryn Beatty, M.D., Columbia University EMBA graduate, Group Medical Practice

---

Study the study group: Boston University offers The Team Learning™ Course. This course is designed to help students operate more effectively in a team-learning environment. The course addresses contracting, feedback, assessment, leadership, and decision-making.

The group dynamic is an important part of the academic experience. Students work closely together, so they must possess managerial, collegial, and leadership skills. The group experience may reshuffle each semester, and it is essential that the group function cohesively. There will always been disagreements among the group members, but these differences of opinion are expected to be resolved in a respectful and team-oriented manner.

I had five years of managerial experience before going back to school. I know how to work with people, whether they are my colleagues or my classmates. When given a group assignment, we work slowly and carefully delegating responsibilities and

coordinating details. Sure, sometimes conflict arises, but we're adults. We manage through it, constructively. After all, we all have bigger fish to fry back at work. No one feels a need to one-up the next person or boss others around. We work well as a team in order to get the job done.

—Kevin McNally, New York University EMBA student, Director, Solomon Smith Barney

Occasionally conflict does occur and the group has to sort out the problems:

I recall one person in my group always had a habit of starting projects on Thursday before Friday class and this became intolerable to the rest of the group. To say the least, we regrouped at the end of first semester.

—Mary Kucharz, JD, University of Illinois EMBA graduate, Assistant Corporation Counsel City of Joliet

Classroom Discussions

Attend a class to experience the highly intellectual and provocative discussions first hand. A morning business law class might discuss the privacy issues and its financial impact on the valuation of Facebook. An afternoon business policy class could address an analysis of the economic crisis in Greece and the devaluation of currencies. Professors move quickly through their lectures, taking students deeply into the subject matter. These highly interactive lectures combine corporate strategy with legal theory, draw upon case studies, and build on the class's knowledge base. At the end of three hours, the lectures and exercises are intellectually draining but immensely satisfying.

Although discussions get heated, the maturity of EMBA students is such that they generally listen more thoughtfully and provide feedback more constructively than the younger students in the traditional MBA.

Their points of view are based on years of experience on the job not from personal theory or summer internships. Sitting in on some of these classes can illustrate for you the depth of student inquiry. The types of questions EMBA students ask professors and each other are more substantive and relevant to real-world experience. With this added maturity of the students, the EMBA degree reflects a high level of sophistication and general practical business knowledge that is notably lacking in the average student in a traditional MBA program. There can be no question that in this complicated and competitive global marketplace the EMBA provides an advantage over colleagues and competitors who have a traditional graduate business degree.

The people who were in my class already demonstrated success and achievement. They were accomplished professionals. In a regular MBA program chances are they would be coming directly from undergraduate school or from limited experience in the business world. They may test well and may have done well as undergraduates but they may not be successful managers, certainly not executive level or successful entrepreneurs. Simply stated, recent undergraduates in business school spout off less-than-credible remarks that would probably be challenged and certainly not tolerated in the EMBA. A summer internship is not sufficient experience to reference during an intense class discussion. Men and women in my program would call you on the carpet. Your classmates will not allow you to shuck and jive your way through some of these cases not really knowing your stuff. My classmates enforced the rigors of the program.

—RP Singh, New York University EMBA graduate, Director of Business Development, Reuters News Service

You will have plenty of time to sleep on Monday morning when you return to work. From Friday to Sunday expect your adrenaline to be on overdrive. Armed with real-work experiences, you will find yourself engaged in intellectual

discourse with some of the best minds in academia. And that's just during breakfast. After a four-hour, intellectually draining marathon over business negotiations you're free to break for lunch or as most choose, snack and sleep. When class ends, sometimes late in the evening, students with stamina will stampede with the professors to the local pub for a beer or two, or three. Others, punch drunk from class, will retire to their rooms.

—Brett Tarleton, Fordham University EMBA graduate, VP, Elkins McSherry Financial Management

Group Presentations

The Executive MBA learning model focuses heavily on sharpening presentation strategies and public speaking skills. Most courses will require a final case analysis, business plan, paper, or group project and a summation in the form of a group presentation.

After delivering a class presentation, the study group is expected to defend its results. Fellow classmates vigorously present their own set of conclusions and thoughtfully examine and argue on points. Defending your work can be intimidating, but the overall exercise has its obvious benefits.

Sometimes the professor asks the class audience to evaluate and grade the quality of each group presentation, from clarity of the case statement to creativity of delivery to overall analysis and concluding results. On occasion the professor requests that study partners grade each other on participation and general performance, sometimes anonymously and other times face-to-face. In such a position students can be professionally merciless, as can the professor for putting them through such an exercise that pits student against student.

I knew going into this program that I would probably have to give presentations. I never knew I would have to give so many. Our professor for global communications, who happens

to be an instructor for Toastmasters, helped me develop some great presentation strategies. He offers the same advice to senior managers from some of Wall Street's biggest and most powerful brokerage houses. I got great feedback from him and my classmates. Now at my company, I'm helping others prepare and deliver presentations.

—Brett Tarleton, Fordham University EMBA graduate, VP, Elkins McSherry Financial Management

Leadership Development

Probably one of the hardest subjects to teach but one that requires the most professor-student and student-to-student interaction is leadership development. No single class teaches the principles of leadership. Instead, the Executive MBA program is in itself a two-year lesson in leadership. While each attendee has leadership potential or actual experience by the mere fact of being in an EMBA program and employed in a management position, the overall experience—working in study groups, delivering presentations, and working with fellow student executives—helps shape these leadership propensities further.

At the same time EMBA programs have paid more attention to delivering course work on leadership. Such case studies and role playing can draw upon real life issues like managing an oil spill in the Gulf Coast or handling corporate mismanagement that leads to financial meltdowns. Real life cases make each member a stakeholder and serve as a highly provocative yet practical learning experience.

Crisis management classes include the following storylines:

- *As CEO of a major airline carrier, how do your short—and long-term goals change in the wake of higher oil prices?*
- *Stock value is at a two-year low. Rumors of accounting irregularities are circulating. As a preemptive move, how do you prepare shareholders?*

Through coursework, students appreciate a deeper meaning of leadership and possess a stronger understanding of the many challenges leaders face in the business world. Coursework allows students to examine issues of self-awareness, teamwork, ethics, and communication. Class exercises enable students to practice effective negotiations, manage change, work through conflict, reach resolution, and address issues of power and authority. Success and money are secondary to discipline, strategy, compassion, and ethics. Students develop leadership qualities and understand the responsibilities that leadership bestows. Two years in an Executive MBA program shapes personal values by allowing students to do the shaping.

A new mantra in MBA programs these days is building corporate and social responsibility. Much of this can be found in EMBA programs. Fordham University's EMBA, for example, sees developing executives who are sensitive to ethical, social, and environmental concerns. Forward-thinking schools are taking these issues—sometimes referred to as the Triple Bottom Line—seriously. According to Ross Geraghty of Top MBA (www.topmba.com), a website for MBA executives and applicants, the Triple Bottom Line has three Ps at its core—people, planet, and profit. Geraghty writes, "business school deans and course creators are in a position to change course structures . . . There are some schools who will, and there are some schools who won't. However, even Harvard Business School's appointment of a new dean, Professor Nitin Nohria, with a background in leadership and ethics . . . suggests that even the great conservative dame of the business school world is paying attention."

The MBA Oath of Responsibility

The Harvard Business School Class of 2009 started a group called MBA Oath (www.mbaoath.org). The group is now a coalition of MBA students, graduates, and advisors who represent over 250 schools from around the world. Its stated goal is "to transform the field of management into a true profession. You can read the whole oath in the Appendix, or at the website or purchase the organization's eponymously-titled book. Here are some excerpts from the oath.

As a business leader . . .

My decisions affect the well-being of individuals inside and outside my enterprise today and tomorrow.

- I will not advance my personal interests at the expense of my enterprise or society.
- I will refrain from corruption or practices harmful to society.
- I will protect the human rights and dignity of all people affected by my enterprise.
- I will protect the right of future generations to enjoy a healthy planet.

I recognize that my behavior must set an example of integrity . . . I will remain accountable to my peers and to society for my actions and for upholding these standards.

That's leadership! A survey reported that at Florida Gulf Coast University 40 percent of the EMBA students were CEOs or presidents. Claremont Graduate University reported that a quarter of its class leads companies.

5.4. Use of Technology

An Integral Component of the EMBA

The most common theme in any business school brochure is how its state-of-the-art, high-tech business school prepares graduates for the electronic twenty-first century. Wired classrooms, virtual private networks, mobile apps, podcasts, iPads, closed-circuit television, and always-on web applications keep students in touch with their classmates, professors, and class work 24-7. Students are expected to own a laptop computer.

With virtual private networks (VPNs) students can decide when to study and can easily interact with classmates and professors. The VPN assures a safe and secure environment to chat, tutor, and exchange files around the world. Private networks enable students who frequently travel, have unpredictable work schedules, or attend satellite campuses to attend classes and augment class work with the use of technology. Through private networks they can access additional resources including sophisticated databases like LexisNexis.

Whether swapping face-to-face class time for lessons in front of a computer diminishes the value of the education is a valid question but also beyond the scope of this book. No doubt technology can enhance as well as diminish the learning experience. Staring at a computer for long periods of time can be a sterile and unrewarding way to learn. A handful of EMBA administrators from different programs felt they had the right mix of face-to-face time with professors and students and computer time to meet the missions of their program.

Computer class: The first distance-learning MBA program accredited by the AACSB (the Association to Advance Collegiate Schools of Business) is at the American School of Business at the University of Baltimore, part of the University of Maryland system.

Wired classrooms allow students to plug and play. Once students are connected in the class, professors may integrate lecture sections on the web for everyone to view and make personal notes in real time. Practically all class assignments from financial modeling to preparation of papers and delivery of PowerPoint or Keynote presentations require the use of a computer. Professors use email to issue and collect assignments.

Eduventures, Inc., a leading independent
e-Learning industry research firm, reports that the
e-Learning market in higher education is an $11
billion business.

Top-ranked Duke University relies heavily on Podcasts, recorded webinars, DVD, and web applications to deliver class content. The Duke University Global Professional MBA requires students to attend the first two weeks of study in the classroom in Durham, while the subsequent ten weeks of learning are completed online through a VPN or a take-home DVD. That is a significant amount of computer time and may not fit the learning needs of all students.

> I always had to have two laptops. I had one for work and one for school. For work we had limited access and needed special software that could not be installed on a non-bank pc. I needed my laptop for emails and ongoing projects, reviews and preparing proposals so I had to have my work laptop. The other laptop was dedicated to school. Here were my papers, school database log-in, and everything relevant for the MBA. I spent a lot of time moving back and forth from the work environment to the school environment, so it really helped to have the ability to switch gears between work and school. Also, carrying them both around the world reduced the amount of time I had to spend at the gym!

> —James Cecere, Duke University EMBA graduate, VP of JP Morgan Chase.

Wharton School on the other hand, minimizes the use of technology. According to one Wharton administrator, the use of technology in place of the classroom dilutes the EMBA program experience. He questions the value of any graduate level education when computer delivery plays such a prominent role in the overall learning experience. As one Wharton graduate contends:

The importance of face-to-face interaction with professors and classmates can't be overstated. Institutions that use too much technology, by default, reduce the interaction between people. Much of my learning experience was generated by my classmates, and trading this interaction for computers is a mistake. Technology can enhance the learning experience but should not drive the learning experience. The personal relationships gained from an EMBA are what can build the foundation that exists even years after you graduate from the program. Too much attention toward technology at the expense of student interaction risks losing the true value of attending the EMBA.

—Shelley Boyce, Wharton EMBA graduate, CEO of MedRisk

Other side of the world: Fordham University EMBA students prepared with Beijing International University MBA counterparts (BIMBA program) via closed-circuit teleconferencing. When it was 11:00 P.M. EST, it was 11:00 A.M. in Beijing.

If people miss the class, we have it on video and, if two or three people cannot make class, rather than dub tapes we literally digitize the lectures on DVD for students to access. While our mission remains face-to-face teaching, we have to recognize the flexibilities technology allows. We attempt to accommodate these busy professionals. We've bridged video conferencing from Dallas, Atlanta, Chicago, Champaign, and Delaware.

—Merle Giles, Director, Executive MBA Program, University of Illinois at Urbana-Champaign

5.5. *Virtual Private Networks*

Virtual private networks connect students privately onto a platform monitored and maintained by a third party. With registration and password access, the network is accessible from practically anywhere on the globe. These private networks come with all sorts of functional benefits including support for closed circuit video conferencing, chat room discussions, one-on-one learning and tutoring, exchanging files, and access to repositories of information from the U.S. government and LexisNexis.

Top vendors of groupware products for higher education include Embanet of Canada and Blackboard in the United States. Each vendor serves an impressive list of university and corporate clients.

Each vendor offers niche applications to support the following features:

1. Complete electronic exchange of e-mail,
2. Workgroup conferencing for electronic discussions, file sharing, and collaboration,
3. Remote access and online information services with an intuitive, multi-tasking interface a private, secure electronic platform,
4. Government and privately-collected business-relevant databases.

How much coursework is devoted to the use of computers?

- Does the program offer a groupware system?
- Is faculty using the system, and how have students found the experience?
- Are there any fees associated with using the groupware system?
- Is a laptop required for the program?

Interview with James Cecere, Duke University EMBA Graduate, Vice President, JP Morgan Chase

What were the classes like in the EMBA program?

Duke is a "Clicks and Bricks" program. In a typical semester you spend two-week residencies either on the Duke Campus or overseas—five residencies total. The class schedule normally runs daily from 8 A.M. to 4:30 P.M. Evenings were spent with teammates working on projects or case studies. On the weekends, in addition to the work you did either on your own or with a team, Duke arranged for various trips that were either cultural or business-focused. We did this in every country we visited.

What exactly did the Clicks and Bricks of the Duke EMBA entail?

Duke utilizes various forms of technology, including Podcasts, DVDs and the Web to deliver learning materials. The web was used as the main communication platform with each student having customized access. We would use either chat rooms or bulletin boards to facilitate discussion throughout the non-residency portion. The formats employed by Duke were reflective of the technology available globally and were sensitive to the time zone. For example, if a chat was scheduled for 9:00 A.M. EST, then it was 1:00 A.M. in Australia! Therefore, the bulletin board was a great place to facilitate discussions. The other added benefit of the bulletin board was that it gave people the chance to clarify their thinking, and people often write a lot differently than they speak. For the distance portion, the professors could not deliver lessons via the Web. Given the challenge of delivering such a level of technology in parts of the world, this is not yet possible. For example,

in Costa Rica, the best linkage available to some of the
students there from their homes is a 15.6k modem line. A
live video presentation over this type of connection would
therefore not be prudent. The solution therefore is for the
professors to record their lessons on either a CD-Rom or
on a DVD, and then provide those to students for review.
Typically, during the distance portion, a "screen cam," as
we called it, would be reviewed, and we would then discuss
it during our class chat session on the Internet or via the
bulletin board. Again, the chat sessions are very much like
instant messaging on AOL; you can carry on a discussion
by typing messages to your group mates.

Some groups, however, did arrange for Net Meetings
given their access to better communication lines (i.e., T1
lines). Duke made this software available and left it to the
students to decide whether or not to use it.

Other neat technologies that were introduced either by
Duke or by students included voice recognition software.
While the success of this technology was somewhat mixed,
the majority made great use of it and found it to be very
helpful.

Describe the integration of technology into the classroom and
overall learning.

Professors focus on delivering the core subject matter
required for the course. This includes the theoretical and
practical application of the varied subjects. There are often
exams or smaller projects due during this period to ensure
that students understand the core requirements of any given
subject. The distance portion then picks up and focuses on
team projects. The professor provides additional learning
materials, such as screen-cams, whereby additional lessons

are provided. From an individual perspective, students will watch these screen-cams and usually will also perform corresponding "homework" from these lessons to ensure additional understanding. As a team, the students will also be given group assignments, usually in the form of case studies, to work through and submit to the professor for a grade. These case studies are meant to allow the teams to apply the core learning materials to a complex scenario. The groups seem to work well with each other, and all primarily utilized the technology provided by Duke on the laptops and the website. Students will typically split up the work amongst the team. One person usually coordinates, or leads, the case study to ensure that it is completed and that all team members participate. Once the project is completed, the project leader will electronically submit the assignment to the professor.

Were there any technology related shortfalls to the Duke program?

The university has made considerable investment in boosting its technology infrastructure. Students are known for quickly embracing new technologies given their backgrounds, and spent a lot of effort consulting with Duke on ways to improve its use and delivery. This was an interesting interaction as one had a community of students from major corporations that were used to leading-edge technology while at the same time you had academics who come from a more traditional environment. While many embraced technology and integrated the use of IT into the curriculum, there was also a resistance and a slower rate of acceptance from some professor. This led to inconsistency in the delivery of material and the utilization of even the most basic technology. Therefore in some classes, students handled a lot of paper.

Also, with Clicks and Bricks, you can run the risk of never growing close and creating bonds with classmates. The risk is overemphasizing the clicks and less the bricks. We forged tremendous relationships, and now have life-long friends from around the world. The structure of the program has the potential to move too far into the "click" space and could potentially threaten this.

How often were you on the Duke campus?

I traveled to Duke for both the first and the last residency. I also opted to head to Duke's campus during the program to work on some projects and to see a professor. I met up with other classmates. While this is not standard (actually, I think it is quite rare) I opted to do this as an opportunity to get together with some other classmates and to focus on a course that I really wanted to ensure total understanding.

CHAPTER 6

The Corporate Perspective

Reliable statistics on corporate investment in workforce training and education is hard to come by. These business expenses hit the bottom line and cutbacks on education become a PR nightmare. Therefore, companies do not like to boast about such investments and instead show the contributions by their charitable arms as forms of giving back to the community and investing in the local populace. Companies are also wary of treating tuition expense reimbursement as an entitlement as they do with health care, day care, and other corporate benefits, as school is looked upon as a personal and expensive decision.

It is no surprise, then, that only 25 percent of workers feel a strong attachment to their employers, and 4 in 10 feel trapped in their jobs, according to Walker Information, an Indianapolis-based research firm. Even before the economy slowed, employee loyalty was on the decline, comments Walker vice president Marc Drizin. "I think most organizations still don't understand why you need to be good to your workers," he says. Workplace discontent affects productivity, and a company is doomed to failure if it loses its skilled workers. When the economy does rebound, the most talented staffers tend to find opportunity elsewhere, thereby reducing the company's competitive edge.

What will drive corporate investment in education and training? The answer is the need for better-trained, skilled workers—and managers. More companies will need to grow their education and development programs utilizing internal departments or collaborating with outside institutions like community colleges and universities and with outside contractors. Emphasis will be placed on the development of future leaders, providing fast-tracking in those organizations that lack competent leadership. A suggested alternative for motivating and growing management is the Executive MBA.

You do not have to be a Fortune 500 company to initiate a corporate reimbursement and training program, either. Companies that buck the trend and invest during economic downturns convincingly outperform when the economy turns around by further investing resources to support the education and training of their best and brightest. *Fortune* magazine's list of best companies to work for list employer training programs and reinvestment as a measure of workplace satisfaction and loyalty. None of these companies are filing for bankruptcy any time soon, as they all represent the top-ranking market positions in their respective industries.

Sweet Corporate Tradition: J.M. Smucker provides 100 percent tuition reimbursement with no limit to the dollar amount.

As a hiring manager in need of recruiting and retaining qualified employees, you must embrace education and training as a core commitment of your company during both good and bad economic periods. This challenge to remain focused on the long-term success of your company and to internalize corporate education is critical during highs and lows of the economy. The Executive MBA course work can serve as a strategic tool and a necessary imperative for competing in the twenty-first century.

6.1. Types of Sponsorship

Benefits policies vary greatly from company to company, and the treatment of tuition assistance is no exception. Some companies treat reimbursement of EMBA outside the tuition reimbursement policy. The traditional MBA overshadows the EMBA, and most companies are simply unaware of the latter's existence and thus fail to appreciate the immediate benefits of such education to the company. Employers that purposely do not offer sponsorship of EMBA students give the following reasons for passing up this valuable opportunity:

- Excessive time away from work,
- High tuition expense,
- Employee flight upon graduation.

Here are some reasons for taking up a program that promises benefits for both your company and your employees.

Time Sponsorship

Class sessions are typically based on an evening or weekend schedule specifically so that they do not interfere with employment. The actual time that EMBA students are away from work is quite limited. When study tours are added to the basic program, the total number of days per year away from the office can range from two and four weeks—little more than most employees' vacation time.

Attendance is required as course work is delivered in a highly concentrated manner. Missing one weekend session can equal missing an entire month's worth of lectures in a traditional program. EMBA students are expected to attend and actively participate in each and every class. The time commitment is critical for success in the EMBA. Employers who permit their employees to leave work in order to attend classes and study tours reap rich rewards from their newly-energized and better-equipped employees, often after only a short time. Employers are, however, required to sign a statement of understanding that the employee will be missing some work time.

Furthermore, most programs expect that employers will minimize the employee's business travel during the duration of the program. Depending on the class schedule, the employer should expect that a student may need to leave work early or miss an entire day once or twice a month. If you are an employer, you can avoid conflict around staff and minimize the disruptions of work absences by addressing the issue ahead of time. You will find that many employees are only too happy to use vacation and personal time to make up for missed work. Responsible, ambitious employees understand that attending school is not shelter from fulfilling work duties.

Before agreeing to be a sponsor, request the EMBA calendar in order to measure student time requirements and the impact that such a schedule is likely to have on your employee's work demands, and plan accordingly. School administrators seldom make adjustments in the academic calendar on behalf of a sponsoring company.

> I work for a non-profit company and didn't feel it was appropriate to approach them for financial sponsorship. I did, however, request for time sponsorship and asked them to look at the schedule and see if they could adjust my work schedule to accommodate the program. They were most accommodating and clearly understood the future benefits that my taking time to attend the EMBA program would have for the organization. They accommodated my hectic class schedule and were appreciative of my hard work in managing dual responsibilities.
>
> —Matt Brooks, Georgetown University EMBA graduate, Director of the Republican Jewish Congress
>
> I was employed for the first year, and then spun off a small division into a start-up company during the second year. I self-financed my tuition, my employer feeling that giving me flexibility in time away from work was a sufficient form of sponsorship.
>
> —Shelley Boyce, Wharton EMBA graduate, CEO MedRisk

Financial Sponsorship

An Executive MBA is an expensive endeavor. Programs range from $40,000 to $145,000 or more in tuition plus travel costs from study tours. The high cost of tuition along with concerns of employee flight upon graduation serve as chief barriers for corporate financial sponsorship. A growing number of applicants are accepting that they must shoulder a proportion of the course costs themselves.

Retaining good employees is always a challenge, if not the most important aspect of the long-term viability of the organization. Organizations continually grapple with the tradeoff between their investment in their employees and the increased marketability of those employees who are recipients of that investment. Providing sponsorship for an EMBA— whether it is financial or a commitment of time—is really no different. Each company has to determine the level of commitment and the return that it wants through a formal retention mechanism. This challenge to push and pull at the same time is what keeps human resource officers up at night.

> I think the EMBA is an incredibly valuable degree. It means that the candidate is someone with tremendous practical experience, the kind of experience I desire in those I hire. I also think the EMBA offers the company, along with the individual, a richer and more thorough perspective on the issues facing an organization in the internal and external environments and, in particular, in the competitive environment.
>
> I plan to offer sponsorship; it is most certainly something we plan to include as we grow. The EMBA attracts better candidates, retains better employees, and results in better performance. We have the good fortune to be located near some great universities.
>
> —Synthia Molina, Former admissions officer for the Drucker School; CEO, Alternative Link, a healthcare intelligence company

JP Morgan Chase offers a tuition sponsorship program and the application process was incredibly rigorous. I was so impressed by the organized sponsorship application and selection process, I told myself that if I can accomplish this then I can accomplish anything. I went into the EMBA with the backing of my colleagues, my boss, and president of JP Morgan Chase. It became such an honor to represent my company in class and to this day, continue to value JP Morgan Chase for sponsoring me.

—James Cecere, Duke University EMBA graduate, VP, JP Morgan Chase

Prior to attending any classes, we ask the candidate to sign a promissory note, which is basically an agreement that they will stay with the organization for three years after getting an EMBA or they will have to pay back some portion of the tuition. Everyone signs the note. When people break the agreement, they are obligated to pay back some portion of the agreement. We will pursue employees who refuse to honor the agreement.

—Hiring Manager, Investment Bank

Employers are reluctant, justifiably, to sponsor employees who may not return to work after graduation. It is a concern for schools as well, as it violates the essential mission of the Executive MBA: to augment and enhance both the employee and employer. It can also compromise future revenues to the school, as it relies on an annual stream of loyal, corporate-sponsored attendees who attend with at least partial funding from their employers.

A contract between employee and employer is usually the most common practice to assure continuity. The results are mixed according to several hiring managers interviewed on this subject. Complications vary from determining a mutually agreeable time commitment after graduation to the practicality of pursuing employees who break contractual obligations on a legal basis. Some corporate officers feel the risk of resignation is simply not worth the investment, while others value the education and training and fully support their employees.

However valid the employer concerns may be, there is no accurate data to measure the actual flight risk. Perhaps it is real, or perhaps it is more the exception rather than the rule. As noted above, a 2010 survey found that EMBA graduates reported significantly higher salaries after they received their EMBAs, suggesting that their employers found their new skills highly desirable. The same survey group reported the higher salary was achieved largely with the same employer. More than nine years after they completed their EMBAs, 40% of the respondents remained at the same place of employment. Quite possibly EMBA students may have more staying power than some companies assume, and they may actually represent a group of employees with uncommon loyalty.

Regardless of the reality, financing the education is an important issue for every stakeholder. Recognizing the sensitivity of this issue, a number of creative and enterprising initiatives have been launched to protect the corporate investment while still give employees the flexibility of growing their career wherever they choose.

Employer-based contractual and financing initiative

If the employer determines a contract is necessary, NYU administrators recommend the terms be set for no longer than three years after graduation. In fact, NYU suggests that when a corporation grants financial sponsorship, employees are more willing to sign such sponsorship conditions. If an employee is reluctant to sign a contract, financial incentives or guaranteed position upon graduation are possible inducements. School administrators also suggest that addressing the commitment to the company early on in the sponsorship negotiation process helps mitigate potential conflict later on down the road.

If an employee chooses to leave the company before an agreed-upon time frame elapses, the following schedule for payback can be added to the contract:

- If the employee leaves the organization immediately after graduation: employee is required to pay back the full cost of the program;
- One year after graduation: employee is required to pay back two-thirds of the program cost;
- Two years after graduation: employee is required to pay back one-third of the cost;
- Three years after graduation: no pay back obligation.

If a sponsored employee leaves or is terminated during the course of the Executive MBA, the company has the following options:

- Require reimbursement to the company;
- Terminate sponsorship and write off money spent to date;
- Continue sponsorship through the duration of the degree.

Corporate write-off: Tuition reimbursement is a corporate expense, so at least there's an educational tax write-off.

A corporate sponsorship program is a generic term describing the formalization of EMBA sponsorship. The employer internalizes a formal process for managing the EMBA student from candidate identification and selection to financing the education and, of top priority, protecting the corporate investment.

6.2. Protecting the Corporate Investment

Over the years I have consulted with a number of companies on their corporate tuition reimbursement programs and the process for candidate selection. No company has the exact same policy, but all offer equitable and above standard practices. They represented an electronics firm in Connecticut, a pharmaceutical start up in New Jersey and California, and a handful of investment houses in New York City.

Corporate education is a hefty investment. Graduate business school is expensive, and the Executive MBA is no exception. However, just as companies do not want to lose talented employees, employees do not want to limit their options upon graduation. Several unique financing strategies perfected in recent years allow employees to exercise their options while also protecting the corporate investment. These newer types of corporate financial sponsorship strategies share a common goal of satisfying each constituency (employer, employee, and university) in an equitable manner.

A corporate sponsorship program encourages the employer to remain committed to employee education and enables the company to continue grooming its workforce with confidence, while still recognizing the reality that its newly-educated workers may wish to pursue employment elsewhere. If a sponsoring employer is fearful of making the substantial EMBA investment only to lose those valuable sponsored employees, these types of creative corporate sponsorship programs can offer a solution to protect that investment.

The fundamentals of any corporate sponsorship program allow an employer of any size to create and coordinate a partnership between a bank or other lending institution and a university on behalf of its employees. The bank serves as an honest broker between employer and the employee in coordination with the university. Acting as a third-party billing system, the bank pays the school and bills the employer until the loan is paid off or the worker leaves the company, whichever comes first. A signed promissory note makes the employee ultimately responsible for the loan.

The employer can start repayments immediately or at a later date, and the life of the loan can extend for as many as five years or more. The schedule depends on the amount of time the employer expects the worker to remain loyal to the company post graduation. If the employee accepts a new job elsewhere the loan can be restructured and amortized over a new payment period with the new employer. If the new employer refuses to accept the loan or the employee drops out of the workforce, the loan then becomes the responsibility of the employee and is amortized over a standard payment period consistent with a traditional student loan.

The most important point is that no large sums of corporate dollars need be immediately committed to either the bank or the university. Instead, terms of the loan are tied to a predetermined employment period consistent with whatever time frame the company deems sufficient to recoup its investment. The employee must agree to the work arrangement of that predetermined number of years. If the work arrangement remains in good standing and the employee remains with the company, the employee is absolved of any financial obligation. If, however, the employee leaves the company early, that employee now assumes the debt. Some companies report saving as much as $50,000 or more on former employees.

Sign here!: These types of programs can also serve as an incentive sign-on bonus, where the repayment criteria can provide a motivation to hire or retain valued employees.

Employer Benefits

- The program serves as a pro-active recruiting tool and appeals to all types and sizes of businesses, including for-profit as well as non-profit organizations.
- The corporate repayment process is spread over a predetermined and negotiable payment period that lasts only as long as the employee stays with the corporation.
- A corporation can spread the cost of the education over a reasonable period of time (three to five years), either once the

student begins or once the student graduates, thus reducing the need for a large immediate capital outlay.

- Employer satisfaction increases, as the payment method provides employees the incentive to stay with the company long term.
- Corporations are relieved of enforcing company restitution agreements if the employee leaves prior to the termination date.
- Corporations do not have to make any financial investment and do not have to provide any funding until the employee actually completes the EMBA.

The payment method enables corporations and universities to work more closely and efficiently as they process applicants. Better coordination between the two can lead to a lower student loan default rate or less painful loan burdens for employees no longer with the corporation.

Employee Benefits

- The employee obtains financial support through a coordinated and streamlined administrative process established by the creation of such a payment method.
- Employees save thousands of dollars in student loan repayment expenses.
- The employee avoids the need to address a sometimes-contested and sensitive issue of tuition reimbursement with the company.
- These programs generate workforce loyalty and goodwill toward the employer.

University Benefits

- Creating these types of financing programs can enhance the diversity of the student mix, as more students are able to participate in the EMBA.
- The payment method eliminates deferred payments and corporate billing requirements, as the university receives its payments directly through the lending institution.

- Academic recruiters can draw from a wider pool of corporate applicants, as the payment method enables most corporations to participate in the EMBA with minimal risk.
- Universities receive payment at the beginning of the program rather than months after students process claims for reimbursement through the corporation. Direct billing provides payment almost immediately, thereby boosting cash flow for the school.

Frequently Asked Questions Concerning Corporate Sponsorship Programs

Describe the process of coordinating a corporate sponsorship program.

First, the lending institution will conduct a credit check to determine eligibility of the employer and employee to participate in the program. Usually the company will make arrangements with its existing bank. Student loans are a safe investment, particularly for business school, and student loan approval rates tend to be high. Once credit reviews are approved, the lending institution and the company agree to the terms of the loan with a promissory note for student signature. The lending institution serves as a conduit to disburse funds to the school and issues monthly payment statements to the company for payment on behalf of the employee.

In essence, a corporate sponsorship program functions as a third-party billing service where the company can participate or not at any point in time depending on whether or when the employee leaves before the end of term of the repayment agreement.

Which schools participate in these sponsorship programs?

Many prestigious graduate business schools have their own arrangements with local or national funding institutions to support the financial arrangement. It is best to work with a lender that may already have a relationship with the university.

How does early departure through layoff, firing, or new employer impact the overall repayment process?

Once the employer discontinues loan payments, the loan balance becomes re-amortized based on the minimum payment and terms provided in the employee's promissory note. The employee then assumes full responsibility for payments and the employer has no future financial or administrative involvement with the loan. The employee may choose to negotiate with a new employer to assume payment. There are no restrictions on having successive employers assume payments on behalf of the employee. If another firm does not assume payment the loan is restructured for the employee to manage.

What are the tax implications for these programs?

Tax laws may vary by state and for employees and employers. Seek consultation from a tax specialist on the tax implications. Update: In recent years changes and interpretations in the tax treatment and deduction rules have benefited students counting on tax breaks from the investment. Chapter 9 explores this topic in greater detail.

Policy Changes

Loan eligibility, participatory requirements, and other policy changes toward corporate sponsorship are common. Be sure to check with the university and financial institution to determine their latest rules and regulations.

6.3. Corporate Sponsorship Considerations

From small to mid-sized businesses to Fortune 500 companies, workforce challenges include who and where to downsize and how and when to attract and retain talented workers. Putting aside the high cost of turnover and on-the-job training, businesses are increasingly recognizing the perils of losing their core asset: Key employees.

Salary increases, bonuses, and promotions are traditional currencies awarded to employees for performance and longevity. These tangible currencies are the cost of doing business and essential to compete in the workplace. Additional currencies of non-direct monetary value for the employee may include comprehensive health benefits and supplemental benefits such as extended leave and daycare.

Top companies such as Google, Apple Computers, McKinsey, Boston Consulting Group, and Disney among others consistently reinvest in their employees, offering and rewarding managers with MBA sponsorships or in-house MBA-style trainings. It is fair to surmise that such institutionalized educational training programs motivate employees. Aspiring mid-level managers compete for open slots for the next enrollment period. Those lucky few who are chosen to attend receive corporate accolades, a letter from the CEO, and admiration from peers in addition to a boost in their credentials and eventual salary grade. The surrounding echo reverberates positively throughout the workforce, as fellow colleagues see the benefits bestowed on prized employees.

In similar fashion the EMBA is also an ideal tool to recognize the contributions and develop the skills of talented employees. It serves as an effective retention tool and an instrument to recruit top performers. It also functions as a method to create positive professional competition among employees and departments. EMBA alumni earn a reputation for scholarship, achievement, and leadership at the company.

Hunting grounds: EMBA classes can even serve as a resource pool for access to a highly motivated, highly educated, professionally trained, and difficult to reach population. Several people interviewed for this book report hiring their EMBA classmates.

Sponsorship does require the company, large or small, to develop a system to recognize and reward its employees. As you will read from Synthia Molina, CEO of a small healthcare intelligence company in California and former admissions officer of the Drucker School at Claremont Graduate University in Claremont, California, she plans to institute a sponsorship program once her company reaches a specified head count and milestone in revenues. On the other hand, an investment banking firm reports instituting a multiphase nomination process and confers scholarships on a select list of EMBA programs. Although the firm does not consider sponsorship an entitlement, it does agree that the EMBA serves as a means to attract and recognize top employees. When a company chooses the right candidates, awarding such prized employees with the chance to attend an Executive MBA program makes great corporate policy.

If you are in a position to introduce or recommend an institutionalized corporate sponsorship program, no matter whether you are an employee or an employer, start with the following *top ten* case statements:

1. An Executive MBA places valuable employees in a fast-track educational training program.
2. The employee can apply newly-learned information and skills immediately on the job for an immediate return on corporate investment.
3. The employee completes the degree within two years or less— unlike a part-time program, which can take as long as five years.
4. Corporate sponsorship can be used to recognize and reward exceptional performance and serve as a potent recruitment and retention tool.

5. Used as a reward, EMBAs allow corporations to enhance company loyalty among the best and the brightest of its middle manager group at minimal cost.
6. Using EMBA sponsorship as a reward, senior managers can create competition to motivate employees.
7. The EMBA can be used as a tiebreaker when evaluating key employees and determining the appropriate career path.
8. Through a highly professional and motivated program, the EMBA presents real business development opportunities for sponsoring corporations.
9. The Executive MBA is the most rigorous MBA an individual can earn. A senior level corporate officer must ask, "How is the competition grooming mid-level managers for the senior level?
10. Are competitors sponsoring candidates for Executive MBAs and, if so, am I being left behind?"
11. The education creates networking opportunities that the savvy employer can treat as a recruitment pool for access to the best and brightest.

6.4. Guidance Through the Sponsorship Creation and Selection Process

From the Fortune 500 to small and mid-tier companies, corporate sponsorship can apply to any sized employer willing to make the investment. There is no specific type of firm or industry ideal for sponsoring employees in the Executive MBA program. Just as any company can be a benefactor of the EMBA, any company can recruit, retain, and reward exceptional employees.

Six Critical Steps to Setting Up a Corporate-Based Sponsorship Program

The following six steps describe how to create a sponsorship program. Use this template to build your own unique sponsorship program:

Step 1: Formulate an Internal Policy

A responsible senior manager from within the company should independently address the notion of an EMBA corporate sponsorship program. The employee should not be the first to present the concept and serve as the impetus for creation.

Step 2: Assemble the Right People

Form a task force to create corporate guidelines on a sponsorship policy. The policy should address topics such as:

- Number of candidates per year,
- Selection process,
- Level of reimbursement,
- Rules pertaining to absenteeism,
- Sponsorship review and termination.

Step 3: Manage the Selection Process

For large corporations with several divisions, determine the number of slots per division that will be made available. Each division head can serve as the point person and submit applicant names for review to the appropriate decision-making committee. Department supervisors can be encouraged to recommend candidates for sponsorship. The company should set objective standards for candidacy. Examples of objective criteria might include a 550 GMAT score or above, outstanding work performance, longevity, or multiple referrals from the department.

Some companies require candidates to provide GMAT scores and application essays and occasionally to undergo an interview, as part of an internal nominating process. Once the applications are submitted, the review committee assembles and reviews the applications. Review committees generally consist of representatives from senior management, corporate officers, and human resource representatives.

Sometimes the president of the company evaluates and identifies likely candidates. A formal interview is normally conducted with all candidates.

Step 4: Reward Process

The president of the company can notify those chosen by letter, and a copy of the letter is placed in the candidates' personnel files. In these circumstances, sponsorship serves as an important recognition of corporate service not a fringe benefit. It can then be identified as separate from the standard tuition reimbursement process.

Step 5: Beta Test

When initiating a sponsorship program, organizations should start small. Initially, when only a few individuals are selected, they can and should provide an appraisal of the program they attend. This information can be extremely valuable for rating various Executive MBA programs. Creating a feed-back process through which students report on the quality of teaching, the class participation, the applicability of the curriculum to the needs of the company, and other criteria is very helpful in evaluating programs for future applicants. Companies can use this comparative data to measure the strengths and weaknesses of various EMBA programs.

Some corporations only sponsor students to certain schools based on criteria of student satisfaction, accreditation, strength of the program, and program relevance to their type of industry. During the beta test, sponsors should be sensitive to diversity issues and include a broad range of employees. Soliciting opinions from a diverse population of attendees will enable sponsors to gather opinions from a wide audience to determine the most appropriate programs to sponsor more effectively. Prospective sponsors should request program presentations from the universities and send evaluators to attend EMBA open houses where feasible.

Step 6: Monitor Progress and Plan Accordingly

During budgetary planning periods, it is important to identify a specific allocation to support executive education. Firms can start small with one or two candidates initially. Since tuition and program fees as well as employee interest, business conditions, and other factors change from year to year, flexibility in budgeting is recommended. In fact, if employee retention issues arise, expanding the program (budgets permitting) may be a good way to address them. The important point is that creating a workable and beneficial corporate policy does require flexibility in execution.

In preparation for a sponsorship program a company should:

- Meet with EMBA program administrators and study the curricula of various schools.
- Determine the type of accreditation the program may possess.
- Review the academic calendar.
- Coordinate a financing mechanism for a corporate sponsorship Program.
- Review the sponsorship program periodically to assure adherence to fair employment practices.

6.5. Corporate Testimonials on the EMBA

Interview with Synthia Laura Molina, CEO, Alternative Link, a Healthcare Intelligence Company, and Former Director of Admissions at the Drucker School, Claremont Graduate University:

What is your opinion of the EMBA?

I think the EMBA is an incredibly valuable degree. It means that the candidate is someone with tremendous practical experience, the kind of experience I desire in those I hire. I also think the EMBA offers the company, along with the individual, a richer and more thorough perspective on the issues facing an organization in the internal and external environments and, in particular, in the competitive environment.

I received my MBA when I was twenty-four years old. I probably would have gotten more out of it if I'd had a little more actual experience. I am now actually deciding whether to pursue a Ph.D. or an EMBA myself. Getting an EMBA is not about getting a degree. It's about getting reeducated in a manner that will serve me, my organization, and our constituents.

In my view, the value of an EMBA also depends on whether the candidate is interested in technical application of MBA course content or in the strategic application of what's taught in the degreed program. I see the EMBA more as a strategist's degree, not a functional degree needed by someone who will just manage a single department within a company. If the candidate is interested in the degree for strategy, leadership and general management, go with an EMBA. Furthermore, from my experience serving as an administrator for the Drucker School, sitting in on EMBA classes, the faculty and students were top of the line.

How has your company profited from the EMBA?

We have two EMBAs and a couple of early—and late-career MBAs in the firm. I think we would be better off if we got some more EMBAs, because the firm is currently facing strategic challenges that may require the insight and competencies uniquely gained from an EMBA.

Recently I had the good fortune to sit in on some EMBA classes at the Drucker School. I could see firsthand the caliber of students and the sophistication of the questions raised in class. I wish I had gone through this route. In fact, I wish my entire team had gone the EMBA route. I have seen the difference in the quality of the discussions. The degree creates tremendous value when a company is going through a particular stage of development and classmates who have been there and are experienced can offer consultation and contacts. The networking opportunities are phenomenal!

As I think of my own situation with this company, I think I'd like to hear from others facing parallel problems in other industries or in the same industry as mine. Hearing firsthand from those "who have already been through it" is as helpful as reading trade journals or working through related case studies. The personal experience of classmates adds a lot to the overall value of the education.

Do you feel every company should encourage the EMBA?

I don't know about every company, but I would say yes in relation to those I've served. Yes, the training from an EMBA is exceptional. One really bad management decision made at the middle management or executive level can have devastating financial consequences, far greater than the tuition required for dozens of EMBAs. If we could get more people educated through EMBA programs, this would undoubtedly improve our corporate performance.

Would you consider sponsoring the EMBA as a competitive advantage for the firm?

Sure. It attracts better candidates, retains better employees, and results in better performance. At my firm we want to reach the point where we can offer a tuition reimbursement program. We are not quite there yet in staff size and in financials. However, it is most certainly something we plan to include as we grow. We have the good fortune to be located near some great universities.

Describe the ideal EMBA candidate for your firm.

The ideal candidate is a functional employee who's already worked in multiple disciplines, has a commitment to betterment, grasps the big picture, and has a strong strategic mind. Many strategic professionals I have known are pretty frustrated on the job because they know they are stronger strategists than the people they report to. The EMBA is an ideal way to get out of this trap. The tactically-oriented boss does not want to lose the strategically-oriented employee, yet the employee is not satisfied intellectually on the job and may be viewed as a threat to the boss. The EMBA can be used as a way to keep the strategic employee engaged and groom him or her for promotion. (In the short run, the tactically-oriented boss may just be happy the employee is too busy with school to run even bigger circles around the boss.)

While you were on the review board at Drucker School, what were some of the characteristics you looked for in an EMBA candidate?

The characteristics were twofold: first, a desire to grow the firm and, second, a desire to contribute value outside the firm and university, in society. What I liked was an understanding of their own limited knowledge (humility) and a commitment to doing something constructive about that . . . about satisfying the desire for knowledge and being a greater contributor (motivation).

At Drucker we looked for strategy, leadership, and general management qualities. We wanted individuals who saw the role of management in advancing society; who understood how to align individual, organizational, and societal needs to gain greater leverage and benefits for all; who were servant-leaders with a real understanding of how the world works. We looked at candidates to identify if they'd faced significant challenges in their lives, and we studied how they overcame those challenges. We looked, in particular, at their character and effectiveness: the marks of real leadership.

Drucker was a comfortable program, a premium product. Class was often held on weeknights and weekends, often at local hotel, with dining included. It wasn't at all easy, but it wasn't made unnecessarily uncomfortable. It fact, the atmosphere was more like a happy family atmosphere. But it also offered a more worldly view. Students were encouraged to go on study tours to Mexico and England. The school has an exchange program with Oxford and some other noteworthy institutions.

The Drucker School offers certificate programs in the form of modules, which can be acquired and combined toward a degree. Topics include strategy, leadership, general management, marketing, and a few others. I think this modular education concept is great for employees seeking a few courses in a concentrated fashion initially and then building a degree over time. I think this concept is great for companies, too, because the employee gains expertise in concentrated areas that can be applied immediately to benefit the companies' bottom lines.

My firm is going through a merger and we could use professional expertise internally. I wish I had more coursework in the MBA on entrepreneurial finance. Facing a hiring decision between a candidate who has an MBA and a candidate with an MBA and graduate certificate, the candidate with the certificate and the option of proceeding at a later date toward an EMBA would be a much more attractive hire. I'd expect this candidate to be not just a problem-solver but the kind of leader with insight that prevents problems to begin with.

Interview with Hiring Manager of a Fortune 500 Investment Banking Firm in New York City

Can you describe for me the EMBA review procedure at your company?

We have a formal committee called the Corporate Education Group which overseas academic issues. Each year we generally have about thirty to forty participants for the EMBA. We get a certain number of individuals from each of our business divisions, which include the investment banking business, the retail business, the treasury business, etc. The process begins with line managers conducting interviews with prospective candidates. They make sure specific corporate criteria are met.

The criteria follow:

- Must be an officer of the organization,
- Must be at least three years with the company at the time of nomination,
- Should generally be someone in a key leadership position who has demonstrated an ability to make a broad contribution to the organization,
- Must be someone who has received "1" or "2" performance ratings: "1" is outstanding and "2" is commendable,
- Must have a minimum GMAT score of 600,
- Should have the consensus of reporting manager and senior VP of department.

After each business comes up with names, they will then put those names forward to me and my team and we then sit down with the corporate steering committee, comprised of senior people in each of our business divisions, and finalize our candidates for that year.

At that point the company has relationships with a certain number of schools. We send a letter of sponsorship to those schools with a list of our candidates for the upcoming year. From that point, candidates have a year to go ahead and get their applications together, get their recommendations together, and fill out the applications to the schools of their choice.

We update the school list periodically but it represents the top schools around the country. If a candidate wants to attend a school not on the list, he can go through the standard tuition process and go to any school he chooses, but this has to be for the regular program and not the EMBA.

How has your company profited from the EMBA?

The more we can do to facilitate the development of our employees through programs like this, the better we find ourselves. We don't do anything after they get their EMBA. Getting their MBA does not mean automatic promotion or salary increase. We find that, when selected in the proper way, these are people who generally take their careers to the next step and often end up in true leadership positions at the bank.

Do you use the EMBA as a recruitment and retention tool?

No, we do not. It is not used as a tool to keep employees if they have one foot out the door. It is not looked upon

---

as a tool to help them move from one business unit to another. It is strictly a development tool.

Do you feel that the EMBA is appropriate for any company to offer?

I do. I think that it certainly has proven to be a great program. It makes people feel more loyalty to the organization, even though it is not meant as a retention tool, and the organization really gets a "bang for its buck" as a result of spending the money on such a program. It is certainly a competitive advantage for us.

(Note: This interviewee specifically requested anonymity.)

CHAPTER 7

Wide Appeal to Different Populations

7.1. Women, Working Mothers, and the Executive MBA

"For a woman to succeed in business," according to feminist historian and author Fannie Hurst, "she has to be twice as good as a man to go half as far."

Government workforce data report that employed women outside the home rose to 66 million in 2009 up from 30 million in 1970. Today over 46 percent of the labor force is female, and that percentage is growing. Women are closing the M.D. and Ph.D. gap and make up more than 47 percent of the students in law schools, according to the American Bar Association. In contrast, women represented just 31% of the entire student population in business schools in 2007, according to a study by the Forte Foundation. As reported by Catalyst, a women in business publication, only fifteen of the Fortune 500 are headed by a female CEO, that is a paltry 3%.

Are gender roles too entrenched in a way that business remains a less acceptable career path for women than the fields of law and medicine? Does the old-boys network in upper management refuse to crack? Perhaps the cost is too far out of reach, considering that, even with an MBA, women will continue to earn less than their male counterparts five years after graduating.

How about the timing? Women who attend law or medical school are generally in their immediate post-college years. The need for practical experience in law or medicine is not as necessary to the educational experience as it is for a business degree. It's rarely possible for women who leave the workforce during their child-bearing years to leave employment again to attend business school full-time, although it's done—though sometimes to the detriment of a career. Attending part-time over five years at night as a primary caretaker for young children is rarely a practical option. Business schools struggle with low numbers of women and are making direct appeals to corporations to sponsor more female employees.

The Executive MBA offers an interesting alternative for women, particularly for women over 30 who are mothers, trying to balance a career with family. Assuming a support structure at home, business school complements work, receives endorsement from an employer, and can be achieved within two years in classes held on weekends with minimal interference with the job and family. It may fulfill a woman's academic aspirations, boost enrollment, and lead to a corporate world better represented by women, particularly in upper management.

Advantages for Working Mothers:

- No career interruptions: Working mothers can continue to maintain full and active employment.
- Monthly or bi-monthly weekend or evening schedule does not interfere with work and permits a more flexible organization of family responsibilities.
- EMBA class assignments, although rigorous, are quite manageable and designed to accommodate work and personal responsibilities.
- An EMBA serves as a balance between career growth and family requirements.
- Technology allows students to conduct research, exchange papers, participate in virtual study groups, and receive online tutoring from the home or office.
- Incidentals and other administrative issues related to school are handled by program administrators.

Overcoming challenges, making adjustments, and meeting requirements necessary to earn an MBA are doable, according to every woman interviewed for this book. Without being singled out for special treatment, women will find that fellow classmates, faculty, and administrators are willing to make accommodations within reason and that they can still meet graduate business school expectations.

If you accept the idea that business school best serves people with experience, then personal and career choices that women have traditionally faced such as postponing family or dropping out of work for business school do not have to be the only options. The EMBA specifically accommodates full-time work, so the degree does not set back career advancement.

Here is a typical schedule in the life of one working mother who attended an Executive MBA program.

- o 6:00 A.M. Wake up and dress for work.
- o 6:30 A.M. Feed husband, daughter, fish, and dog.
- o 7:30 A.M. Take daughter to daycare.
- o 8:00 A.M. Arrive at work.
- o 9:00 A.M. Meet with CFO to develop cash flow and discuss
- o pro forma for a business planning project.
- o 10:00 A.M. Review financials for noon meeting with auditors.
- o 11:00 P.M. Receive call from classmate to briefly discuss Porter's
- o Five Forces and plan evening study group.
- o 12:00 P.M. Meet with auditors to review previous quarter performance.
- o 1:30 P.M. Grab lunch.
- o 2:30 P.M. Review the evening study outline just sent by email from classmate.
- o 3:00 P.M. Prepare for morning presentation, review MS
- o PowerPoint presentation.

○   4:00 P.M. Attend unexpected meeting and conclude preparation for morning meeting.
○   5:30 P.M. Pick up daughter and dinner.
○   6:30 P.M. Eat dinner with daughter and husband and leave clean up for husband.
○   7:30 P.M. Watch conclusion of Disney movie with daughter.
○   8:00 P.M. Enter study room, shut door, and conference call classmates to discuss assignment on Merck-Medco case. Draft outline, discuss timeline, and delegate parts.
○   10:15 P.M. Take a break and prepare lunch.
○   10:30 P.M. Read Economics chapter and go online to post questions for professor.
○   12:00 A.M. Go to sleep.

Interview with Darcy Sementi, University of Illinois EMBA graduate, VP Sales and Marketing, Personal Care

Why did you choose the EMBA?

I am the breadwinner in the family and quitting my job was not an option. Some of the schools I looked at had no part-time program and, while others did, I did not want to see this education go beyond two years. The greatest barrier to the EMBA is the cost, but I did get sponsorship from my employer. I found the program schedule accommodating.

You gave birth during the program. How was this handled?

I gave birth to my son two days before our study tour to Europe. I did not miss a class outside of Europe. My pregnancy was a surprise, and the first person I ended up telling about my pregnancy was my administrator. I was afraid that missing the trip to Europe would prevent me from graduating. He was so supportive and eased my worries. He assured me the professor would work something out. Leading up to the trip there were case study assignments, and I fully participated in the evaluation and preparation of the case. I was fully involved with all the work but did not make the trip to present the results. In lieu of not making the trip, instead I wrote a paper on international business.

What was it like being a working parent who just delivered a child midway through the program?

I was the only woman with four men in my study group. We encountered a couple of dynamics. First, I live twenty minutes south of Champaign and work here in Champaign. The understanding I made between my husband and me was that one night a week I was gone for my study group. We made Wednesday night the study group and would meet with the group until late in the evening. I would also have every other Saturday away from my family. Whenever you have a collection of people, over time you develop group dynamics, and I clearly became one of the two leaders of the group. I did my fair share of the work. I never needed or relied on others to pull my weight. What did happen with our group is that the guys would occasionally meet one other time during the week and even got a tutor for the stats class.

My first child was nine months old when I started the program. My second child came midway through the program. The first year of the program I would study once my daughter went to sleep, up until midnight. Finding time to study was the biggest challenge of all. During the second year of the program, my daughter was staying up later, and I could not wait to begin studying when she went to bed. So she would sit at the kitchen table and do "homework" with mommy. My mindset in the morning is to go to work. I could not study in the office. I utilized every waking moment before and after work to find time to study. That for me was the biggest challenge.

How did you manage study groups?

To help keep me disciplined, I made a schedule each week of everything I had to prepare and get done for family, for work, and for school. On Wednesdays, the study group would meet in our office, and we would begin studying at 5 P.M., and at 6:30 P.M. eat pizza or sandwiches. If I could stick with my schedule then I could meet the challenges of class. A few times I did need to go outside of my schedule, and this was during the semester when we were studying accounting.

Did school scheduling make things easier or harder for you?

Professors were incredibly accommodating and would check ahead of time to make sure tests or projects were not due the same day; they spread them out. We would never have more than two tests or projects on the same day. Kudos to the program administrators for their help in making this manageable for all of us.

I have no regrets about the program. It helped me in my career transformation. The networking is phenomenal. The CFO [of my company] is a classmate, and he would not have hired me if it were not for our interaction and relationship in the program.

What advice do you have for women considering going back to business school?

Consider the Executive MBA! I recommend doing it sooner as opposed to later. There is a big difference in terms of time commitment and manageability when your son or daughter is nine months old as opposed to two years old. It was so much easier when they are younger. They don't know you're leaving them for school, and you can get away with studying a lot more because they sleep a lot and are a bit more manageable.

There is a big paradigm shift in our thinking today in society toward women being the breadwinner and the husband being the stay home dad. When my husband takes our children to the park, mothers are in the park asking if he has a day off from work. The role reversal alone presents a challenge for women.

Women can step up and take the role of supporting the family while the father stays at home and, at the same time, if you want to take a sabbatical from work and be a stay home parent with the intention of returning to the work force, then the EMBA should be considered as an option. It will depend on how the university feels about this.

We are family: According to an EMBA administrator from NYU Stern School of Business, families are invited to certain student weekends, attend workshops, meet families of other classmates, and even stay overnight during some residencies.

Family friendly: Schools want to be family friendly. The University of Chicago receives high marks for this, as an EMBA graduate, quoted in *BusinessWeek*, mentioned. "From Day One the school included my family in everything."

While there is no hard-and-fast statistic on the number of mothers attending business school, the Executive MBA clearly presents an interesting opportunity for either parent wishing to advance his or her professional education. The message is clear: Maintain a professional career and manage a family while earning an MBA. The Executive MBA may be the perfect mechanism to help address an important gender gap in the managerial workforce and in professional education.

Financial aid for women:
Business Professional Woman's Foundation
1718 M Street, NW, #148
Washington, DC, 20036
(202) 293-1100
www.bpwfoundation.org

Catalyst Inc. (Headquarters)
120 Wall Street, 5th Floor
New York, NY 10005
phone: (212) 514-7600
fax: (212) 514-8470
email: info@catalyst.org
www.catalyst.org

Questions for women to consider while evaluating EMBA programs:

• How many women are currently enrolled in the program?
• How many of the program faculty are women?
• Will there be guest lectures given by businesswomen?
• What effort has the school made to recruit female students and faculty to the program?

7.2. Doctors and the Executive MBA

Practicing medicine also means running a business, a necessary skill that is neglected by medical schools. A doctor is a service provider, and patients are the customers. Part of a physician's daily practice is dealing with the administrative requirements of managed care, a burdensome and complicated reimbursement system. More so today than ever before, the doctor must pay attention to the bottom line, manage a staff, negotiate contracts, meet a payroll, market the practice, and remain competitive. These are all business—not medical—issues.

Four types of doctors attend the Executive MBA program:

1) The doctor who seeks departmental status for a hospital or board
2) The doctor who works in a business environment (e.g., a pharmaceutical company)
3) The doctor who seeks to leave medicine for a career change
4) The doctor who is member of a group practice.

An Executive MBA course schedule can accommodate a physician's schedule, and the program profile in the back of this book lists schools designed solely for the medical professional, although a non-medically-oriented EMBA is also possible. Medically-associated EMBA programs also draw professors from schools of public health, law, and medicine.

Business school teaches the physician practical business concepts from how to read and understand the significance of a P&L statement, a balance sheet, and a cash flow statement to negotiating managed care contracts and streamlining operations for a more profitable and efficient private practice. The degree can also provide a foundation in finance and marketing for understanding the challenges of your own practice, hospital, or pharmaceutical company. The business degree is an extremely practical degree for physicians.

Is there a doctor in the house? Five EMBA programs are structured for physicians, and most programs have at least one medical professional in the classroom.

Interview with Kathryn Beatty, M.D., EMBA Student at Columbia University, Private Pediatric Group Practice in New Jersey

What events led you to decide to attend business school?

I went to medical school early in life at UNC Chapel Hill. I started my practice in Princeton in1995. During my time in the practice, I became the eighth partner and started becoming aware of the business aspects and pediatrics around Princeton was growing. By the time I hit my fourth year in the practice, we had twelve physicians and were increasing by fifty percent. Now that we have thirteen physicians, are opening a new practice, have a staff of sixty, and have the potential to build satellite office, business management was essential. Pediatric population growth is fifty percent annually, and there is practically no competition. I realized that no one in the practice knew the business management perspective. We do an excellent job as physicians, but no one had formal training in business management. There were many aspects of the practice that were ignored, so my goal in going to business school was to get a more educated approach to handling business challenges facing the practice.

Generally speaking, there is definitely a sense of status quo in medicine. By the nature of our trade, we are conservative people. We don't take risks or experiment the way some do in business; therefore, when I come up with new ideas, there tends to be resistance and fear.

What were your original intentions for going to business school, and is it meeting your expectations?

As a partner, I get a financial statement at the end of every year that summarizes my performances and its impact on the bottom line. Normally I would file this in my circular file somewhere on my floor. I did not even know how to read this. When you are trained to be a doctor, you are trained on delivering medicine. You are completely focused, and that's what your patients expect. If you find yourself in the ER, you care less whether the physician knows the difference between an income statement and a balance sheet, how they relate to one another, and relationship to cash flow. You want the illness taken care of immediately. That is how physicians are trained and they are trained really well, but, in fact, to have a business in the future there is no way you can do so unless you know how to manage your business especially in the changing world of health care.

So what I had hoped to accomplish was to go to a program where I would meet people from different industries and with different perspectives. I want to hear from people who work for pharmaceutical companies and insurance companies and find what their thinking is and understand how they approach challenges where they work using tools we learn in school. Such things as cost accounting we never even thought of at the practice. We have many departments and could figure out where we are losing money and make things work. With managed care we are on a fixed income and the goal is to decrease your expenses to make money on that fixed income. The old school of pediatricians is not going to work in this new system, and we must find new ways to approach this system. Even though I am only two semesters into my MBA, I feel I have already achieved an understanding of where I can begin applying many of these principles at work.

Since I am learning so much, I gain a lot of personal growth. So far I am very excited about my MBA experience even if not everything I learn will have direct application at where I work; nonetheless, from a personal standpoint I am learning so much more than my peers.

Why the EMBA over the MBA?

It had to with my family, my practice, and when I can attend school. I could not cut back on my job because my colleagues and patients depend on me, and I don't feel I could adequately fulfill my job if my patients can't depend on me.

The only way I could add an extra dimension to my work and family is one of these Friday-only programs. This way I am still a full-time employee who is defined as four days a week and use school as my day off. It's a crazy schedule; I have three full-time jobs. There are schools that have MBAs for physicians. I did not want to be in a program with physicians, I need an outside vantage point. I need a more generic perspective. I like and needed the diversity of the program.

Do you see a career change down the road?

Not in the near future. There are few M.D./MBAs out there, and the demand for them is certainly there, but I love to take care of children and want to build a practice as efficient as our medical skills are excellent.

Describe the pros and cons:

Pros: Enormous personal and professional growth as well as exposure to subjects I never imagined I would enjoy or feel a need for. Case in point, Macro Economics, Micro Economics. Taking management classes opened my eyes to new ways of thinking. Even coming up with a core ideology of a business, mine included, makes complete sense when you read about the concept. But actually doing one is a different story and with everyone uniting behind it. I always look forward to learning new things and meeting new people from diverse backgrounds and industries—hearing about how their industries function, overcome challenges, adjust to market pressures. Even learning how companies began like the creation of FedEx is fascinating. I never look at the "Intel Inside" campaign the same way now that I know the deep-rooted strategy it employs.

The cons: Time commitment, although for me this is not a problem. I am so motivated to be in school and learn this material. It is a huge time commitment from 8 A.M. to 6:30 P.M. and twelve to twenty hours of homework a week. There is a lot of teamwork, and we all work together nicely sometimes picking up the slack for one another. In medical school it is so competitive and everyone tries to outdo the next person.

In business school there is a lot of teamwork and cooperation. As a physician in the real world, you should act in a team mindset, call to get advice or look things up when necessary, but that is not what they teach you in medical school. They don't encourage knowledge sharing; you can't ask; and the posting of everyone's grades for the public to see is a shameful system in medical school.

In my practice, I make a point to show new physicians and ancillaries around the office, give an orientation, take them under my wings, and all this helps set the tone for a collegial practice environment. But that is not the general mindset in medicine, so this is an example of another pro with MBA.

How do you manage working with your team if you are not living in the area?

The EMBA model allows for flexibility even with commuting to school. On my team I have one guy from Virginia, another from Pennsylvania, someone from Baltimore, two of us live in Princeton, New Jersey, and one who did live in Charlotte, North Carolina, until he moved to Manhattan. We have a team call once a week to work things through, and the few times we have to combine efforts for a presentation we work it out on a Thursday before school through a virtual private network where we Instant Message in virtual team conference rooms. Everything is online. Professors will post all material online, administrators will communicate with us and send us materials online.

The administration is really supportive. They recognize that we work full-time and that the job has given us the day off to attend school. In addition nothing is static. People change jobs, people lose their jobs, get married, all sorts of transitions, and they are supportive and help you as you work your way through these transitions. It's all much different than when going to school in my twenties. Also your peers value the experience the same way. We are here to learn, we want to be here and we lead busy lives. We will put everything we can into school and assignments and draw from the experience of people who have a focus or strength in that subject.

Is medical school failing to address the needs of doctors? Or is an MBA necessary for M.D.s?

I don't believe every doctor needs an MBA. There are plenty of practice management classes for physicians that are offered all the time. They look at staffing, accounting, etc. I am sure I could get a lot out of these weeklong sessions, but I wanted a broad overview of the education piece by piece, and I value education immensely so that for me the only real option was the MBA. I did not want a couple of specific questions answered, because I don't even know what questions to ask. This way I am getting exposed to areas I never ever would have considered.

My route is definitely not necessarily the route for physicians, but, when I counsel kids in my practice who say they want to become doctors, I tell them not to just take science classes. I tell them to take accounting, operations management, and marketing. Learn about different areas of business and apply this to medicine. Some guys in my practice have taken business classes as undergraduates, and they are bit savvier when it comes to questions concerning the business side of being a physician. In medical school it would be helpful to have one or two business classes, but where is the time, and when you are trained to save lives, no one really cares about those business issues.

How many women are in the program?

Of the sixty-five classmates about twenty-five percent are women.

What advice do you have for working women?

Think very hard about whether you will have the time to do it. Where will you get the time to attend class and complete the homework? I don't give up time to spend with my children to study, which means I stay up even later at night, but I am a bit unique and I know my study habits. Not everyone can function this way.

You must ask, "Why am I doing it?" and look at your life to determine if you can get everything out of the experience and still do a good job at work and go to soccer practice. A lot of women are leaving the workforce to stay at home. Most of my peers are dads, whose wives do not work. There are fewer dads that stay home. Many women are making the decision in their early thirties, so if they are married they have small children. With a career and children the option of adding school on to that is just not there. I think there a lot of women who are still single in their early thirties and do not necessarily want to add more to their plate and be a 100% career workaholic, and so adding on additional responsibilities is in the opposite of the direction in which they want to go. I think the workaholic mom does not want to add more. A stay home mom that once had a career is a possibility, but the business school may want you currently employed, because they want you to and you'll want to apply what you learn on the job.

Anything else you wish to add?

So much of the world is the business world, and I should be tired come Friday. Instead I am so motivated to learn and look forward to sitting in class discussing complicated business topics. I cannot say enough about this wonderful experience. I love my classes, my professors, and my classmates. I should have taken an accounting class not an organic chemistry class while preparing for medical school. Doctors are getting squeezed by the insurance companies, and physicians need to understand the business issues in order to compete and push back these HMOs which are making health care decisions and profiting from them, while leaving the physician in a compromised position both in delivery and financially.

Interview with Howard Birenbaum, M.D., MBA Graduate of Loyola University Maryland's online program, Director, Division of Neonatology, Greater Baltimore Medical Center

As a doctor, how did you decide to pursue an MBA?

I was an employed physician in a community hospital in Baltimore, Maryland, where I served as the director of a newborn intensive care unit. It became clear to me that I needed to understand the business side of hospital-based medicine. My experience was that a majority of the financial decisions of the hospital were made by non-physicians who may not always understand the importance of how their financial decisions were impacting our clinical services. A wall between management and medicine always existed and the prevailing attitude was: "You take care of the patients, and we'll worry about the money." Well, that did not always work well for me, and it seemed an easier task to learn the business side of medicine, get an MBA, get the credibility to work better with the CFO and COO rather than always compete. So I had been thinking about this for a long period of time.

A typical MBA program was not an option. I needed an income, and the hospital would not support me while [I was] at school. The staffing issues simply did not allow me to just pick up and attend classes throughout the week. What was important to me was not to join a program that was physician-based. I am learning a lot from people in my group. They represent a wide range of backgrounds. I learn a lot from people in marketing and finance. Granted, the question does come up as to whether I need to understand all there is about accounting or supply chain management. Medicine is so diverse that you bump into these business school issues all the time.

I joined an organization called American College of Physician Executives which has an affiliation with schools including University of Massachusetts, Carnegie Mellon, and Stanford, I believe, where you could get an MBA or a Master in Medical Management (MMM). I was not interested in programs that were exclusively for physicians. I wanted more diversity of business issues. Locally, Loyola has a regional EMBA that a lot of physicians attend and the price and distance were amenable to me. The other MBA program nearby was University of Baltimore. The University of Baltimore had the first approved web-based program.

I attend the Merrick School of Business at the University of Baltimore. By attending the University of Baltimore, benefits include the close proximity to work and home; the tuition costs are manageable since it is part of the Maryland state system; and there were no travel demands. I can work exclusively with classmates and professors over the web. The program overcame many issues that I was facing with other programs. Also my long-range plan is not to run an HMO or run a hospital so I found the curriculum a nice fit.

How do you see the MBA helping you as a doctor in your day-to-day work affairs?

The MBA augments my ability regarding issues at the hospital. The MBA helps me in approaching budgetary issues in the department and hospital-wide. The formal curriculum of an MBA prepares me to not just analyze and address business issues but present them to my team and the hospital at large. When you are working in a setting where you are primarily a clinical person, you are looked at for your expertise as a clinician not necessarily as a business person, and I try to advocate for my patients not only in the craft as a deliverer of medicine but also to know the business side of the practice of medicine—to understand the larger environment that we live in today so that we will be able to continue to deliver care now and for the future. I feel my MBA is enabling me to understand these deeper issues and communicate our clinical needs more effectively to hospital administration.

You have to keep in mind that the typical doctor began in premed and remains on a focused track studying medicine. I never took an economics course, a topic that branches into so many segments of society. I was never exposed to such practical business issues—ever.

How did you prepare to go back to school?

As a physician you are an avid learner. You never stop learning. The profession has state requirements, and good physicians will stay on top of the learning process. You never stop learning, and you never really leave school, as medicine remains a constant learning process. Since the program is web-based, you don't have the luxury of time in the classroom setting, and instead to be successful you have to be disciplined. The program allows for more time to graduate, but I will be graduating within two years. So to answer your question, I was never not in the learning mode, so going to back to school in this sense was easy. The challenge was adjusting to the demands and discipline that the rigors of the program present and the delivery method.

Can you describe the program?

There is a traditional MBA program, a web-based program and a weekend program that allows attendees to mix and match to accommodate their schedules. By not being in a classroom setting, you do lose that aspect and the groups formed over the Internet rather than a real team setting, face to face; you lose this benefit. I do like classroom settings;

I do like the opportunity to see the body language. Then again, there are plenty of business models where projects are handled across the world by virtual workgroups. The program is primarily text-based, not a lot of visual presentation, no streaming video or lecture via DVD or CD-ROM. I have been pleasantly surprised by the quality of the lectures and caliber of the professors. My interaction with them is online. Not hearing the professors speak or getting feedback live from classmates is something important and missing. Our textbooks are linked to web exercises, lecture notes, and our textbooks are standard with the business school traditional program.

What advice do you have for your medical peers thinking about an MBA?

Do your homework. You want to ask yourself what you as a doctor want to gain from the MBA. I know some physicians who have the MBA and are not doing much with it. One physician told me that he uses it to recognize the bad decisions by hospital administrators. Most that I am aware of don't make a career change. They use it to help with the business side of medicine for their private practice or department. Using the MBA to do your work better, to manage the people you are responsible for, to develop budgets, build business plans. The MBA helps immensely in this area. As a physician I have seen plenty of balance sheets and pro forma but was never able to make sense of them. The MBA helps the physician present an idea and use research and analysis to back it up in order to form a cogent and presentable business argument.

A lot depends on what type of physician you are. If you are in a business office practice, you'll hire an office manager. If you are a physician like me in the hospital, you want to take a look at the delivery of care in other ways. As a member of the American Academy of Pediatrics, I have an opportunity to lobby and support legislation and understand how government works. All of this revolves around business from government policies on third-party payers to understanding each decision and the consequences of these decisions. Trying to balance quality of care and fiscal responsibility and make the right decisions when faced with finite resources and ongoing demands in our nation's health is a constant challenge. My MBA affords me the opportunity to study these complicated business issues.

No one in medical school teaches you how to go about setting up and running a practice. You study for four years, intern, and then do a residency. No one teaches you the business side of all this. There are some medical schools that offer dual M.D./MBA, it makes sense.

What tricks or rituals do you employ to manage all this?

My kids are all grown up, and my spouse works full-time. Also I have arranged working twenty hours in the hospital at a time, and that gives me free more time at the other end of the week for my studies. But just as people find time to exercise and work out, I find time for school.

From my perspective, what was important to me was not joining a MBA program that was physician-based. I am learning a lot from people in my group. They represent a wide range of backgrounds. I learn a lot from people in marketing and finance. Medicine is so diverse that you bump into these business school issues all the time.

(Note: Loyola University Maryland does not offer an EMBA but rather a distance-learning program. Dr. Birenbaum's personal experience pursuing an MBA as a top physician offers valuable insight for any medical professional considering an MBA.)

Tuition Tax Deductibility of Medical Professionals

Can a physician take the cost of an EMBA as a tax deduction? The answer to this has real economic significance, and, fortunately for physicians, the answer may be clearer cut for them than for other EMBA candidates. A nurse who claimed that the cost of her MBA was a legitimate deduction challenged the IRS's initial ruling against her and won in 2009. Lori Singleton-Clarke argued that she qualified for the deduction because her MBA study helped her deal with physicians who may have infringed on hospital rules. "I didn't want to feel outmatched by surgeons who didn't want to talk to me," she noted. While the implications go beyond those in medicine, physicians who deal with hospital administrators and insurance companies can find themselves in a similar boat and can prepare a solid case for their deduction building on Singleton-Clarke's example.

Questions for doctors to consider while evaluating EMBA programs:

- Do you have a program specific to medical professionals?
- How many physicians are enrolled in the existing class?
- How many of the faculty are board-certified physicians or other licensed medical professionals?
- How much time must I be away from the practice?
- Can I speak to a graduate who is also a practicing physician?

7.3. Lawyers and the Executive MBA

Whether practicing law in a firm or as counsel to corporate or government agency, you find that the subjects of law and business are closely connected. A background in both has its obvious benefits, particularly in the corporate boardroom. Many lawyers who are seeking career change or fresh focus on the principles affecting business may find the Executive MBA a practical opportunity. In the corporate world legal counselors are often drawn into strategy sessions and asked to advise on business matters that may be beyond the scope of their legal expertise but rather delve into marketing, finance, and operations. In law school students are taught to attack problems with a "win or lose" attitude. Business philosophy is built on partnership and cooperation. The business world seeks out synergies and builds partnerships that are mutually rewarding. Sometimes these partnerships are with your biggest competitor (for example, Apple Computers and Microsoft or Amazon and book publishers). Therefore, it's understandable, particularly for corporate lawyers, to desire a business degree to help become more conversant with the broader scope of the business world.

Interview with Mary J. Kucharz, JD, University of Illinois EMBA graduate, Assistant Corporation Counsel, City of Joliet

Describe the similarities to and differences of business school and law school.

Similarities included the workload. I went to law school fulltime, and I consider the EMBA a full-time program, similar workload with demands to complete papers and come to class fully prepared. The bonding that took place in law school is also like the EMBA. You are often put into work groups or units and you take the same classes and develop a rapport. In the EMBA, you are all taking the same classes and form a strong bond as you break into study groups of four to five people throughout the two years. Networking with classmates is great and you are in a position to build an even stronger bond.

The differences are that in law school outside of class you meet with students in the afternoon, hang out in their apartments, etc. In the EMBA it is difficult to meet or talk, particularly during the daytime while people work. The biggest difference is the availability of fellow students and turnaround time to talk and pass information to classmates. I found professors to be accessible in both.

With regard to law professors your contact is face to face. In b-school, you'll do more communication by phone and email, and most professors are willing to meet before class or stay late for one-on-one.

The EMBA is competitive, but we also root for each other. In law school the mindset is different. Team and study groups are encouraged in the EMBA. Working together through the problem. The study group represents the teamwork in the working world. Law school is less team oriented.

What got you thinking about the MBA and ultimately the EMBA?

I faced many different non-law related projects at work and met many non-legally oriented people in government, so I felt I needed more exposure beyond the legal world. I wanted to learn the business ways of attacking a problem, not just the legal ways of attacking a problem. I thought about a traditional MBA, going back to school at night but did not want to drag it on for a number of years. I knew some people who had gone through the Executive MBA program through the University of Illinois. When I started thinking about getting my MBA, I compared the learning model of the EMBA to various MBA programs in the Chicago area and felt the EMBA was the best fit.

Did you consider an MBA earlier in life? Has the degree changed your career in any ways?

I considered an MBA prior to law school back in the mid—to late-1980s and decided not to pursue an MBA but rather to pursue a law degree.

I can't say that my pursuit of an MBA was for a career change. In law school you are taught to attack problems in a certain way. In law school your focus is very "win or lose," which is not how things are, it's not the rule outside the legal world. My first and foremost objective was to enhance and broaden my way of thinking, to attack problems I encountered every day. Secondarily, the possibility to make a career change and make me more marketable outside the legal world was a consideration. A career change was not top of mind but I can't say it did not play into my thinking when deciding to pursue an MBA. Business school taught me to economize the language and build structured condensed paragraphs. While in law school briefs contained boilerplate language and too much content that really is not necessary. I feel stronger and more competitive in my writing and thinking compared with many lawyers I meet on a regular basis.

While I have not pursued a career change with any vigor, I do now teach undergraduates and graduates in the business school, and I am not sure if that door would have opened for me if I had not gotten an MBA. I don't and never have desired to teach law classes. I have always wanted to teach business classes, organizational behavior, and human resources classes.

Why did you choose the University of Illinois?

Once I decided to go through the EMBA program, knowing I could achieve my MBA within two years even though workload was grueling, I then began looking at different schools that offer the EMBA.

When I began my search, the University of Illinois was forming satellite campuses to accommodate people not necessarily on or near the main campus. I looked into Notre Dame, Northwestern, and the University of Illinois. Most of my information came from the school or friends who had attended their programs. I liked the University of Illinois for the fact that I was in driving distance to the Champaign campus and could still have the face-to-face with students and professors. If I did not want to go to the satellite site, I was also able to go to the main campus. I was impressed with the program administrators, their backgrounds, and the well-recognized and proven faculty. I was impressed with the style, setup and warmth of the program.

Any thoughts on why we don't seem to hear as much about the EMBA as we do about the regular MBA, and where did you turn for information?

Correct, the EMBA is not well known. Most people who attend business school are right out of school. The EMBA's focus is not people who have been out of school for two or three years. It is marketed to people who have been in the workplace for several years, and getting to them is sometimes a hard reach. This is hard group to market to. They are not found in job fairs but in corporate offices. They are not walking through a university campus but a corporate campus. The EMBA must get out to social organizations, professional organizations, etc. Marketing the EMBA through the school is not the way to go. Good, formalized information on the EMBA is not readily available, and what is available cannot compete with the extent of literature for the traditional MBA.

What were the biggest challenges while in school, working, and with your family?

Work was the biggest challenge, because finding a free moment to talk to a classmate was always difficult. When one classmate had a free moment, he would call only to find it hard for the person on the other line to talk. Coordinating with classmates during the workday to go over a test was simply difficult. Scheduling time was difficult because, with four to five people in a study group, it was not easy to coordinate time for everyone to meet. My study group worked a lot by phone, because of distance and timing, and this was a bit hard to manage sometimes. Some people were out of town or had late meetings, etc. We often tried to coordinate before we left class.

Personal life was bit easier because I don't have children, but do have two senior parents at home and a husband. I saw other classmates with children struggle a bit more to coordinate and manage school, family, and work. Everyone has to be on-board. There will come moments when you get up from the dinner table and make it clear it's time to study when people around the table had included you in their evening plans. It's an adjustment when you can't do the things you like at night or on the weekends due to school. You have to be willing to make those adjustments prior to going into the program. You must sit down and discuss this commitment with your family, husband, children, and so on. You need their buy-in because there will be times when you miss events and family affairs, but the upside is you are done in two years.

What sorts of tricks or rituals did you employ to get through the EMBA?

If I was at work and had homework to do, I would not come home until my schoolwork was done. If I came home, the schoolwork would not get done. It was a lot harder to hide at home. Since I live nearby, I would shut my office door at 5 P.M. and study till 9 P.M. if I had to. This was the best way to complete homework. I employed the same strategy in law school. My advice is to remove yourself from distracting environments, which usually means that home is not the place to get your work done. You shouldn't do this every night, but devote a good solid four or five hours to study which then frees up time later in the week to be with your family and friends. I would put a calendar together and coordinate with my husband. When I knew he was working late, I would stay at work late and study. We would try to match our schedules. Also, don't give up the things that you would use to reduce stress. If you are a runner, keep running. If you work out: don't stop. Try to maintain the stability and familiarity of your life prior to the EMBA, otherwise your life will be turned upside down. I was a runner and kept my routine throughout school. There were a few things I refused to cut out that were important to me like exercising, and I built a routine that included my daily dose of running on pavement or on a treadmill.

On average how much homework did you have?

Each day I was always working on something for school, but this may have been less than an hour like an edit of a draft of a paper, or making some phone calls, or reading a chapter. On certain days I would devote a solid four to five hours studying, but every day you'll end up doing something school-related. Sunday afternoon was big study day for most people. On a weekly basis, I easily studied between fifteen and twenty hours.

There were two other lawyers in my class, one in my study group, neither of whom practiced law. Both had been out of the legal profession for a long time.

Do you have any complaints about the experience? Did anything not work well?

Our program created study groups based on proximity to each other. This makes sense but does not always work well if not everyone gets along. Driving distance should not really be a factor, because it does not address the balance or mix of skills for the group.

The worst thing is to mix people with different work ethics and life perspectives, because it creates a problem not just for the party but the entire study group. The downside of this is it can cause a lot more stress and tension in an already tense and stressful environment. A study group that does not mesh is not good. One person in my group had a habit of starting projects on Thursday before Friday class, and this was the worse approach for me.

How did you find the faculty?

I thought they were exceptional. Many were proven professionals with real work experience, while others were thought leaders in academia with great research credentials. Our professors were so well versed in current events, on top of new developments in the business world, we were constantly in touch with world events, and I also felt we functioned as a global business program. We tied classes together well with current events.

I understand the University of Illinois offers student support through tutoring, work support, and other administrative assistance. How did this help you?

The program offered a range of administrative and academic support while we were away from work and in class. They had a fax machine, printers, Internet access, etc., and all were readily available with staff willing to assist while we were in class. We were also assigned teaching assistants, and they would meet before, during, and after class if necessary. Let me tell you there were some classes that called for TAs. We needed them, and they were available. Granted, I did not use TAs until well into the program.

Can you describe a personal experience in the program or how the program has advanced your career?

One of the best parts of the whole program was the international section. To me the international business component was a huge selling point of the program. Prior to heading to Europe, we had a class that prepared us for the numerous meetings and reviewed and rehearsed the study questions with corporate executives. We worked so hard leading up to the trip and during the trip: jumping from one boardroom to the next, one factory floor to the next or over to government offices.

Trust me, the trip to Europe was not a vacation, a boondoggle. It was a hands-on trip, walking through the factories at Volkswagen and talking to corporate heads of Lufthansa; meeting with corporate officials of IBM and P&G in Frankfurt, Germany. Still to this day we marvel over what we saw and were able to accomplish. The trip exposed us to the bare roots of industry and of specific companies. Studying real business cases in the actual company being affected opens your eyes and mind. The EMBA program truly is a hands-on experience into the corporate world in Europe.

What did you go through to get corporate sponsorship, considering you are a lawyer?

My employer agreed to pay no matter whether it was an MBA or EMBA, although I had to fight hard to get HR to approve a lawyer for an MBA. I had to put together a huge presentation on why it made sense in my current position. They did end up paying for it. Some of my classmates report that their corporate pushed them toward the EMBA over the MBA, possibly because of timing and exceptional delivery of education.

Any final thoughts you would like to share about your experience in the EMBA?

The ages ranged from twenty-eight to early fifties, but I can see why the program is not for everyone. It is clear to me that the older students were the ones well prepared. They were committed, dedicated students, and they clearly had the drive, motivation, and overall desire to carry on this challenging two years of work and school. As a lawyer, what I appreciated in the program was the life experiences and work experiences I heard from my classmates. When someone is working for fifteen years, this person possesses a world of practical experience that just makes the classroom experience much richer. You will not hear these stories from someone who graduated from college and decided to go back to school a few years later.

If I am able to say the following without getting in trouble or be ridiculed, the EMBA was so much fun. It was such a worthwhile experience. If you can call b-school fun, trust me the experience was a lot more fun than law school.

Questions for lawyers to consider when evaluating EMBA programs:

- Where do I go next after achieving the MBA?
- How many lawyers are enrolled in the existing EMBA class?
- How many members of the faculty are practicing lawyers or come from the law school?
- How much time must I be away from the practice?
- Can I speak to a graduate who is also a practicing lawyer?

CHAPTER 8

The Admissions Process

8.1. The Career Record

> The ideal candidate is a critical thinker, a strong
> communicator, a motivator, and demonstrates the
> collegiality of a team player but can also act and think
> independently. The candidate should have charisma,
> style, leadership, and uniqueness necessary to stand
> out. The person will have experienced success as well
> as failure and knows and understands both winning
> and losing.
>
> —NYU EMBA Program Administrator

When considering an application for acceptance into the traditional
MBA program, admissions officers place strong emphasis on
undergraduate grades, overall GPA, type of major, class rank, and
GMAT scores. These quantifiable and very recent attributes serve as
an objective comparison among applicants. Once the record is set,
there is not much one can do to influence the application process
beyond the recommendations, essays, and (for some schools) the
interview. Acceptance into the Executive MBA program also requires
the undergraduate degree, grades, and GMAT scores. However, less
emphasis is placed on these aspects, and more emphasis is placed in
areas meant to reflect personal and professional attributes as an adult.

These attributes tend to be applicant's control and best reflect where he is today and not as he once was during those years in college a decade or more ago. The overall package presented is best described as each applicant's *career record*.

New to GMAT: One less essay and one new
section called Integrated Reasoning.
With the data given, let's see how well
you connect the dots.

The career record is an aggregation of professional and personal history summarized in a series of steps that include essays, interviews, evaluations, and the business school application. The career record best represents a total picture of a working professional applying to an EMBA program. Each component of the career record deserves careful attention, and no part should be treated as less import than the next, although admissions officers agree that certain aspects of the career record receive more weight than others, as illustrated in the pie chart below.

Career Record

- Work history,
- Written essays,
- Evaluations,
- Interviews,
- Academic transcript,
- GMAT scores.

The Career
Record

Work History	23%
Written Essays	19%
Evaluations	21%
Interviews	23%
Academic Transcript	7%
GMAT Scores	7%
	100%

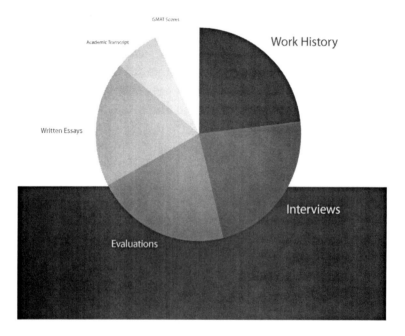

As you will see, if an applicant approaches the entire admissions process from the perspective of the career record, the process works very much in favor of the applicant. As most applicants are in their thirties, their careers are still in an early stage, and much of the story of their careers remains unwritten. What applicants will write about what they have already done will be what they feel is most relevant and, of course, puts them in the most favorable light. Admissions officers repeatedly express the desire to look for reasons to admit candidates not reject them, so applicants should not be discouraged by bad grades or test scores that would prevent applying for an EMBA placement.

Academic achievement vs. work achievement: Over the years business schools have concluded that there is a weak correlation between academic success and business success.

8.2. The Admissions Process

Applicants should follow these general steps as a guide through the entire application process:

- Begin by narrowing the number of schools. Gather information about the school on its website, from brochures, and from the appendix of this book. If possible, attend an open house.
- The program descriptions and associated literature can help capture the feeling or mission of the program. Give consideration to what image the program is trying to convey and how it goes about doing it. Does the program have a quantitative focus, a leadership focus, a diversity focus, a global focus?
- At the open house—most likely held in the evening or on a weekend—administrators, professors, and current students will highlight program particulars and address your questions and concerns.
- At the reception listen to what other prospective students have to say, particularly about other open houses they may have attended. Current EMBA students will be on hand; a private conversation can be very helpful.
- Meet administrators for an informal, preliminary review to discuss the program further, address issues concerning time

away from work, sponsorship, and travel. This book offers many helpful questions at the end of each chapter to prepare you for the meeting. At this exchange, applicants who are deciding whether to apply need not try to sell themselves.

- It is important to be open and receptive to advice including the recommendation to postpone the application for whatever reason or to consider the full-time program or another business school's EMBA program that is closer to your strengths.

- Request the opportunity to observe a class. When you attend class, speak to students about the pros and cons of the program. Discuss how the classroom and workload affects personal and professional life. Sit in on some classes and get a sense of how various programs differ.

- Complete the application. The application will include biographical data, at least two essays, at least two professional evaluations, undergraduate school transcript, a resume, a corporate table of organization identifying the applicant's position in the organization, a proof of sponsorship form—if required, and GMAT scores. An interview is usually scheduled after the school receives the application.

- At the formal interview it is now time to sell yourself. It is important to highlight all the positives you learned while investigating the program. Applicants should demonstrate a genuine interest in the program and the people who represent the program. Universities like to publish high attendance rates of those they accept, so they should feel confident that an offer made becomes an offer accepted.

Timing

Submit the application as early as possible as most schools have rolling admissions. The sooner the application is received, the sooner the school will provide notification of their decision. With rolling admission, applicants can expect notification within four to six weeks.

Electronic applications

Read the application instructions carefully. The electronic application reduces paperwork, but complete the application carefully and be sure to print a copy, if that is at all possible. You will have to mail your undergraduate transcript and your evaluations under separate cover.

Deadlines

Meet all application deadlines. Be sure to include the application fee, take the GMAT exam on the dates the school recommends, and play by their rules for scheduling interviews.

Review committee

Admissions officers consist of program administrators and selected faculty as well as members of the advisory board. Each member of the committee measures your application against a set of criteria defined by your career record, the committee's expectations, and, of course, other applicants.

8.3. Work History: Experience Matters

A major corporate complaint, heard even more frequently during times of budgetary constraint, concerns justifying the high five—and six-figure salaries of inexperienced, newly-minted MBA graduates. Business schools mistakenly inflate graduate salary expectations. Students leave campus with little practical experience to offer and expect six figure salaries. Hiring managers increasingly grow frustrated with these attitudes and prefer employees who can bring practical, valuable experience to the company, not just a diploma.

Experience matters according to corporate recruiters, career counselors, and even business schools. By definition, the Executive MBA requires a minimum of seven years work experience, preferably in a managerial role. Throughout the EMBA application process from writing the essays to interviews and employer evaluations, the applicants are expected to provide intimate details describing their work history. It is essential to make admissions officers feel confident that the prospective student will nicely round out the classroom environment with a unique set of skills and work experiences to share with fellow classmates.

Experience matters for a whole host of reasons not withstanding the absolute value of the education. For example, two years' experience working for a union would probably enable an applicant to address labor-relation issues better than any single course in business school. The working world is a wonderful introduction to both business theory and practice, although the theory may not be as apparent or understood. Real-life experience is the textbook that students take with them to class: The bigger the book, the more prepared for classes, exams, and projects.

Administrators encourage applicants to discuss international travel and overseas experience working with people of different cultures. This is especially true for programs with an international focus. Language skills should be clearly noted on the application and during interviews, as they attest to the worldliness of the candidate. When describing your work history, highlight your ability to work in groups and delegate responsibilities. Prove your organizational skills and illustrate your leadership abilities through essays and interviews. Describe how you thrive in team environments and respond to challenging situations. Emphasize your strengths and the lessons learned during good and bad times throughout your career.

Experience also means professional education. Attending professional conferences or achieving special certifications adds experience as a working professional. Be sure to include any of the following:

- Attended training programs and conferences.
- Taken graduate courses,
- Earned certifications like CPA, CFA, CHA,

- Written business plans and competitive analyses,
- Lectured to graduate students and professionals,
- Published articles or books.

While administrators advise applicants to discuss their accomplishments openly, they also know that life is paved with uncertainty. Applicants should take the time to consider thoughtfully some challenges faced on the job and be prepared to articulate lessons learned from overcoming these challenges. In fact, failures and disappointments are part of reality and need to be confronted. A bankruptcy, layoff, or dissolution can offer substantive insight into professional experience that demonstrates how you handle adversity. Overcoming adversity and moving onto the next big thing makes an applicant a more rounded person and demonstrates maturity and perseverance.

8.4. The Interview

An interview is essential. A face-to-face rather than a phone interview is strongly encouraged. The interview can last for more than an hour in either a one-on-one or panel format. The applicant will be asked a broad range of questions that pertain to professional capabilities and ambitions. It is a good idea to sketch out a five-year plan for after graduation prior to the interview. Some important considerations for preparation include professional attire, understanding the audience, having some working knowledge about what the interviewers want from a candidate, and being able to articulate achievements clearly. Interviewees should have their resume available for reference. Note taking during the interview is acceptable. Treat the interview as if it were a high profile meeting.

Why are manhole covers round? Interviewers may want to explore the candidate's thinking process and ability to formulate a cogent response rather than necessarily provide the right response.

Admissions officers are interested in the whole person. They will ask a series of getting-to-know-you questions such as what is important in life outside of work and how you spend your time when you are not working. Candidates should also feel free to discuss personal issues that are relevant including religion, family, and volunteer work. Share your interest in hobbies. Are you a marathoner? Do you play a musical instrument? If a particular program has an international focus, describe your international experience, familial roots, and languages spoken.

Sounds like the working world: An admission advisor was overheard saying: "We won't care which school you attended as an undergraduate or that you have perfect GMAT scores. We don't want boring people in the program. We want interesting people that can make the class as enriching as possible."

Applicants will want to ask questions in return but should avoid asking questions that can be answered in the school's literature. Taking the lead from comments made by the interviewer, you can feel free to continue discussion on a given topic. Keep the conversation interesting and on a professional level.

Interview Discussion Points:

- Work experience,
- Conflict resolution and problem solving,
- Relationship with peers and superiors,
- Personal successes and failures,
- Professional successes and failures,
- Ability to manage change,
- Extracurricular activities: volunteer work, hobbies, and other personal and professional accomplishments.

Sample Interview Questions:

- Tell me about yourself, or how would you describe yourself.
- Why have you chosen this particular program?
- What are your interests outside of work?
- What are your plans after graduation?
- Where do you see yourself in five years? ten years?
- What are you looking for in the Executive MBA?
- What are your greatest strengths/weaknesses?
- Who recommended our program to you?
- What would you do next year if you do not get accepted into business school?
- Why should I choose you over another applicant?
- What questions do you have for me about the program?
- What do you do in your spare time? Hobbies? Last book read for pleasure?
- Tell me about your most challenging experience at your company and what you learned from it.
- Tell me about a stressful experience and how you coped with it.
- How would you describe your personal philosophy?
- What is the biggest failure you've had to deal with?
- What have your supervisors criticized most about your performance?
- If you could change one thing about your personality with a snap of your fingers, what would it be?
- Tell me about your most satisfying experience at your company.
- Tell me about an experience working with a difficult colleague.
- Tell us about an ethical business situation you faced.

Sample questions to the interviewer

- Are there any major changes anticipated at the school for the upcoming year?
- What industries do graduates come from?

- What do you consider the greatest strengths and weaknesses of the program?
- How would you describe the EMBA teaching methods?
- What is the percentage of students who change careers after graduation?

It never hurts: Send a note of thanks to the people you met, especially to those at programs under serious consideration.

8.5. Professional Evaluation

Letters of recommendation or evaluations speak critically to professional qualifications, maturity, and burgeoning managerial skills. If a colleague or superior cannot speak confidently about an employee's abilities and provide the needed backing to support the application, the applicant should reconsider applying or look elsewhere for support. Not only must the applicant feel prepared for matriculation, but colleagues must feel the same way about the applicant. It is important to demonstrate to business schools that you are ready, not only in your opinion but also in the opinion of your superiors. A weak employer evaluation or letter of recommendation will sink the entire application.

The EMBA application includes evaluation forms that the people you select for evaluation must complete. Generally two independent evaluations are required. They can be in the form of a letter of recommendation, an evaluation form, or both. The evaluation form consists of a table addressing a range of abilities meant to measure your overall intellect and skills. The evaluator is asked to rate you on a scale of 1-5 on writing, analytics, teamwork, competence, and ability to manage work and school.

If only the form and not a letter of recommendation is requested in the application, a 200- to 300-word essay by the evaluator explaining how the program will benefit from your attendance will be looked upon favorably by admissions. If a letter of recommendation is required, it usually consists of a set of questions. Here is a sample of these questions.

- How long have you known the applicant and in what capacity?
- In your opinion, what is the candidate's motivation and suitability for a career in management? Comment on both strengths and weaknesses.
- How have the applicant's professional responsibilities changed during the time that you have known him/her?
- Please provide any comments regarding the applicant's aptitude for graduate work and a career in management.

Select someone who can speak about your business and strategic acumen. Consider a counterpart who has seen your growth and can speak first-hand regarding your influence at the company. If that person can attest to your successes and failures, that can be extremely helpful.

It is private: Provide evaluators with a form and return-stamped envelope. You are not entitled to review what was written by your evaluators, unless they offer to share that information.

A Closer Look at the Evaluation Form

The evaluation form includes a set of questions that address your ability to complete a master of business administration degree while working full-time. You are judged from "exceptional" to "poor" on such characteristics as maturity, leadership, analytical skills, communication, organizational, and interpersonal skills.

Choose Your Evaluators Wisely

The evaluation is a critical piece of your career record. It gets to the heart of your professionalism and core capabilities in the eyes of those who work and evaluate you on a daily basis. Their evaluation of you will significantly influence the review committee. Of course, the process is slightly biased, as you will seek evaluations from those people who you feel will best fulfill the duty. You will select people best able to appreciate and articulate your strengths effectively. They must rate your skills critically and stand by their recommendation for your inclusion into the program.

Whom to ask for a recommendation: A close boss or peer is always helpful. Former colleagues and clients, past or present, are other suggestions. Even consider people you may have come in contact with over the years while serving on the board of a charity, hospital, or university.

It is critical to seek evaluations from colleagues who are willing to devote the time and are sensitive to the application due date. People with impressive credentials who are not necessarily familiar with the candidate are not good people to solicit. Admissions officers frown on these types of high-profile reviews and will remark on this. At the same time, your evaluators should know why you want to return to school, what you hope to gain from the education, and how your education will benefit the company.

For your supervisor, address how you plan to make up for missed work and deal with work emergencies during class time. Tell your supervisor how you feel about this exciting opportunity and how his or her input in the evaluation is so critical for acceptance. Make your intentions known to colleagues, as they will be the ones putting out the fires while you sit in class or travel overseas. Demonstrate your gratitude for the time and effort spent on the evaluation with a nice gift for helping you get into business school.

8.6. The Essay

The essay is an opportunity not only to demonstrate strong writing skills but also to bring out personal depth as a constructive thinker. It also allows admissions officers to become acquainted with the applicant as a person. It is important to write relevant, concise, and informative essays that highlight aspects of your character that reflect on you both as a person and as a professional.

You are required to complete one to three essays. The essay questions should be read carefully to determine which responses will result in the strongest return. The exercise is an important opportunity to impress your readers about your career history—highlighted and punctuated by real-life examples of growth and overcoming challenges. At the same time, it is an important opportunity to elaborate on areas that you feel may be weak in your application.

The Four Important Steps to Writing a Strong Essay:

1. Relevant Content

- Consider the topic content carefully.
- Use your resume to identify salient points.
- Create an outline with examples specifically relating to the core subject that addresses the essay question.

2. Professional Style and Mechanics

- Write short, declarative sentences.
- Edit the resulting essay carefully (multiple drafts are common).
- Review the final product.

A cautionary note: Your essay should reflect the style and mechanics of good English grammar. Avoid a common error of business professionals in using terms, phrases, and jargon that may come naturally to you after years of conditioning at your company.

3. Mark of Distinction

- Humanize the essays. It's okay to be professional while also being self-deprecating.
- Emphasize humility. Learning from peers and taking criticism are qualities that make you a professional. The uniqueness one personifies comes from understatement rather than overstatement.
- Demonstrate that you recognize the quality of the competition even in a situation where you came out on top.

4. Answer the Question

- Zero in on the question, underline the core parts of the essay question, and build a response with supporting data.
- Exercise caution and care. A common complaint from admissions officers when reviewing essays is how careless some applicants can be when it comes to answering the essay question.
- Take the essay seriously. Recognize that the essay is for acceptance in the Executive MBA program and that the essay question should be answered with specificity. Be creative in your thoughts but not in the writing.

Some Pointers from Georgetown

The admissions department of Georgetown University's McDonough School of Business provides some basic pointers about essays. Some of them may seem obvious, but more people overlook them than you might expect.

- Spell-check before submitting an essay.
- Do not abbreviate any acronyms, especially military or government-related ones.
- Address something interesting in your background that is not career-related but which will make you stand out among the applicant pool.

- Make sure that essays reflect the correct name of the school to which you're applying when you use the same essay to apply to multiple schools.
- Avoid generalizations; try to provide specific examples of your accomplishments.
- Adhere to the specified length of the essay.

Sample Essay Questions:

- How are you different from the next applicant? Describe how your experiences in and out of work will enhance the overall classroom experience.
- Why have you chosen to pursue an MBA now, and where do you see yourself five years from now?
- Recall a professional project that you found both challenging and rewarding and in which you take some pride. Describe any concerns that you had in relation to your ability to be successful in this project and how you faced up to the challenge of bringing the project to a successful conclusion.
- Explain why you have decided to apply to our program at this point in your career. How does our program suit your career endeavors and any future goals that you have set for yourself?
- State why you believe the EMBA program would be advantageous to you and your company at this stage in your career. Discuss personal and professional qualities that you feel will contribute to the program. Describe your main qualities as a leader and elaborate on your professional strengths and weaknesses.
- Over the past two years we have seen business leaders indicted and once-mighty companies now in bankruptcy. Have you ever faced an ethical dilemma, and what measures did you take to resolve the issue?
- Is there anything else you would like the admissions committee to know about you?

Essay #1: Question and Sample Response

- Describe a challenging professional experience that makes you prepared to accept increasing challenges in your profession.

Essay Response:

Terminating the existence of a company through a vote to dissolve is an unpleasant experience, as I learned firsthand after four years of hard work as CEO of a technology company. The decision to dissolve came 24 hours after failing to secure a needed final round of venture capital. The board called for a non-judicial dissolution: termination through vote by shareholders, as called for in the corporate by-laws. Most corporate dissolutions are non-judicial (not involving a court), unless fraud was involved. Since I never went through this before, I had no idea what to expect. I soon learned that the dissolution process grows in complexity with legal and tax requirements.

Being charged with carrying out the dissolution process requires a team of experts including lawyers, accountants, board members, directors, and key employees. Ultimately, the minutiae involved with completing the process fell on the shoulders of a few unlucky individuals, including myself. Due to the inclement mortgage meltdown so many companies were on the verge of collapse many more dissolution filings are expected in the coming months. Reflecting on this experience, I realize I learned a great deal and hope never to experience this failure again.

Once the vote to dissolve was affirmed, I formed a working group with input from accountants, lawyers, and the board. Collectively, we wrote a working document that outlined the tasks necessary to complete the dissolution process. The document specified tasks with key assignments, expectations of each working group member, compensation, if we could collect any, and the establishment of deadlines in order to keep the process moving forward. We gave ourselves twenty-five days.

Forming the Working Group

It is important to be surrounded by mature, professional adults, each with thick skin willing to face the un-pleasantries ranging from angry creditors to negotiating with unsavory liquidators. The working group must be trustworthy and reliable, because it is now operating a cash business as assets are sold and critical schedules are met. I was very proud of the people on my team for their hard work and dedication to bringing this painful experience to closure. Unfortunately, it is essential to take measures to avoid theft or fraud. I read a report in the *Wall Street Journal* about employees of a failed business reportedly taking thousands of dollars worth of hardware after receiving notice that their company would be ceasing operations. I had to be extra cautious because I needed the assets to compensate both my working group, pay creditors, and remain above board under and maintain our pride.

We issued a corporate policy about corporate theft to all sixty employees on the same day of the announcement to dissolve. However, we didn't want to take any chances. So, in the days leading up to this announcement, we surreptitiously took inventory and where we felt it necessary, inconspicuously removed valuable assets. The profile of our working group included persons knowledgeable with the internal accounting system, aging summaries, and banking records. So, it was important that the team knew the passwords and account tracking numbers and had familiarity with these systems. We maintained the policy of always having a trustworthy key person on hand These systems generate a wide range of extremely valuable reports from account/receivables to creditor aging reports. Equally valuable is the capability to produce collection sheets, mail merges, and various other administrative reports that can save enormous amounts of time and money, facilitating communication with creditors and shareholders. I also called the bank to determine who outside the team had access to the accounts and blocked them. I had to collect all checkbooks and restrict check-writing privileges to a key person in the working group.

Posting Legal Notices

We posted legal notices to the state, the public and any interested parties overseas. In New York, a Certificate of Dissolution must be filed with the New York State Department and be accompanied with a statement from the tax commission. The fee was $25 paid by a personal check. Our general counsel handled the processing. Once filed, this act sets in motion the official legal dissolution process.

State law requires public notification in the county of the corporation. A public announcement in the form of a legal notice must appear at least twice over a two-week period in a newspaper of "considerable circulation" as I read in the fine print of the company by-laws. Although state laws vary on this subject, a company may be required to post a notice in every area where a corporate office is located. Since we held offices in Dublin and Paris, international law required overseas notices in their local newspapers.

Dealing with Shareholders and Creditors

The most difficult component of this process was informing the remaining shareholders and creditors of the dissolution directly. My general counsel prepared notices to shareholders and creditors, and we distributed them by mail. I had to notify some in person. Many friends and family were terrible disappointed, if not financially ruined.

Sadly the situation with angry creditors, many of whom became friends over the years, turned ugly. On a number of occasions we felt harassed, bullied, and uncomfortable dealing with them. The best communication method, I quickly learned, was to encourage this irate group to submit all questions, comments or complaints in writing. I set up a forwarding address for all communications, and we never gave out our home phone numbers or home addresses.

Handling the Liquidation

Technology changes rapidly, and at that time the market was saturated with computer hardware and office equipment. One company reportedly fetched a Dell 6900 server for $1,500 at auction. We purchased a similar system two years ago for $40,000. Depreciation on computer equipment is nearly 100 percent at the end of eighteen months. I was deeply concerned at how I would be able to compensate my team for their efforts. In the end we broke even, thankfully.

Liquidating assets was highly stressful. Buyers get impatient, sometimes nasty and can take advantage of your weakened bargaining position. However, money collected means money to pay down credit obligations. I kept a journal listing each item, the final sale price, and the party to whom it was sold. Sale of assets has obvious tax and legal implications, and the board and accountants expected a full report.

Heading Home

On the twenty-fifth day of this process I presented the board with a document of all working group activities. This report was my last formal contact with all board members. I kept my head held high as I presented a three-page document describing the remnants of the company and the performance of these final days. Nobody was happy with the ultimate demise of the company, and some were understandably bitter after losing significant investments. But I stood with pride in front of this committee and concluded with a final word of thanks to each and everyone one of them. I expressed my deep appreciation and gratitude for their unyielding support over the past four years.

My dreams of success have been delayed. The subway is full of people with similar stories, some who lost more and some who lost less. What I lost in money I gained in knowledge. The short subway ride home was just long enough to start thinking about my next business plan.

Essay Critique:

Pros

- Clearly states a significant, challenging problem. Speaks with enormous confidence and experience;
- Addresses a professional failure that turned into an terrific learning experience;
- Demonstrates corporate leadership and effectiveness;
- Highlights seniority and delegation capability;
- Narrative includes real world examples intertwined with legal and financial theory and concepts;
- Good use of bullets to lay out the narrative;
- Able to humanize an incredibly difficult professional and personal experience;
- Humble, credible, and likeable character and well written Document.

Cons

- Reads very much like a textbook description of how to dissolve a corporation—what pre-existing knowledge did this person turn to and build upon to help carry this procedure forward?
- Does not directly address the question of how could the lessons learned add value to the next step in a greater role.
- In this case, the person has already reached senior level.
- What does "companies on the verge of collapse, exacerbated by the tragic events of September 11, 2001" have to do with the experience? Writer gets tangential
- Overkill on insignificant details like posting legal notices— unnecessary information

Essay #2: Question with Sample Response:

- The ability to work in a team environment is a crucial component of our program and to most business careers. For this essay you are to place yourself in a hypothetical group whose assignment is to submit a final report and present a group project to the class. What strengths will you bring to the group? What weaknesses will the group help you to overcome?

Essay Response:

The end of the semester is approaching and the final project has been assigned in our business ethics class. Working in groups of four, we are to demonstrate how corporate corruption has impacted the investment community within the past year and instigate the latest financial meltdown. When working in a group, each individual has certain strengths to contribute to the project and certain weaknesses that the group effort should be designed to overcome. I will discuss mine.

Each member of the group has been assigned to report on an area of the project. Team member 1 will document how investor sentiment has changed over the course of the year since corporate corruption has been reported in the media. Team member 2 will analyze the changes investors are making with their portfolios. Team member 3 will investigate how companies are changing their corporate policies and practices to meet new compliance requirements. As the final member of team, I will present a case study of several companies, each of which has been found guilty of misconduct and a violation of ethical practices. Each study will involve a complete analysis of the company's actions after it was charged.

My investigative skills and my knowledge in using technology efficiently will enable me to uncover specific information quickly. My determination will help keep the group focused through tense times. For example, one of my supervisors at Barclay's suddenly fell ill, and I was assigned to handle the bulk of her projects. I had to constantly remain focused, especially when I had to perform on the job in stressful circumstances. Through diligence, the projects continued successfully. My determination paid off.

My understanding of the securities industry and keen analytical sense will prove invaluable when I review how a company I am researching reallocated its assets and liabilities. I have been credited by my co-workers as having a positive attitude and strong interpersonal skills. These traits will help facilitate my interaction with my team when we are under pressure to finish the project productively and on schedule. I will also be able to resolve conflicts among my team members and make sure we are working in unison. My leadership ability will prove useful if my colleagues should need guidance on the project or an unrelated issue.

My ability to work under pressure will be constructive in times when unexpected events should occur (and they always do). Just such an instance occurred when one of my associates informed me that he had entered an incorrect order for a client; the number of shares exceeded the client's request. I immediately took the appropriate steps to cancel and correct the trade without inconveniencing the client. I recall when I first began in banking I had committed a similar mistake. Although my boss chastised me, he did express his gratitude for how I was able to remedy the situation without harm. In this case, my underling has not made an effort to find a solution nor address any solutions. I will be sure to speak with him directly about this in the upcoming review.

As a closet perfectionist, I sometimes fixate on a minor flaw, reluctant to move on until I am positive that my work is perfect. Most of the work that I do involves managing a team responsible for processing time-sensitive banking transactions and financial decisions. While I have always met deadlines, my constant review for perfection causes me to sometimes belabor a point. At Barclay's one of my responsibilities was to ensure that all the securities information was correct. I checked and rechecked reports, and while my superiors commended me for the errors I had uncovered, I felt that I could have moved faster if I were not as meticulous. Moreover, while I can be trusted to complete my project for the team, I am sometimes uncomfortable when relying on others to do the same and tend to want to oversee others' efforts myself. In my past group work on various projects I was never actually disappointed by a group member, and I know that by continuing to work in groups with highly astute individuals I will learn to be more trusting and overcome this flaw.

It is important for me to receive an education that not only disseminates knowledge but also focuses on the dynamics of maximizing the practical application of this knowledge in the corporate arena. I believe team interaction is an integral part of the business world. I am positive that my work ethic and attributes mentioned above will make me an essential part of any team. I want to continue my education at the university because I strongly believe that attending through the Executive MBA program ideally incorporates the importance of team dynamics as an integral part of its educational philosophy.

Essay Critique:

Pros

- Addresses the question,
- Integrates practical business experience into the response,
- Draws narrative back to focus on the value of the education from specific university,
- Identifies personal habits that the author describes as weaknesses like a "closet perfectionist",
- Comes across professionally as the mess-up results in repair through constructive feedback,
- Narrative includes real world examples and practical operational experience.

Cons

- No need to repeat the question as done in first paragraph,
- In the third paragraph, why so confident the group will respond to efforts? Writer has not established such credibility for leadership.
- Improve the general flow of the document—it could be tightened.

- Important thoughts are scattered. For example, in the first paragraph, I expected the applicant to address his own actions as stated in the closing remark.
- Incomplete chronology—not clear what is present and what is past: He goes from describing himself as a banker managing a team to being a front-line staff person.
- Needs better transitions between stating his qualities and giving work-related examples that demonstrate those qualities.
- Does not appear to delegate well—is the applicant capable of calling for assistance and seeking team support?

8.7. The GMAT

According to the Graduate Management Admissions Council (GMAC), approximately a quarter of a million GMAT tests are administered each year throughout the world. Up to one-quarter of these tests are from repeat test takers who, according to GMAC, on average add no more than 30 points to their score. GMAT scores are used by nearly 1,300 graduate management programs throughout the globe and an estimated 900 schools require GMAT scores from their applicants.

According to GMAC, the GMAT serves as a requirement for the following reasons:

- Measures one's verbal, mathematical, and analytical writing skills;
- Predicts performance in the first year of business school;
- Compares one applicant to the next through an unbiased, quantitative measurement;
- Maintains business school accreditation.

Most test takers will add to the list "increased anxiety, unnecessarily." Business school teaches the student discipline, teamwork, analysis, evaluation, and corroboration. These principles are consistent with the professional world. The GMAT exam is individualized and a race against the clock. The test ignores realities of the business world. Regardless of the merits, or lack thereof, the GMAT remains a requirement that must be taken seriously.

> "The admissions process for EMBA programs has already become more simplified as many institutions are dropping the GMAT requirement. Increasingly, academic institutions take the view that, if a competing school in their market drops the GMAT requirement, they have to eliminate it as well in order to compete for students. We at Fordham's EMBA Program require the GMAT for admissions and will continue to do so."
>
> —Dr. Francis Petit, Associate Dean, and Mary Kate Donato, Director, Fordham University Graduate School of Business

The good news is that behind closed doors most EMBA administrators will admit that the GMAT receives low attention in the process for acceptance. Some people are exceptional test takers, others are not. Your career record is what will ultimately influence your acceptance into a program.

Obviously, scoring high on the GMAT can help strengthen your career record. Applicants are encouraged to do their best, take a few practice exams, and even consider a prep course. Taking the exam seriously and preparing as best as possible serves a number of other important purposes:

1. Test scores may be used as a criterion at your company in the competition for corporate sponsorship and in some cases as a criterion for how much funding you get from your employer.
2. Good test scores may tip the hand in your favor, if you are tied with another comparable applicant.
3. The test may serve as a benchmark for improvement. Based on the scores, consider voluntarily taking one or more classes to brush up on writing or math skills. Admissions officers will look favorably at the initiative and motivation.

4. Test preparation sets the tone for disciplined study habits prior to returning to school. A prep course can help instill good study habits.

For additional questions concerning taking the GMAT, please refer to the FAQs in the Appendix.

Interview with Dr. Francis Petit, Associate Dean, Fordham University

What do you look for in an EMBA applicant?

At Fordham, we would look at the level of work experience of each applicant. How many years of experience do they have in each position and have they grown professionally in each of those positions.

They do not have to be at a certain level like CEO or VP, but we do look at a set amount of work experience. Our essays address the growth issues, and we expect thoughtful consideration on professional growth so we look at their essays in great detail. We also want to understand why they want to come to Fordham University. We also look at their goals short term and long term to see how these goals would apply to Fordham's Executive MBA program and how the program would help assist in achieving those goals.

Tell me more about what you look for in the essay.

In our essay questions we try to see what led them to where they are now in their career and lives. Then we try to identify why they feel Fordham's EMBA is the best fit. Maybe it's the weekend format or the potential international residency or specific faculty. We like to see specific things about the program that attracts the candidate. Not just saying the curriculum is outstanding, we are not interested in the generic but want to read about specific characteristics of the program that best fits their career life-long goals.

Not only do we want to make sure we want the candidate, but we want to make sure they want Fordham's program. We also want to be sure that whatever they want from the program is something that Fordham can deliver. It has to be a match on both sides.

Describe the ideal EMBA candidate.

The ideal candidate is someone with at least seven years or more of work experience. Significant management responsibilities are certainly a plus. Company sponsorship would be great although there seems to be less of that these days and many people are willing to pay out of pocket to attend these programs. We also want to see someone who really wants the degree, the program, and all that it has to offer. We saw EMBA enrollment surging during good years and less so during the economic slowdown when there is less financial sponsorship available. The lack of sponsorship matters. However, even during this uncertain economy, prospective students, even if they are not sponsored, are willing to self-sponsor themselves for the EMBA. They want the EMBA, and they want it now.

Why would a university offer the EMBA, since many do not?

There are some significant reasons to offer the EMBA. Generically speaking, universities offer the EMBA because it serves a particular market, more specifically the higher level executive; a gap in the delivery of education to certain populations. Because of travel schedules or family, not everybody can go to class at night. Not everybody can drop out of the workforce and go full-time, either. The EMBA definitely serves a population who want the convenience as well.

It is also great for the university. It helps the university create contacts with the corporate world, through the student and the employer. The spillover into other opportunities includes developing non-degreed programs and custom, specific corporate programs.

Why do business schools not offer the EMBA?

Universities have limited resources. Like starting a business, you have to put a lot of resources in at the beginning to get the program going, and some schools are not in a position to do that. Also, it depends on the market is serves. It may not make sense to have more than one EMBA for a market. The general population may not support two programs.

Fill in the blank: The EMBA does XX really well and XX not well.

For strengths, as opposed to going to an MBA part-time in the evening or attending regular program, the EMBA is cohort-driven, so the strengths include the relationships and camaraderie of the group. The EMBA is a cohort-driven program. Obviously, there is a lot of teamwork as a result. Given that most EMBAs are together for a full one, two, or three days per session, there is definitely a much higher chance for group dynamics to develop. If the group dynamics are done well, they could help sell the program because referrals are a necessary and helpful way to recruit applicants.

Not so well, is that the EMBA is a lot more laborious and there are so many student needs. For example, every student may have a different billing scenario for their sponsoring companies, and managing this can be labor intensive and challenging to meet each need of every student.

Do you see any trends in the delivery of education, particularly as it relates to the EMBA?

I think group work has a big emphasis in the EMBA and will continue to be big. You learn from your faculty but you can learn so much more from your counterparts and from cross industries. I see the use of technology increasing as an instrument to assist in the learning as something that continues to grow. Face-to-face lectures combined with technology represent the best of both worlds.

More universities need to be sensitive to traveling concerns of their students. More travel is geared toward the EMBA. Traveling on study tours is more prevalent in the EMBA program, although MBAs in the traditional program also have travel opportunities.

Can you describe the relationship between the administration and EMBA and administration and faculty?

Of course, the student is the customer. Administration does wear two hats. The EMBA student has needs, and the program director must lead the program. The administrator, dean, and assistant dean have to show leadership. However, they also must know customer relationship management skills with the students and must be seasoned in order to effectively work with the faculty. With respect to the faculty, they are critical to the EMBA. Students expect top-notch faculty who can do very well teaching executive students.

Describe the personal character of the EMBA?

The EMBA student is more catered to than those in the traditional MBA. They are paying a higher price, and thus their expectations are higher by definition. Student complaints about faculty tend to be along the lines of teaching quality, grading, or the submission of grades. Schools select faculty differently. Either the director of the program selects the faculty or the Chair of the department selects the faculty.

What advice would you give a prospective student considering the EMBA?

I would begin by determining if the company will sponsor you. This way you know if you can take the time away from work and are aware of the financing options. In terms of admission standards, there is less emphasis placed on the GMATs, although it is better to have a good GMAT score; but the work experience counts a lot. I would advise this person to pick the programs that he or she likes. Certainly develop relationships with the key people in the program, and let them know that you are very interested.

Some programs are growing; Columbia started two new programs, one with LBS and one with Berkeley, and that means a lot of seats to fill. Start with support from the office, and see what's out there.

Say you have a candidate who is not strong enough, has borderline work experience, and low GMAT scores, what would you suggest?

The GMAT can always be taken over. Obviously more work experience counts.

The age range of those in the EMBA range has grown. There are younger people getting into good EMBA programs. They are twenty-eight and twenty-nine years old, and the separation between the EMBA and MBA has grown gray. Indicate to the school of choice and your strong interest to attend.

Sponsorship is cyclical with the economy. The better the economy, the more corporate sponsors available. However, even if you are not sponsored by your company, do not let that stop you from considering the EMBA.

Does the EMBA offer a unique opportunity for women?

I think it is always harder for women because maternity issues can hurt women in the job market, unfair as this is. Every school wants to increase the enrollment of women in the school. If a woman goes through the EMBA, chances are she has a young family or no children, or her children are grown up. Increasing the number of women in the workforce as well as their pay is an important societal issue. If financial sponsorship were offered more often and other special funding opportunities were directed at women, you may see the number of women working toward an MBA grow.

As a movement, at what stage is the EMBA?

Schools with EMBAs are still entering the market, and some offer more options. Some may offer a more competitive price. The movement is still growing; it has not reached maturity yet. Many top schools with brand recognition are partnering with schools outside the U.S. to extend the brand within a geographic area and penetrate new markets. Prospective students, especially outside the U.S., are very brand oriented.

CHAPTER 9

Financing the EMBA

9.1. Planning the Investment

As with any investment, planning is important. The entire business school experience can cost an additional several thousand dollars beyond tuition in GMAT preparation fees, application fees, equipment, books, and travel fees. While your employer may generously cover certain fees, the organization may not cover others. So the first step will be to identify all of the associated costs. You will want to determine how much you can handle financially, while relying on other sources of funding to cover the difference.

The Planning the Investment form found in the Appendix outlines many of the fees associated with an Executive MBA program from start to finish. Begin by exploring which schools you want to target and enter their estimates into the form. Then, sit with your employer to determine which fees may be reimbursable.

9.2. Building the Case for Corporate Sponsorship

Having determined that the EMBA as the most appropriate fit for your career, the next step is to pursue corporate sponsorship. The tuition expense of sponsoring the EMBA is the greatest challenge for an employer to buy in to, and this may not be easy. Even with a corporate policy supporting tuition reimbursement, rules can change, particularly during difficult economic periods. Tuition is one of the first items discontinued when a company's revenues begin to fall.

Seeking financial sponsorship may be a challenge (a recent *Wall Street Journal* article noted that only 59% of companies currently offer employees any sort of financial support for education), or it may be warmly welcomed and enthusiastically supported.

Before seeking tuition reimbursement, it is incumbent upon you to review the corporate policy. Quite possibly, the tuition reimbursement policy will not address the Executive MBA specifically but rather either full-time matriculation or the more traditional part-time program. This ambiguity can be an advantage, because there might be sufficient flexibility in the policy to accommodate the EMBA, even though it is not expressly mentioned. After all, is the Executive MBA a part-time or full-time program? Depending on your situation, base your argument for support on the reasons described below.

EMBA is a full-time program. Here's why:

- Graduate in two years much like a full-time program,
- Earn the same number of credits,
- Required to take many of the same core courses,
- The diploma will read "Master of Business Administration."

EMBA is a part-time program. Here's why:

- Classes are held over weekend or evenings,
- Same classes as part-time program,
- Same number of credits,
- Course is completed earlier or, at most, slightly later than a two-year traditional program.

So which is it, full-time or part-time? Several MBA administrators define it as part-time while most EMBA administrators define it as full-time. Naturally, go with the most generous corporate policy accommodating either scenario. Remember, the Executive MBA program usually requires additional fees like overseas travel and the purchase of a laptop, which may not be reimbursable by your employer.

Some policies only reimburse up to a certain number of credits or up to a fixed tuition amount each semester.

Three factors are critical when seeking corporate sponsorship. First, become thoroughly familiar with the benefits policies as written, particularly with regard to what is explicitly excluded. Second, get a good understanding of the degree of flexibility written into the policy to accommodate a variety of programs and circumstances. Third, and perhaps the most critical, stay sensitive to the personalities of those managers from whom you need support and approval. You will need at least one manager to advocate for your support.

Employees may need to educate employers on the benefits of an Executive MBA. Refer to the top-ten case statements in Chapter 6 when pitching sponsorship benefits to your employer.

9.3. Sources of Funding

An Executive MBA program at Ohio University costs above $30,000 in total, while at Columbia University in New York City the costs can reach $150,000. By the way, don't assume that costs at comparable institutions will be the same. While Ohio University's EMBA is among the least expensive, at its sister school, University of Ohio, the total cost is more than two-and-a-half times higher, $79,000. Student loans, personal savings, or corporate sponsorship are means to finance this expensive education. As discussed earlier, corporate support may be limited in what it will and will not cover. Before leaving a current employer for a willing sponsor or cashing personal assets to pay for school, check with human resources regarding corporate loans, scholarships, or employer participation in a corporate sponsorship program.

Public Funding (Student Loans)

To become eligible for student loans, the Free Application for Federal Student Aid (FAFSA) must be completed. FAFSA can be obtained by going to *www.fafsa.org*. The information you provide FASFA is then examined by the federal government to determine a level of financial need. FAFSA then provides a Student Aid Report (SAR), which determines the level of eligibility. Funding eligibility applies to Stafford loans, both subsidized and unsubsidized, and other loans such as the William D. Ford Federal Direct Loan Program and the university-administered Federal Perkins Student Loan. Because you work full-time, eligibility for these loans is based on your income.

Once the FAFSA process is complete, the school will require a financial aid application. Information such as the previous year's IRS 1040 form, financial aid transcripts from schools attended previously, and a photocopy of identification is required. The result of this process is eligibility for unsubsidized Stafford Loans, usually administered through a local lending institution. Unlike undergraduates, graduate students are not eligible for government subsidized loans, which carry a lower interest rate and have other student-friendly features.

Stafford Loans provide up to $20,500 per year. Graduate Stafford loans have a fixed interest rate of 6.8% through 2013. Unsubsidized loans charge interest from the time the loan is disbursed until the loan is repaid in full. The standard repayment term is 10 years, but other options are available. One helpful place to get details about this program is www.staffordloan.com.

As a total of $20,500 per year is not enough for most traditional or Executive MBA programs, other private sources will become essential. Business school loans are available from lending institutions, and most banks offer a low interest educational private loan, though the repayment period may be shorter than it is for a Stafford. Surfing the Internet using a search engine will help identify banks that provide this service.

Special Programs for Veterans (the GI Bill)

Military veterans can also explore possible GI benefit programs. The post-9/11 GI Bill covers graduate degrees as well as tutorial assistance and test reimbursement. GI Bill benefits are based upon the highest in-state tuition charged by a public university in the state where the school you're applying to is located.

The relatively recent Yellow Ribbon program allows schools to expand their financial commitment to veterans by extending education benefits above and beyond those provided by the Montgomery GI Bill. The Yellow Ribbon program is, however, restricted to veterans who served in the armed forces after September 10, 2001. Prospective students who are veterans should check with Veterans Affairs to determine their eligibility for any VA support program. More information is available at www.gibill.va.gov/post-911.

Corporate Sponsorship Program

Unique and creative EMBA financing programs enable employers to become actively involved in sponsoring employee education while protecting the corporate investment. These educational financing methods were created to minimize conflict by streamlining the payment process and protecting the interests of all parties: university, employer, and employee.

The financing mechanism through a corporate sponsorship program protects the employer from assuming full risk for loan repayment should the employee decide to leave the current employer during the repayment period. The portability feature of the loan allows the student to transfer the loan to the next employer or accept personal repayment responsibility.

Many universities actively participate in these sponsorship programs and prospective EMBA students are encouraged to inquire at the appropriate student loan office. Also, human resource departments and employee education program administrators can readily determine their level of participation and with which universities they have relationships. Certainly inquire about the possibilities of developing a corporate sponsorship program for the Executive MBA, if none should exist at your place of employment.

Corporate sponsorship programs offer a fair and equitable option for employee education. These types of programs have received positive reviews and strong endorsements from participating universities, corporations, and students. A detailed review of this financing method is discussed in Chapter 6.

Private Funding

Check with school officials for university-based funding opportunities in the form of scholarships, fellowships, and grants. Qualifications range from academic achievement, financial need, veteran status, ethnicity, gender, and even certain disabilities. Admissions Committees select recipients based on academic and professional performance as well as on personal qualities such as leadership, integrity, and community service. Scholarships range in value from set percentage of the total tuition to a fixed amount.

Working full-time should not stop you from pursuing any free money. You probably have a family or mortgage to support, and schools recognize that not every student is an investment banker. School-sponsored scholarships are available at most schools. Georgetown University's McDonough School of Business, for example, offers Diversity Scholarships of $10,000 to $15,000 for qualified applicants.

Individual or corporate donors create "named" scholarships for students meeting a specific need, like the ones listed above, or an area of academic study. Quite possibly, the school to which you apply may offer a scholarship from your employer. These named scholarships may require an additional level of effort on your part such as an additional class, internship, or project in the field. Accessing a scholarship generally requires a formal application, an essay, and an interview with a review committee. If you think you have a chance, meet the eligibility requirements, and can afford to make the time investment, by all means pursue any and all scholarships available.

Tax Deductibility

People who plan to self-finance an EMBA inevitably ponder the issue of tax deductibility. Companies can write off any contributions they make to an employee's EMBA education as a business expense, but things are more complicated for an individual. The most critical piece of advice that many sources offer is that you should consult with a tax expert on the subject and focus on IRS Publication 970, which covers a myriad of tax benefits for education. The precise implications of some of the guidelines there, however, remain murky at best, and, if you decide to deduct the cost of your EMBA, you cannot expect your deduction to simply sail through the auditing process. You will need to be prepared to make your case to the IRS.

That said, there are some basic guidelines that can help you as you explore your financing of an EMBA.

- Deductibility for an education expense comes down to the reasons for the need for the education and who is requesting the need.
- The cost of an education can be deducted if:
  - o The education maintains or improves skills you require in order for your employment or trade *or*
  - o The education is an expressed requirement from your current employer as a condition for your retention or maintaining or improving your status at your current place of employment.

If your education is to prepare yourself for some *new* trade or business, then the expense is *not* deductible. This includes changing careers or simply earning a higher salary. The tax ruling specifically makes the point that your intent in undertaking your education is not relevant.

Questions to consider:

- What is my employer's policy on tuition payment or reimbursement?
- Will my employer financially support this endeavor?
- Would the corporation be willing to participate in the Corporate Partnership Program?
- Will my employer support my time commitment to the program?
- How much money in loans will I need?

APPENDIX

EMBA Self-Assessment

Personality and work demand questionnaire

Take this quick self-assessment to determine how your learning style and lifestyle will fit with the demands and expectations of attending an Executive MBA program. Answer each question based on whether you agree or disagree with the statement. Assign points to each sentence based on the following scale:

1 point: I strongly disagree with this statement.
2 points: I disagree somewhat with this statement.
3 points: I agree somewhat with this statement.
4 points: I agree with this statement.
5 points: I strongly agree with this statement.

Keep in mind that this assessment is meant to gauge your compatibility, your learning style, personality, and lifestyle with the Executive MBA learning format. Although the results should not dissuade you from pursuing an MBA, the fact remains that the EMBA learning model is not suitable for everyone and that alternative learning models like a traditional MBA are available.

Learning Style:

1 to 5

I consider myself to be a disciplined student.		
I was a disciplined student as an undergraduate.		
I do not procrastinate when I have work to do.		
I prefer to work with others in a group or team.		
I actively participant in meetings.		
I rarely need assistance from teaching assistants.		

Section Subtotal _____

Impact on Employment:

1 to 5

I cannot afford to stop working and become a full-time student.		
My preference is to remain employed while going to school.		
I generally don't have commitments during the weekend.		
My work schedule allows me time to meet with groups in the evening.		
I can count on my colleagues to cover for me when I am away from work.		

Section Subtotal _____

Family and other responsibilities:

I can manage being away from home on a consistent basis for the next two years.		
Being outside the country for extended periods of time is not a problem for me.		
My spouse is supportive of my academic endeavor.		
My absence will not affect the quality of my home life.		

Section Subtotal _____

Personality:

I have an outgoing and enthusiastic personality.		
I typically seek out adventure and challenging experiences.		
I enjoy debating and discussing my views with others.		
When I have a project to complete, I meet the deadline.		
I am able to work well with others.		
I am disciplined and diligent both as a professional and as a student.		
I am able to motivate myself.		
I am able to focus my attention.		
I consider myself to be an organized person.		
I am able to manage my time efficiently.		
I consider myself to be patient both with my work and other people.		
I would like to attend an EMBA program.		
I express my ideas and opinions well to others.		

Section Subtotal_____

Total Score _____

If you have 27-54 Points: You may want to look into a part-time MBA program.

If you have 55-87 Points: Consider a full- or part-time MBA program.

If you have 88+ Points: Congratulations—You are the ideal EMBA candidate.

Planning the Investment

Use this schedule to scope out costs and other associated fees to consider for planning the investment.

EMBA Cost Preparation Form

Preparation fees

Item	Estimated Cost	Reimbursable (Yes/No)
Preparation course, optional	$1,000	
GMAT fee	$250	
TOEFL fee	$150	
Editor of essays, optional	$150 per hour	
Transcript (from schools attended)	Varies	
Application fees vary	Varies, on avg. $150	

Program Fees

Item	Estimated Cost	Reimbursable (Yes/No)
Tuition Varies		
Residencies Varies		
Hotel		
Air		
Car		
Food		
Computer laptop $1500, average		
Internet subscription		
Books $200 to $300 per semester		

Questions to Consider Before Requesting Sponsorship

Work schedule:

Depending on the program, classes may cut into the 9 to 5 work schedule.
- Are you willing to give up vacation and personal time for class time?
- How much work time will you be missing?
- Does your job permit time away like this?
- Are your co-workers willing to cover for you?

Relevance to work:

Employers will look to determine the need or relevance of an MBA toward the job title you hold.
- Is there direct applicability to your current job?
- Is the degree preparing you for some other position in the company?
- Have you been at the company long enough?

Levels of sponsorship:

Employers may base reimbursement on a variety of conditions.
- Are associated fees, like preparation courses, books, and travel reimbursable?
- Can a company laptop be borrowed?
- Does the reimbursement vary depending on tenure at company?
- Are you reimbursed based on the grade you earn per class?
- Can you receive partial reimbursement upfront?
- Is there a limit on how much you will be reimbursed per semester, per year?

FREQUENTLY ASKED
QUESTIONS

What is the Executive MBA?

An Executive MBA w are a highly motivated group of middle to senior level managers with a minimum of seven years of work experience (schools vary on how much work experience they require a candidate to have) who must maintain employment while attending classes. The Executive MBA builds upon the collective experience of the classroom while applying practical and theoretical principles to the education. Employers receive immediate payback, as students apply class lessons directly in the workplace. It is considered one of the most practical forms of graduate business education available. Other types of MBA programs are the traditional full—and part-time programs; distance-learning programs; and customized, in-house corporate or industry-wide programs.

How do I know which program is right for me?

The EMBA learning model varies by class schedule and delivery format. Some programs emphasize e-Learning and staggered class scheduling to allow students from anywhere in the world to attend, connect, and communicate with classes and classmates. Characteristics that contrast one EMBA program from another include scheduling, program concentration, managerial experience, location, content delivery and flexibility, study tours, generally accepted time away from work, and financial sponsorship requirements.

Can I still apply to the full—or part-time program if I don't get accepted into the EMBA?

If you request this arrangement, some schools may accommodate and roll over the application to the regular full—or part-time program. Others will require a separate application and additional fee or may require you to attend a second interview. As the use of online applications increases, schools may become more amenable to requests to rollover the application to a full—or part-time program.

What happens if I receive sponsorship and then lose my job?

This is a difficult and complex question. Obviously, this depends on the arrangement you worked out with your employer. Indeed, if your employer pays full tuition and pays the school directly, the school then becomes a creditor on the unpaid balance. If you are being reimbursed, the employer may clear your balance upon dismissal and not pay future semesters or even refuse to pay anything. If the company goes bankrupt or files for Chapter 11, then life may get even more difficult. Your best bet is to meet with your school administrators and seek possible options. Student loans may be necessary.

Will the school help me find a new job when I graduate?

An EMBA is designed for the employee established in his or her career and place of employment. As we know, there are no guarantees in life; and, therefore, people lose their jobs, change careers, or drop out of the workforce for a range of reasons. However, job changing is not the goal of the EMBA degree. Your university can help you secure employment and career direction in several ways.

The career services office is one option. Although corporate recruiters are more interested in recruiting newly-minted MBAs for entry level positions, the career office could help. A better avenue for job opportunities might be classmates and alumni—both serve as a great job bank. Some schools contract with executive recruiters and placement agencies to assist EMBA graduates in securing placement.

Will the lack of sponsorship put me at a disadvantage?

EMBA program administrators find this question difficult to answer because they need to balance your credentials with considerations such as what financial and professional support you will have. Although they will give your application an unbiased evaluation, not having financial and time support from an employer can prevent a student from performing well and completing the program. Every administrator agrees that time away from work (time sponsorship) is crucial for acceptance.

Will I need to complete prerequisite coursework and what expenses might be involved?

If you have been out of school for many years, you may need a refresher in calculus or general accounting. Most programs offer a one—to two-month preliminary review prior to the official start date. There is no harm in taking a refresher course, particularly since it's included in the tuition. Unless you can make the case otherwise, take prerequisites to get your mind back into the books.

Do most EMBA courses include teaching assistants in addition to the professors?

Professors have graduate students and Ph.D. candidates who also serve as teaching assistants. As future instructors themselves, these candidates usually jump at the opportunity to work with Executive students.

What is the typical number of hours required per week for class preparation?

Obviously, time commitment varies per student, per class, and per semester. You must ask yourself if you are a quick or slow learner, reader, and writer. Everyone learns at a different pace. It all depends on the individual.

A J.P. Morgan vice president and NYU graduate states that after a ten-hour workday, she studies two to three hours each night and an additional three to four hours each day on the weekends. She explains, "The workload ebbs and flows per class and per semester, much like work demands can vary. You find your rhythm and you manage—just don't procrastinate."

The Executive MBA Council recommends a minimum 15-20 hours a week for classroom work, computer and research efforts, and assignments. Study groups working collectively on assignments can ease the demand a bit.

How are GMAT scores weighted in the admissions process?

Take the exam seriously, although not all EMBA programs require the GMAT. Scores do play a role in the acceptance process, but they signify only one of many aspects that represent your career record. In addition to maintaining accreditation, schools use the GMAT to gauge a candidate's need for preparatory classes prior to the first semester. No one wants to get caught behind the schoolwork, but schools can use the GMAT to identify and engage students in refresher classes like algebra, writing, calculus, or general accounting prior to the first semester.

No matter what scores you earn on the exam, keep in mind that even top-ranked schools accept all ranges. Don't allow the GMAT to dictate your future. Be mindful of your career record when preparing the strongest application possible.

What is the Computer Adaptive Test (CAT)?

CAT relates to the GMAT. In a computer adaptive test, the computer screen displays one question at a time, which is drawn from a large pool of questions, categorized by content and difficulty. Based on a correct response, the questions become increasingly more difficult. The trick is to answer the first several questions correctly so that you then maintain a range of scoring based on the threshold of questions previously answered correctly.

How do the GMATs and CAT work?

The GMAT exam consists of three main parts, the Analytical Writing Assessment, the Quantitative Assessment, and the Verbal Assessment. The exam time lasts three-and-a-half hours, but plan up to four hours to complete the entire exam. The test begins with two separate writing exercises and allots 30 minutes to each one. Then there is a Quantitative Section and a Verbal Section each of which take 75 minutes to complete. The entire exam including the essays is keyed into the computer.

How long are GMAT scores valid, and how often the test be taken?

The scores are valid for three years, and the test can be taken as many as a five times. A written request for more must be made to GMAC. Visit their website for details are *www.gmac.com*.

How much does the GMAT cost?

The cost seems to increase periodically. The registration fee to take the exam is currently $250, rescheduling fee of $50, a cancellation fee of $80, and a $28 fee to issue scores to each additional school beyond the set initial number. Be sure to cancel the test at least seven working days prior to the scheduled appointment.

I have hobbies outside of work. Does this make me a better candidate?

Yes, it does. It has been rumored, for example, that, if you can play a musical instrument, then you are almost automatically accepted into NYU. Don't be shy to boast about your skills, interests, and hobbies. If you speak another language: speak up!

If I have prior experience in a subject area, is it possible to have that related class waived?

Waiving classes is not recommended unless the class is in your profession, like accounting. A test may be required to determine your proficiency in a particular subject.

What is the "capstone", and does every program require it?

Capstone is the generic term used to represent a summation of coursework in the form of a year-end exam or final project. The exam evaluates your accumulation of knowledge by working through cases drawn from various coursework. As a final project, students working in teams develop business plans for their sponsoring organizations. Projects may include a new market entry strategy, a product development project, or an organizational assessment with appropriate change management.

What if I am not from a math-oriented or accounting profession?

The EMBA trains you in management—there is no avoiding these core classes, but support for such classes will be made available. Diversity in education is equal to diversity in the classroom. Business schools don't stock up on specific disciplines. Being an engineer is not a ticket into a program, if you are one of eighty engineers applying. You may have to distinguish yourself from the flock of other engineers who may be applying. The obscurity of your background or professional strengths may be exactly what the program needs.

My job requires frequent travel. Can I make up missed classes?

The class structure makes it impossible to make up a missed class. Too many missed classes in a semester may result in a failing grade. It is best to talk to your professors and administrator to make arrangements long before classes are missed. One option is to determine if the facility supports video conferencing, recording, or closed circuit television. Another option is to postpone the grade until the class is taught again with another EMBA group or to attend a comparable class in the regular or evening program. Missing classes diminishes the EMBA experience. You will miss some exhilarating classroom discussions and terrific guest speakers and cause potential disruption to your working group. Administrators, professors, and classmates will strongly advise that you not miss any classes, as they will all count on your contribution in the classroom.

Is it possible to sit in on one or two classes as an observer prior to applying?

As a passive observer—yes, and it is encouraged. Talk to the program administrator, who will set up a time to allow you to sit in on a class and interact with students. No matter how intriguing the discussion may be, sorry, you can't interact while class is in progress.

What are the different types of accreditations?

Be mindful of a school's certificate of accreditation. The form of accreditation and the type of granting body may matter in the eyes of your current or future employer. It can even affect your level of sponsorship. Check with human resources, as they can usually provide you with information as to the types of accreditation accepted by the industry. The American Assembly of Collegiate Schools of Business (AACSB) accredits most graduate-level business schools in the U.S.

Accreditation organizations vary in scope and purpose. Some accrediting bodies focus locally, while others do so internationally. Some focus on the organization and delivery of the curriculum (the AACSB), while others focus on the measures the schools use to continuously improve the academic quality delivered (the Association of Collegiate Business Schools and Programs or ACBSP). For admissions standards and accessibility there is the Graduate Management Admission Council (GMAC). The sister to the GMAC in Europe is the Brussels-based European Foundation for Management Development (EFMD)— *www.efmd.be* that offers European Quality Improvement System

(EQUIS) accreditation and the AMBA accreditation from the London-based Association of MBAs—*www.mba.org.uk*. Most others address distance learning and evaluate in-house corporate training programs or specialized executive training.

Who is the American Assembly of Collegiate Schools of Business (AACSB)?

The AACSB, the Good Housekeeping seal of approval for business schools, is a not-for-profit organization founded in 1916 to drive quality into the undergraduate and graduate business school curriculum. In addition, the organization attempts to standardize the quality of educational institutions, confirming business degrees including the Executive MBA. According to the website *www.aacsb.edu*, the AACSB has accredited 593 institutions: 473 in the United States and 120 from outside the US. Each year the organization publishes a set of guidelines that address the function, operation, and delivery of a business education. It also encourages faculty diversity. Section FD.2 of the AACSB accreditation guidelines states, "The school should demonstrate continuous efforts to achieve demographic diversity in its faculty." This principle applies to undergraduate as well as graduate programs.

What is the role of the EMBA Council in EMBA education?

The EMBA Council supports EMBA program administrators through its periodic benchmarking survey, which compares peer schools on quality and standards, and through other forms of professional development. The council also works closely with the many accreditation organizations mentioned above.

CLASS SCHEDULE AND PROGRAM CURRICULA

The following class schedule and sample curricula are used to illustrate the intensity of a typical day in school and profile the next two years in the Executive MBA.

Sample Class Schedule

Fordham Business School Executive MBA Program

Classes:

Financial Management of Multinational Companies
International Business Law and Ethics
Marketing Strategy

Friday

International Business Law and Ethics	1:30-5:00
Financial Management of Multinational Companies	7:00-10:30

Saturday

Financial Management of Multinational Companies	8:30-12:00
Marketing Strategy	1:30-5:00

Sunday

Marketing Strategy	8:30-12:00
International Business Law and Ethics	1:30-5:00

The Executive MBA (EMBA) curriculum is all about generating the most value in the shortest period of time. The program focuses on building each student's personal portfolio—a balanced set of skills that are immediately applicable in the workplace. Drawing from various disciplines and emphasizing the global nature of management, the EMBA gives students the necessary tools to succeed no matter what path their career takes.

Sample EMBA Curricula

Wharton School Executive MBA

MBA for Executives First-Year Curriculum

Conceptual Framework for General Management

Leadership Essentials   Management of People at Work
(includes Field Application Project)
Foundations of Leadership and Teamwork
(includes Ethics Module)
Management Communication

Analytical Foundations   Managerial Economics
Statistics for Managers
Decision Models and Uncertainty (1/2 semester)

Core Business   Finance
Foundations   - Corporate Finance
- Macroeconomic Analysis and Public Policy
Accounting
- Financial Accounting
- Managerial Accounting Analysis (1/2 semester)
Operations
- Operations Quality and Productivity (1/2 semester)
- Operations Supply Chain Management (1/2 semester)
Marketing
- Marketing Program Design (1/2 semester)
- Marketing Strategy (1/2 semester)

MBA for Executives Second-Year Curriculum

Conceptual Framework for General Management (continued)

Leadership Essentials   Government and Legal Environment of Business (includes Field Application Project)

Analytical Foundations   Strategy
—Competitive Strategy (1/2 semester)
—Global Strategic Management (1/2 semester)
International Seminar

Electives *(20 chosen from nearly 200)*

Sample Elective Selection Corporate Development: Mergers and
Acquisitions
Corporate Finance
Entrepreneurship through Acquisition
Financial Derivatives
Formation and Implementation of
Entrepreneurial Ventures
Geopolitics
International Finance
Investment Management
Managing Organizational Change
Marketing Research
Marketing Strategy
Mathematical Modeling
Negotiation and Conflict Resolution
New Product Development
Pricing Policy
Real Estate Investments
Risk and Crisis Management
Strategic Planning and Control
Topics in Health Care
Venture Capital and the Finance of Innovation

George Washington University Executive MBA

Opening Residency	
EMBA 202	Executive Leadership Development
Core Courses	
EMBA 214	Data Analysis and Decision Making
EMBA 290	Organizational Behavior
EMBA 216	Marketing Management
EMBA 222	Financial Accounting
EMBA 261	Human Resource Management
EMBA 210	Managerial Economics
EMBA 221	Strategic Management & Leadership
EMBA 220	Operations Management
EMBA 224	Managerial Finance
EMBA 226	International Economics
Summer International Residency	
EMBA 240	International Business Strategy, Practice and the Multinational Corporation
Advanced Topics	
EMBA 254	Managerial Accounting
EMBA 262	IT Strategy
EMBA 212	Corporate Political Strategy
EMBA 250	Financial Strategy
EMBA 230	Management of Technology & Innovation
EMBA 290	Executive Communication
EMBA 264	Marketing Strategy
EMBA 257	Entrepreneurship & New Venture Creation
EMBA 266	Business Law
EMBA 267	Ethics & Corporate Governance
EMBA 268	Negotiations
Closing Residency	
EMBA 270	Strategy Formulation & Implementation

Northwestern University, Kellogg Graduate School of Business Management

(Descriptions for **Core Courses** or **Elective Courses**)	(Descriptions for **Core Courses** or **Elective Courses**)
Live-In Week 1	**Live-In Week 2**
Analytical Approach to Uncertainty	Negotiation Strategies
Operating Strategies for the General Manager	Strategic Crisis Management
Teambuilding	
Term 1—Fall	**Term 4—Fall**
Financial Reporting Systems	Law and the Corporate Manager
Leadership and Organizations	Macroeconomics
Marketing Management	Management of Organizational Change
Statistical Decision Analysis	Strategic Financial Management
Term 2—Winter	**Term 5—Winter**
Foundations of Strategy	Corporate Governance
Managerial Economics	Economics of Competition
Managerial Finance I	Electives—One
Marketing Strategies	Electives—Two
Creating and Managing Strategic Alliances	
Term 3—Spring	**Term 6—Spring**
Accounting for Management Planning & Control	Electives—Three
Managerial Finance ll	Electives—Four
Consumer Insight and Marketing Strategy	Ethics and Leadership
Operations Management	Capstone Course

Fordham University Executive MBA

Term	Class	Dates	Venue
Fall	• Managing the Transnational Firm (3)	August 5-8	Outside ** Conference Center
	• Managerial Global Economics (3) • International Communication Negotiations (3) • Quantitative Methods and Decision Analysis (3)	September 10-12 October 1-3 November 5-7 December 3-5	Lincoln Center Campus
Spring	• Management Elective (1.5) • Contemporary Ethical Issues in Business (1.5)	January 6-9	Outside ** Conference Center
	• Financial Environment (3) • Financial Accounting/Financial Statement Analysis (3) • Marketing Management and Strategy (3)	January 28-30 February 4-6 March 4-6 March 25-27	Lincoln Center Campus
Summer	• Managerial Accounting (3) • Contemporary Issues in U.S. and International Business Law (3) • ICS in the Transnational Firm (3)	May 13-15 June 3-5 June 24-26 July 8-10	Lincoln Center Campus
Fall	• Global Finance (3) • Transnational Management and Systems Operations (3) • Managing Innovation and Change (3) • International Trade and Development (1.5)	September 9-11 October 1-3 November 4-6 December 2-4	Lincoln Center Campus
Spring	• Personal Leadership Development (3)	January 5-8	Outside ** Conference Center
	• Business Policy (3) • International Field Study (3) • Elective (3) • Research for Final Project (1.5)	January 27-29 February 17-19 March 2-4 April 13-15	Lincoln Center Campus
	• Transnational Application (3)	**April 21-27**	**TBD**

**FOUR-DAY RESIDENTIALS with OVERNIGHT accommodations

Duke University Fuqua School of Business Executive MBA

Term Schedule

- **Term I**

Orientation
Integrative Learning Experience I (ILE I)
Leadership, Ethics, and Organizations (LEO)
Global Markets and Institutions (GMI)

- **Term II**

Probability and Statistics
Financial Accounting
Managerial Economics

- **Term III**

Integrative Learning Experience II (ILE II)
Decision Models
Marketing Management
Managerial Accounting

- **Term IV**

Global Financial Management
Operations Management
Corporate Strategy

- **Term V**

Leadership and Development

- **Term VI**

4 Electives

- **Term VII**

Optional Concentration (consists of a 2-course credit special project)

Cornell University The Johnson School

Alternate weekends (Saturday-Sunday)

First Year Curriculum

Term 1: July. December
Residence
Week: 🖉   Leadership
🖉   Managerial Statistics
🖉   Managing and Leading in Organizations
🖉   Marketing Management
🖉   Financial Accounting

Term 2: January. May

Residence
Week: 🖉   Managing Through Influence
🖉   Managing Operations
🖉   Economics
🖉   Managerial Finance
🖉   Business Strategy

Second Year Curriculum

Term 3: July. December
Residence
Week:
🖉   Marketing Strategy
🖉   Cases in Finance
🖉   Advanced Strategy
🖉   International Finance
🖉   Managerial Cost
🖉   International Business Project

Term 4: January. May

Residence
Week:
🖉   Manufacturing Strategy
🖉   Financial Statement Analysis
🖉   Electronic Commerce
🖉   Elective Set
🖉   Driving Strategic Capability
🖉   Managerial Decision-Making
🖉   Enterprise and Private Equity Project

THE MBA OATH

As a business leader I recognize my role in society.

- My purpose is to lead people and manage resources to create value that no single individual can create alone.

- My decisions affect the well-being of individuals inside and outside my enterprise, today and tomorrow.

Therefore, I promise that:

- I will manage my enterprise with loyalty and care, and will not advance my personal interests at the expense of my enterprise or society.

- I will understand and uphold, in letter and spirit, the laws and contracts governing my conduct and that of my enterprise.

- I will refrain from corruption, unfair competition, or business practices harmful to society.

- I will protect the human rights and dignity of all people affected by my enterprise, and I will oppose discrimination and exploitation.

- I will protect the right of future generations to advance their standard of living and enjoy a healthy planet.

- I will report the performance and risks of my enterprise accurately and honestly.

- I will invest in developing myself and others, helping the management profession continue to advance and create sustainable and inclusive prosperity.

In exercising my professional duties according to these principles, I recognize that my behavior must set an example of integrity, eliciting trust and esteem from those I serve. I will remain accountable to my peers and to society for my actions and for upholding these standards.

This oath I make freely, and upon my honor.

To learn more about the MBA Oath and their publication please visit: http://mbaoath.org/

About QS

QS is the world's leading network for top careers and education. Our mission is to enable motivated people to fulfill their potential by fostering educational achievement, international mobility, and career development. QS links graduate, MBA, and executive communities around the globe with the world's leading business schools, universities, and employers through a variety of platforms including websites, events, e-guides, and technical solutions.

Responding to the needs of the market, the QS World Executive MBA Tour was launched in 2002 to help managers, executives, and experienced professionals meet the world's top Executive MBA programs in a relaxed and friendly environment.

In 2003, the QS TopExecutive Guide (available in both print and electronic versions) and the QS TopExecutive Online Newsletter were launched to accompany the Tour, with the mission of continuing to raise the awareness of the "EMBA alternative" to senior professionals as well as corporations.

The QS TopExecutive Guide reports on pertinent and timely topics that are of interest to EMBA candidates such as the ROI of the Executive MBA degree, course content, career development, and work/life balance, with a dedicated focus on Women and the Executive MBA.

Today, the QS World Executive MBA Tour takes Executive MBA programs to 21 cities in Latin America, North America, Europe, Asia, and the Middle-East.

In the last two years, over 95 Executive MBA programs have participated in the Tour and as we continue to grow, we aim to inform experienced professionals on the flexible/modular study options available in the market, promote lifelong learning and leadership development, and most importantly, encourage talented individuals to take the Executive MBA plunge and invest in themselves.

To learn more about:

- The QS World Executive MBA Tour:
  http://www.topmba.com/emba
- The QS TopExecutive Guide:
  http://www.topmba.com/qs-topexecutive-guide-online
- QS Ltd: http://www.qs.com

EMBA World and QS are proud partners advising students and employers on graduate business education since 2004.

US EMBA Program Directory

Alabama

Auburn University
College of Business
Executive MBA Program
Suite 503 Lowder Building
Auburn University AL 36849
Phone: (334)844-4060

www.emba.business.auburn.edu

Birmingham-Southern College
Division of Business and Graduate
Programs
Masters in Public and Private
Management (MPPM)
900 Arkandelphia Road
Box 549052
Birmingham AL 35254
Phone: 205-226-4841

www.bsc.edu
graduate@bsc.edu

University of Alabama
Manderson Graduate School of
Business
Executive MBA Program
P.O. Box 870223
Tuscaloosa AL 35487-0223
Phone: (800) 365-8583

www.bama.ua.edu

Arkansas

**University of Arkansas at Little
Rock**
College of Business Administration
Executive MBA
Reynolds Business Building, Dean's
Office
2801 S. University Ave.
Little Rock AR 72204-1099
Phone: (501) 569-3356

www.cba.ualr.edu

Arizona

Arizona State University
College of Business
MBA for Executives Program
Tempe AZ 85287-4906
Phone: (480)965-5300

www.cob.asu.edu
emba@asu.edu

**Thunderbird School of Global
Management**
Executive MBA in Global
Management
15249 North 59th Avenue
Glendale AZ 85306-6000
Phone: (602) 978-7384

www.thunderbird.edu
emba@thunderbird.edu

Grand Canyon University

Ken Blanchard Executive MBA
Program
3300 West Camelback Road
Phoenix, AZ 85017
Phone: 877-800-3044

www.gcu.edu/embaworld
admissionsonline@gcu.edu

California

University of California, Berkeley
Haas School of Business
Berkeley-Columbia Executive
MBA Program
545 Student Services Building
#1910
Berkeley, CA 94720-1910
Phone: 510-643-2188

www.berkeley.columbia.edu
emba@haas.berkeley.edu

Chapman University
The George L. Argyros School of
Business and Economics
Executive MBA
One University Place
Orange, CA 92866
Phone: (714) 997-6745

www.chapman.edu
emba@chapman.edu
Claremont Graduate University
Claremont Graduate University
Peter F. Drucker Graduate School
of Management

The Executive Management
Program
1021 N. Dartmouth
Claremont CA 91711
Phone: (909) 621-8193

www.cgu.edu

Golden Gate University
School of Business
Executive MBA Program
536 Mission Street
San Francisco CA 94105
Phone: 415-442-6594

www.ggu.edu

Loyola Marymount University
Executive MBA Program
Center for Executive Learning
1 LMU Drive, MS 8386
Los Angeles, CA 90045-2659
Phone: (877) LMU-8585

www.lmuemba.com
emba@lmu.edu

Naval Postgraduate School
Graduate School of Business and
Public Policy
Executive MBA
555 Dyer Road
Bldg. 330, RM 339
Monterey CA 93943-5103
Phone: 831-656-2463

www.nps.edu/academics/gsbpp/emba
wdhatch@nps.edu

Pepperdine University
Graziadio School of Business and
Management
Executive Master of Science and
technology management
400 Corporate Pointe, 3rd floor
Culver City, CA 90230
Phone: (310) 568-5541

www.bschool.pepperdine.edu

Saint Mary's College of California
Graduate Business Programs
Executive MBA Program
380 Moraga Road
Moraga, CA 94556
Phone: (925) 631-4500

smcmba@stmarys-ca.edu
www.saintmarysmba.com

San Diego State University
College of Business Administration
MBA for Executives Program
Executive Managent Programs
San Diego, CA 92182-8232
Phone: (619) 594-6010

www.sdsu.edu
emba@mail.sdsu.edu

University of California, Irvine
Graduate School of Management
Executive MBA Program
200 GSM, Room 230
Irvine, CA 92697-3125
Phone: (949) 824-4622

www.gsm.uci.edu

**University of California,
Los Angeles**
John E. Anderson Graduate School
of Management
UCLA Executive MBA Program
110 Westwood Plaza, Rm A101f
P.O. Box 951481
Los Angeles CA 90095-1481
Phone: (310) 825-2032

www.anderson.ucla.edu
emba.admissions@anderson.ucla.edu

University of San Francisco
School of Business/ Graduate
School of Management
Executive MBA Program
2130 Fulton Street
San Francisco CA 94117-1045
Phone: 422-422-2508

www.usfca.edu
exmba@usfca.edu

Colorado

Colorado State University
College of Business
Executive MBA Program
1445 Market Street, Suite 280
Denver CO 80202
Phone: (303) 534-3191

www.DenverMBA.com

University of Colorado
Three Campus Consortium
Executive MBA Program

P.O. Box 480006
Denver CO 80248-0006
Phone: (800) 228-5778
Fax: (303) 623-6228

www.colorado.edu

University of Denver
Daniels College of Business
Executive MBA Program
2101 South University Boulevard,
Suite 684
Denver CO 80208
Phone: (303)871-4402
Fax: (303)871-2822

www.dcb.du.edu

Connecticut

University of Connecticut
School of Business Administration
Executive MBA Program
368 Fairfield Road U-41EM
Storrs, CT 06269-2041
Phone: (860) 486-0260
Fax: (860) 486-1699

www.sba.uconn.edu
emba@sba.uconn.edu

University of New Haven
Executive Master of Business
Administration
300 Boston Post Road
West Haven, CT 06516
Toll-free: 1.877.TOP.EMBA
Phone: (203) 932-7386
Fax: (203) 932-7261
www.newhaven.edu
emba@newhaven.edu

Yale School of Management
Yale MBA for Executives
Leadership in the Healthcare
Sector P.O. Box 208200
New Haven, CT 06520
Phone: (203) 432-0345
Fax: (203) 432-0342

www.mba.yale.edu

Delaware

University of Delaware
College of Business and Economics
Executive MBA Program
103 MBNA America Hall
Newark DE 19716
Phone: (302) 831-2221
Fax: (302) 831-3329

www.emba.udel.edu
e-mba@udel.edu

Florida

Embry-Riddle Aeronautical
University
Executive MBA Program
Business Administration
Department
600 South Clyde Morris Blvd.
Daytona Beach FL 32114-3900
Phone: (904) 226-7946
Fax: (904) 226-7984

www.embryriddle.edu

Florida Gulf Coast University
College of Business

Center for Leadership and
Innovation
EMBA Program
24311 Walden Center Drive, Suite 100
Bonita Springs FL 34134
Phone: (941) 948-1812
Fax: (941) 948-1814

www.fgcu.edu

Florida International University
College of Business Administration
Executive MBA Program
University Park
Miami FL 33199
Phone: (305) 348-1036
Fax: (305) 348-6331

www.fiu.edu

Jacksonville University
Executive MBA Program
2800 University Boulevard, North
Jacksonville FL 32211
Phone: (904) 745-7437
Fax: (904) 745-7463

www.ju.edu
mba@ju.edu

Rollins College
Roy E. Crummer Graduate
School of Business
Executive MBA Program
1000 Holt Avenue - 2722
Winter Park FL 32789-4499
Phone: (407) 646-1579
Fax: (407) 628-6336

www.crummer.rollins.edu

University of Central Florida
College of Business Administration
Executive MBA Program
Executive Development Center
P.O. Box 161400
Orlando FL 32816-1400
Phone: (407) 823-2446
Fax: (407) 823-3153

www.bus.ucf.edu
execdev@bus.ucf.edu

University of Florida
Warrington College of Business
Administration
Florida MBA Programs
134 Bryan Hall
P.O. Box 117152
Gainesville FL 31611-7152
Phone: (352) 392-7992
Fax: (352) 392-8791

www.floridamba.ufl.edu

University of Miami
School of Business Administration
Executive MBA Program
P.O. Box 248505
Coral Gables FL 33124-6524
Phone: 305-284-2510

Phone: 800- 531-7137 (USA
ONLY)
Fax: 305-284-1878

www.bus.miami.edu/grad
mba@miami.edu

University of South Florida
College of Business Administration
Executive MBA Program
Tampa Fl 33620
Phone: 813-974-4876
Fax: 813-975-6604

www.coba.usf.edu
emba@coba.usf.edu

University of South Florida
College of Business Administration
MBA Program for Physicians
4202 E. Fowler Avenue BSN 3403
Tampa FL 33620
Phone: 813-974-2615
Fax: 813-975-6604

www.coba.usf.edu
emba@coba.usf.edu

Stetson University
Celebration Center
Executive MBA Program
Business Administration
Department
800 Celebration Avenue, Suite 104
Celebration, FL 34747
Telephone: (321) 939-7603
Fax: (321) 939-7606

www2.stetson.edu/emba
emba@stetson.edu

Georgia

Emory University
Goizueta Business School
Executive MBA Program

Office of Admissions
1300 Clifton Road NE
Atlanta GA 30322
Phone: (404) 727-6311
Fax: (404) 727-4612

www.goizueta.emory.edu

Georgia State University
J. Mack Robinson College of Business
The Executive MBA Program
University Plaza
35 Broad Street
Atlanta GA 30303-3083
Phone: (404) 651-3760
Fax: 404-651-2757

www.robinson.gsu.edu

Georgia State University
J. Mack Robinson College of Business
GEM EMBA Program/E-
Commerce Institute
35 Broad Street, Suite 400
Atlanta GA 30303-3083
Phone: 404-463-9300
Fax: 404-463-9292

www.eci.gsu.edu

Kennesaw State University
Michael J. Coles College of
Business
Executive MBA Program
1000 Chastain Road
Kennesaw, GA 30144
Phone: 770-420-4622
Fax: 770-420-4444

coles.kennesaw.edu

Mercer University
Stetson School of Business and
Economics
Executive MBA Program
3001 Mercer University Drive
Atlanta GA 30341
Phone: 678-547-6162
Fax: 678-547-6337

www.mercer.edu

**The Georgia Institute of
Technology**
Dupree College of Management
Executive Master's in Management
of Technology
The Dupree College of
Management
755 Ferst Drive, Room 340
Atlanta GA 30332-0520
Phone: 404-894-1462
Fax: 404-894-1464

www.mot.gatech.edu
emsmot_staff@list.gatech.edu

The University of Georgia
Terry College of Business
Executive MBA Program
Athens GA 30602-6262
Phone: 706-542-1964
Fax: 706-542-7374

www.terry.uga.edu
executive_programs@terry.uga.edu

Hawaii

Hawaii Pacific University
Business Administration
Weekend MBA for Business
Professionals
1164 Bishop Street, Suite 911
Honolulu HI 96813
Phone: 808-544-0279
Fax: 808-544-0280

web1.hpu.edu
businessadministration@hup.edu

University of Hawaii at Manoa
Shidler College of Business
Executive MBA Program
2404 Maile Way, B-201
Honolulu HI 96822
Phone: (808) 956-8135
Fax: (808) 956-3766

www.shidler.hawaii.edu
emba@hawaii.edu

Iowa

The University of Iowa
Henry B. Tippie School of
Management
Executive MBA Program
C140 John Pappajohn Business
Building
Iowa City IA 52242-1000
Phone: (319) 335-1039
Fax: (319) 335-3604

www.biz.uiowa.edu

Idaho

Boise State University
The Executive MBA Program
College of Business and Economics
1910 University Drive MS 1600
Boise, ID 83725-1600
Phone: (208) 426-4034
Fax: (208) 426-1300

emba.boisestate.edu
emba@boisestate.edu

Illinois

Bradley University
Foster College of Business
Executive MBA Program
FCBA-Room 123 1501 W. Bradley
Avenue
Peoria, IL 61625
Phone: 309-677-4425

www.bradley.edu

Northern Illinois University
College of Business
Executive MBA
DeKalb, IL 60115
Phone: (815) 753-0257
Fax: (815) 753-1668

www.cob.niu.edu
emba@niu.edu

Northwestern University
Kellogg School of Management
Executive MBA Program
James L. Allen Center

2169 Campus Drive
Evanston, IL 60208
General Phone: (847) 467-7020
Admission Line: (847) 491-EMBA
Fax: (847) 467-3773

www.kellogg.northwestern.edu/
programs/emba.aspx
emba@kellogg.northwestern.edu

University of Illinois at Urbana Champaign
College of Commerce and Business
Administration
The Executive MBA Program
218 Commerce West
1206 S. Sixth Street
Champaign, IL 61820
Phone: (217) 333-4510
Fax: (217) 333-3242

www.theexecutivemba.com
emba@uiuc.edu

Roosevelt University
Walter E. Heller College of
Business Administration
MBA In International Leadership
430 South Michigan Avenue
Chicago, IL 60605-1394
Phone: 312-281-3281
Fax: 312-281-3290

www.roosevelt.edu
cma@roosevelt.edu

The Lake Forest Graduate School of Management
280 North Sheridan Road

Lake Forest, IL 60045
Phone: (847) 234-5005
Fax: (847) 295-3656

www.lfgsm.edu

The University of Chicago
Chicago Booth School of Business
Executive MBA Program
Gleacher Center
450 North Cityfront Plaza Drive
Chicago, IL 60611
Phone: (312) 464-8750
Fax: (312) 464-8755

chicagobooth.edu/execmba
xp@chicagobooth.edu

The University of Chicago
Executive MBA Program - Europe
Woolgate Exchange
25 Basinghall Street
EC2V 5HA London, UK
T +44 (0) 20 7643.2210
F +44 (0) 20 7643.2201

chicagobooth.edu/execmba
europe.inquiries@chicagobooth.edu

The University of Chicago
Chicago Booth School of Business
Executive MBA Program - Asia
101 Penang Rd
Singapore 238 466
Phone: 65 6835 6482
Fax: 65 6835 6483

chicagobooth.edu/execmba
asia-po@lists.chicagobooth.edu

Indiana

Purdue University
Executive MBA Program
425 West State Street, KCTR-208
West Lafayette, IN 47907-2056
Phone: (765) 494-7700
Fax: (765) 494-0862

www2.krannert.purdue.edu
keepinfo@krannert.purdue.edu

University of Notre Dame
Executive MBA Program
126 College of Business
P.O. Box 399
Notre Dame IN 46556-0399
Phone: (800) 631-3622
Fax: (219) 631-6783

www.nd.edu

The University of Indianapolis
Executive MBA
Graduate Business Programs
Executive MBA Program
University of Indianapolis
1400 East Hanna Avenue
Good Hall 108
Indianapolis, Indiana 46227
Office 317-788-4905
Cell 317-698-2683

mba.uindy.edu/pages_programs/
executive_mba.php
mba@uindy.edu

Kansas

Benedictine College
Executive MBA
1020 N 2nd Street
Atchison KS 66002
Phone: 800-467-5340 x2589

www.benedictine.edu

Wichita State University
W. Frank Barton School of Business
Executive MBA Program
1845 Fairmont
Wichita KS 67260-0048
Phone: 316-978-3230
Fax: 316-978-3767

www.wichita.edu

Kentucky

University of Louisville
Executive MBA in Healthcare
College of Business and Public
Administration
University of Louisville
Louisville KY 40292
Phone: 502-852-4679

cm.cbpa.louisville.edu

Louisiana

Louisiana State University
E.J. Ourso College of Business
Administration
James C. and Cherie H. Flores
MBA Program

3307 CEBA Building
Baton Rouge LA 70803
Phone: 225-578-8867
Fax: 225-578-2421

Tulane University
A.B. Freeman School of Business
New Orleans Executive MBA Program
Stewart Center for Executive
Education
4112 Goldring/Woldenberg II
New Orleans LA 70118-5669
Phone: (504) 865-5481
Fax: (504) 865-6758

www.freeman.tulane.edu
executive.ed@tulane.edu

University of New Orleans

College of Business Administration
Executive MBA
368 Business Building
New Orleans LA 70148
Phone: 504-280-3215
Fax: 504-280-6007

www.business.uno.edu/emba

Massachusetts

Boston University
School of Management
Executive MBA Program
Boston University Executive
Leadership Center
595 Commonwealth Avenue
Boston MA 02215
Phone: (617) 353-8470

www.bu.edu
emba@bu.edu

Northeastern University
Graduate School of Business
Administration
Executive MBA Program
350 Dodge Hall
360 Huntington Avenue
Boston MA 02115
Phone: (617) 373-5992
Fax: (617) 373-8564

www.emba.neu.edu
gsba@neu.edu

Suffolk University
Frank Sawyer School of
Management
Executive MBA Program
8 Ashburton Place
Boston MA 02108
Phone: (617) 573-8304
Fax: 617-994-4239

www.sawyer.suffolk.edu
kpolito@suffolk.edu

Maryland

Loyola College in Maryland

The Joseph A. Sellinger, S.J. School
of Business and Management
Executive MBA Program
The Graduate Center - Timonium
Campus
2034 Greenspring Drive
Timonium MD 21093
Phone: (410) 617-5064
Fax: (410) 617-2005

www.loyola.edu

University of Maryland
Robert H. Smith School of
Business
Executive MBA
Van Munching Hall
Suite 2417 College Park, MD
20742
Phone: 301-405-2559
Fax: 301-314-9862

www.rhsmith.umd.edu/emba/

Michigan

Michigan State University
The Eli Broad Graduate School of
Management
The Weekend MBA
The James B. Henry Center for
Executive Development
3535 Forest road
East Lansing MI 48910
Phone: 517-355-7603
Fax: 517-432-0466

www.bus.msu.edu
wmba@bus.msu.edu

Michigan State University
The Eli Broad Graduate School of
Management
The Weekend MBA
120 North Business Complex
East Lansing MI 48824
Phone: 800-746-6781
Fax: 517-432-0466

www.bus.msu.edu
wmba@bus.msu.edu

Northwood University
The Richard DeVos Graduate
School of Management
Executive MBA Program
3225 Whiting Drive
Midland MI 48640-2398
Phone: (800)- MBA-9000
Fax: (517) 837-4800

www.northwood.edu
mba@northwood.edu

University of Michigan

University of Michigan Business
School
Executive MBA Program
710 East University Avenue
Ann Arbor MI 48109-1234
Phone: 734-615-9700
Fax: 734-615-9701

www.emba.bus.umich.edu
wmbsemba@umich.edu

Minnesota

University of Minnesota
Curtis L. Carlson School of
Management
Carlson Executive MBA (CEMBA)
4-106 Carlson School of
Management
321-19th Avenue South
Minneapolis MN 55455
Phone: (800) 922-3622
Fax: (612) 625-1012

www.carlsonschool.umn.edu/cemba
cemba@umn.edu

University of Minnesota
Curtis L. Carlson School of
Management
Vienna Executive MBA
US Operations: International
Programs
4-104 Carlson School of
Management,
321-19th Avenue South
Minneapolis MN 55455
Phone: 612-626-8182
Fax: 612-624-8248

www.carlsonschool.umn.edu/cemba
cemba@umn.edu

University of Minnesota
Curtis L. Carlson School of
Management
Warsaw Executive MBA
US Operations: International
Programs
4-104 Carlson School of
Management, 321-19th Avenue
South
Minneapolis MN 55455
Phone: 612-626-8182
Fax: 612-624-8248

www.carlsonschool.umn.edu/cemba
cemba@umn.edu

University of St. Thomas
Graduate School of Business
Executive MBA Program
1000 LaSalle Avenue, TMH 455
Minneapolis MN 55403-2005
Phone: (651) 962-4230
Fax: (651) 962-4232

Missouri

Rockhurst University
Helzberg School of management
The Executive Fellows Program
1100 Rockhurst Road
Conway 207
Kansas City MO 64110
Phone: 816-501-4091
Fax: 816-501-4614

www.rockhurst.edu

Saint Louis University
John Cook School of Business and
Administration
Boeing Institute of International
Business
John and Lucy Cook Hall, Suite 332
3674 Lindell Boulevard
St. Louis MO 63108
Phone: (314) 977-3898
Fax: (314) 977-7188

mba.slu.edu
biib@slu.edu

University of Missouri-Kansas City
Henry W. Bloch School of Business
and Public Administration
Executive MBA Program
217 Bloch School
5100 Rockhill Road
Kansas City MO 64110-2499
Phone: (816) 235-5295
Fax: (816) 235-2351

www.umkc.edu

Washington University in St. Louis

John M. Olin Business School
Executive MBA Campus Box 1158
One Brookings Drive
St. Louis MO 63130-4899
Phone: (888) 273-6820
Fax: (314) 935-7161

www.olin.wustl.edu/emba
emba@wustl.edu

North Carolina

Duke University
The Fuqua School of Business
The Duke MBA-Global Executive
P.O. Box 90127
Durham NC 27708-0127
Phone: (919) 660-7804
Fax: (919) 660-8044

www.fuqua.duke.edu
globalexec@fuqua.duke.edu

Duke University
The Fuqua School of Business
The Duke MBA- Weekend
Executive
Box 90127
Durham NC 27708-0127
Phone: 919-660-7804
Fax: 919-660-8044

www.fuqua.duke.edu
wekendexec@fuqua.duke.edu

Duke University
The Fuqua School of Business
The Duke MBA-Cross Continent
1 Towerview Drive
Durham NC 27708
Phone: 919-660-7804
Fax: 919-660-8044

www.fuqua.duke.edu
cross-continent-info@mail.duke.edu

Queens University of Charlotte
McColl School of Business
Executive MBA
1900 Selwyn Avenue
Charlotte NC 28274
Phone: 704-337-2489
Fax: 704-337-2522

www.mccollschool.edu
mccollemba@queens.edu

**The University of North
Carolina-Chapel Hill**
Kenan-Flagler Business School
Executive MBA evening Program
McColl Building CB3490
Chapel Hill NC 27599-3490
Phone: (80) 453-9515
Fax: 919-962-0551

www.emba.unc.edu
emba@unc.edu

**The University of North
Carolina-Chapel Hill**
Kenan-Flagler Business School
Executive MBA weekend Program
McColl Building CB3490

Chapel Hill NC 27599-3490
Phone: (800) 453-9515
Fax: 919-962-0551

www.emba.unc.edu
emba@unc.edu

**The University of North
Carolina-Chapel Hill**
Kenan-Flagler Business School
OneMBA Global
Executive MBA Program
McColl Building CB3490
Chapel Hill NC 27599-3490
Phone: (800) 453-9515
Fax: 919-962-0551

www.onemba.org
onemba@unc.edu

Wake Forest University
Babcock Graduate School of
Management
Fast Track Executive MBA Program
Wake Forest Road-Worrell
Professional Center, Room 2119
PO Box 7368
Winston-Salem NC 27109-7368
Phone: (336) 758-4584
Fax: (336) 758-5830

www.mba.wfu.edu
evening.exec@mba.wfu.edu

Nebraska

University of Nebraska at Omaha
Executive MBA Program
RH 120
6001 Dodge Street

Omaha NE 68182-0424
Phone: (402) 554-2448
Fax: (402) 554-2298

cba.unomaha.edu/xmba

New Hampshire

**University of New Hampshire
Whittemore**
School of Business and Economics
Executive MBA Program
McConnell Hall
15 College Road
Durham, NH 03824-3593
Phone: (603) 862-1367
Fax: (603) 862-4468

www.mba.unh.edu
emba.program@unh.edu

New Jersey

Farleigh Dickinson University

Samuel J. Silberman College of
Business
MBA in Management (for
Executives)
1000 River Road, COBA
Mail code:H324A
Teaneck NJ 07666
Phone: (201) 692-7206
Fax: (201) 692-7209

www.fdu.edu
grad@fdu.edu

**New Jersey Institute of
Technology**
School of Management
Executive Program-MS/
Management
University Heights
Newark NJ 07102-1982
Phone: 973-642-7499
Fax: 973-596-3074

www.njit.edu

**Rutgers - The State University of
New Jersey**
Executive MBA Program
180 University Avenue
Newark NJ 07102
Phone: (973) 353-5015
Fax: (973) 353-1424

www.emba.rutgers.edu
remba@andromeda.rutgers.edu

New Mexico

University of New Mexico
The Robert O. Anderson
School and Graduate School of
Management
Executive MBA Program
Albuquerque NM 87131-1221
Phone: (505) 277-2525
Fax: (505) 277-0345

www.mgt.unm.edu
emba@mgt.unm.edu

Nevada

University of Nevada, Las Vegas
College of Business
Executive MBA 4505 S. Maryland
Parkway
Box 456001
Las Vegas NV 89154-6001
Phone: 702-895-3904
Fax: 702-895-4090

cob.nevada.edu

New York

Baruch College-CUNY
Zicklin School of Business
Executive Programs
17 Lexington Avenue
Box 1215 New York NY 10010
Phone: (646) 312-3100

zicklin.baruch.cuny.edu
exprogbus@baruch.cuny.edu

Baruch College-CUNY
Zicklin School of Business
Executive MS in Finance
17 Lexington Avenue
PO Box X-13-282
New York NY 10010
Phone: (646) 312-3100

zicklin.baruch.cuny.edu
exprogbus@baruch.cuny.edu

Binghamton University
School of Management
State University of New York
Executive MBA Program
Binghamton NY 13902-6015
Phone: (607) 777-2538

som.binghamton.edu
goodhart@binghamton.edu

Columbia University
Executive MBA Program
1125 Amsterdam Avenue, Room 404
New York NY 10025-1717
Phone: (212) 854-2211

www4.gsb.columbia.edu/emba
emba@columbia.edu

Columbia University
Executive MBA - Global (London
Business School)
1125 Amsterdam Avenue, Room 404
New York NY 10025-1717
Phone: (212)854-2211

www.emba-global.com/
emba@columbia.edu

Cornell University
Johnson Graduate School of
Management
Executive MBA Program
142 Sage Hall
Ithaca NY 14853-6201
Phone: 607-255-4251

www.johnson.cornell.edu
emba@cornell.edu

Fordham University
Graduate School of Business
Executive MBA Program
c/o Fordham University
33 West 60th Street 4th Floor
New York, NY 10023
Phone: 914-332-6011
Fax: 914-332-7107

www.bnet.fordham.edu
admissionsgb@fordham.edu

Hofstra University
Frank G. Zarb School of Business
Executive MBA Program
100 Hofstra University
Hempstead NY 11549
Phone: 516-463-6700
Fax: 516-463-5100

www.hofstra.edu
mba-emba@hofstra.edu

New York University
Leonard N. Stern School of
Business
The Executive MBA Programs
Management Education Center
44 West 4th Street, Suite 10-66
New York NY 10012-1126
Phone: (212) 998-0789
Fax: (212) 995-4222

www.stern.nyu.edu
executive@stern.nyu.edu

**New York University/HEC Paris/
London**
TRIUM Global Executive MBA
Program
44 West 4th Street
Suite 4-100
New York NY 10012-1126
Phone: 212-998-0442
Fax: 212-995-4222

www.triumemba.org
info@triumemba.org

Pace University
Lublin School of Business
Executive MBA Program
One Pace Plaza
New York NY 10038
Phone: (212) 346-1870
Fax: (212) 346-1872

www.pace.edu
emba@pace.edu

Rensselaer Polytechnic Institute
The Executive MBA Program
Pittsburgh Building
110 Eighth Street
Troy NY 12180-3590
Phone: (585) 475-2229
Fax: (585) 475-7164

www.rit.edu
gradinfo@rit.edu

Rochester Institute of Technology
College of Business
Executive MBA Program
107 Lomb Memorial Drive

Rochester NY 14623
Phone: (585) 275-3439
Fax: (585) 244-3612

www.ritexecutive.com
emba@simon.rochester.edu

Syracuse University
School of Management
MBA and MS programs
222 CHM
Syracuse NY 13244-2130
Phone: (315) 443-3006
Fax: (315) 443-9517

whitman.syr.edu
emba@som.syr.edu

University At Buffalo
School of Management
The Executive MBA Program
108B Jacobs Management Center
Buffalo NY 14260-4000
Phone: (716) 645-3200
Fax: (716) 645-3202

www.mgt.buffalo.edu
mgt-emba@buffalo.edu

University of Rochester
William E. Simon Graduate School
of Business
Executive Programs Office
Box 270107
Rochester NY 14627
Phone: (716) 275-3439
Fax: (716) 244-3612

www.simon.rochester.edu

Ohio

Baldwin-Wallace College
Executive MBA Program
Kamm Hall
Berea OH 44017
Phone: (440) 826-2064

www.bw.edu

Bowling Green State University
College of Business Administration
Executive MBA Program
369 Business Administration Bldg.
Bowling Green OH 43403-
Phone: 800-BGSU-MBA

bgsumba.com
mba-info@cba.bgsu.edu

Case Western Reserve University
Weatherhead School of
Management
Executive MBA Program
10900 Euclid Avenue
Cleveland OH 44106-7166
Phone: 216-368-6411

www.weatherhead.cwru.edu

Cleveland State University
Executive MBA Program
1860 E. 18th Street, MH308
Cleveland OH 44114-
Phone: (216) 687-6925

www.csuohio.edu

Kent State University
Graduate School of Management
Executive MBA Program
Room 306, College of Business
Administration
Kent OH 44242
Phone: (330) 672-3622
Fax: 330-672-9495

www.business.kent.edu

Ohio University
Executive MBA Program
Copeland Hall
Athens OH 45701
Phone: (740) 593-2028
Fax: (740) 593-0319

www.cob.ohiou.edu

The Ohio State University
Max M. Fisher College of Business
Executive MBA program
110 Pfahl Hall
280 West Woodruff Avenue
Columbus OH 43210-1144
Phone: (614) 292-9300
Fax: (614) 292-6644

fisher.osu.edu

The University of Toledo
College of Business Administration
Executive MBA Program
1029 Stranahan Hall
Toledo OH 43606-3390
Phone: (419) 530-3622
Fax: 419-530-7260

www.business.utoledo.edu
emba@uoft02.utoledo.edu

Xavier University
Graduate School of Business
Executive MBA Program
Cincinnati, OH 45207-3221
Phone: (513) 745-3412
Fax: (513) 745-2929

www.xavier.edu/xmba

Youngstown State University
Williamson College of Business
Administration
Executive MBA Program
Youngstown OH 44555
Phone: (330) 742-3069
Fax: (330) 742-1459

www.wcba.ysu.edu

Oregon

University of Oregon/Oregon State University/Portland State University
Oregon Executive MBA Program
18640 NW Walker Road, No. 1008
Beaverton Oregon 97006-1975
Phone: 503-725-2250
Fax: 503-725-2255

www.oemba.org
oemba@oemba.org

Pennsylvania

Drexel University
Bennett S. LeBow College of
Business
Executive MBA Program

206 Matheson Hall
3141 Chestnut Street
Philadelphia PA 19104
Phone: (215) 895-1604
Fax: (215) 895-1602

www.lebow.drexel.edu
emba@drexel.edu

La Salle University
School of Business Administration
Executive MBA for Science and
Technology
1900 West Olney Avenue
College Hall Philadelphia PA
19141-1199
Phone: 215-951-5113
Fax: 215-951-1886

www.lasalle.edu
emba@lasalle.edu

Saint Joseph's University
Erivan K. Haub School of Business
Executive MBA Program
392 Mandeville Hall
5600 City Avenue
Philadelphia PA 19131-1395
Phone: (610) 660-1692
Fax: 610-660-3303

www.sju.edu
embba@sju.edu

Temple University
The Fox School of Business and
Management
Executive MBA Program
1515 Market Street, Suite 614

Philadelphia PA 19102
Phone: 215-204-1483

www.fox.temple.edu
melissa.wieczorek@temple.edu

University of Pennsylvania
Wharton MBA Program for
Executives
G21 Jon M. Huntsman Hall
The Wharton School
University of Pennsylvania
3730 Walnut Street
Philadelphia, PA 19104.6340
Phone: 215.898.5887
Fax: 215.898.2598

wharton.upenn.edu/mbaexecutive
mbaexec-admissions@wharton.
upenn.edu

University of Pittsburgh
Katz Graduate School of Business
Executive MBA Program
Mellon Financial Corporation Hall
4227 Fifth Avenue, 5th Floor,
Masonic Temple
Pittsburgh PA 15260
Phone: 412-648-1607
Fax: 412-648-1787

www.business.pitt.edu/katz/emba/
EMBAprogram@katz.pitt.edu

Villanova University
College of Commerce and Finance
Villanova University Executive
MBA Program
601 County Line Road

Radnor PA 19087-4523
Phone: 610-523-1793
Fax: 610-523-1798

emba.villanova.edu
vemba_info@villanova.edu

Rhode Island

The University of Rhode Island
College of Business Administration
Executive MBA Program
210 Flagg Road Kingston RI
02881
Phone: (401) 874-5000
Fax: (401) 874-7047

www.cba.uri.edu
mba@etal.uri.edu

South Carolina

Winthrop University
School of Business Administration
Executive MBA Program
Thurmond Hall
Rock Hill SC 29733
Phone: (803) 323-2409
Fax: (803) 323-2539

www.winthrop.edu
mbaoffice@winthrop.edu

Tennessee

The University of Memphis
Fogelman College of Business and
Economics
Executive MBA Program

400 BA Building
Memphis TN 38152
Phone: (901) 678-4866
Fax: (901) 678-5433

www.memphis.edu/executivemba
mgillnsn@memphis.edu

**The University of Tennessee at
Chattanooga**
College of Business Administration
Executive MBA Program, dept. 6056
615 McNally Avenue
Chattanooga TN 37403-2598
Phone: (800) 532-3028
Fax: (423) 785-2329

www.utc.edu

**The University of Tennessee at
Knoxville**
Executive MBA Program
704 Steely Management Center
Knoxville TN 37996-0575
Phone: 865-974-8519
Fax: 865-974-4989

www.emba.utk.edu
kkarl@utk.edu

**The University of Tennessee at
Knoxville**
Physician Executive MBA program
711 Steely Management Center
Knoxville TN 37996-0570
Phone: (888) 446-5458
Fax: 865-974-0929

www.pemba.utk.edu

The University of Tennessee at Knoxville
Professional MBA Program
606 Steely Management Center
Knoxville TN 37996-0570
Phone: 865-974-1660
Fax: 865-974-4989

promba.utk.edu

The University of Tennessee at Knoxville
Executive MBA Program in Taiwan
606 Steely Management Center
Knoxville TN 37996-0570
Phone: 865-974-1660
Fax: 865-974-4989

promba.utk.edu
lemba@utk.edu

Vanderbilt University
Owen Graduate School of Management
Executive MBA Program
401 Twenty-first Avenue South
Nashville TN 37203
Phone: 615-322-3120
Fax: 615-343-1499

www.mba.vanderbilt.edu
emba@owen.vanderbilt.edu

Texas

Baylor University (Dallas)
Executive MBA Program (Dallas)
The Cooper Aerobics Center
12230 Preston Road

Dallas TX 75230
Phone: (972) 458-2327

www.baylor.edu/demba
emba.dallas@baylor.edu

Baylor University (Waco)
Hankamer School of Business
One Bear Place #98013
Waco TX 76798-8013
Austin Campus
7700 W. Parmer Lane
Austin TX 78729

www.baylor.edu
emba_info@baylor.edu

Rice University
Jones Graduate School of Management
The MBA Program for Executive
P.O. Box 1892
Houston TX 77251-1892
Phone: 713-348-6060
Fax: (713) 285-5131

www.rice.edu

Southern Methodist University
Edwin L. Cox School of Business
Executive MBA Program
P.O. Box 750333
Dallas TX 75275-0333
Phone: (214) 768-2630
Fax: (214) 768-3956

www.cox.smu.edu
mbainfo@mail.cox.smu.edu

Texas A&M University
Lowry Mays College and Graduate
School of Business
Mays Executive MBA Program
219 Wehner Building
4356 TAMU
College Station TX 77843-4356
Phone: 979-845-0361
Fax: 979-862-6296

emba.tamu.edu
emba@tamu.edu

Texas Christian University
MJ Neeley School of Business
Executive MBA Program
TCU Box 298545
Fort Worth TX 73129
Phone: 817-257-7543
Fax: 817-257-6049

www.emba.tcu.edu
emba@tcu.edu

The University of Texas at Austin
The McCombs school of business
Option II MBA Program
P.O. Box 7337
Austin TX 78713-7337
Phone: (512) 471-4487
Fax: 512-475-8747

www.bus.utexas.edu
inquiry@optionii.bus.utexas.ed

The University of Texas at Austin
The McCombs school of business
Executive MBA in Mexico City
ITESM-CCM

P.O. Box 7337
Austin TX 78713
Phone: (512) 471-5893
Fax: 512-475-8747

www.mccombs.utexas.edu
emba@bus.utexas.edu

The University of Texas at Dallas
School of Management
The Executive MBA Program
P.O. Box 830688, HH15
Richardson TX 75083-0688
Phone: 972-883-2562
Fax: 972-883-6381

som.utdallas.edu

The University of Texas at Dallas
School of Management
The Professional MBA Program
P.O. Box 830688, HH15
Richardson TX 75083-0688
Phone: 972-883-2597
Fax: 972-883-6381

som.utdallas.edu

The University of Texas at Dallas
School of Management
The Global Leadership Executive
MBA Program
P.O. Box 830688, HH15
Richardson TX 75083-0688
Phone: 972-883-2373
Fax: 972-883-6164

glemba.utdallas.edu
glemba@utdallas.edu

Tulane University
A.B. Freeman School of Business
Houston Executive MBA Programs
Stewart Center for Executive
Education
1700 West Loop South, Ninth Floor
Houston TX 77027
Phone: (713) 586-6400
Fax: (713) 586.6410

www.freeman.tulane.edu
executive.ed@tulane.edu

University of Houston
C.T. Bauer College of Business
Executive MBA Program
334 Melcher Hall, Suite 250
Houston TX 77204-6021
Phone: (713) 743-4700
Fax: (713) 743-4706

www.uhemba.org

University of North Texas
College of Business Administration
Executive MBA
Box 311160
Denton TX 76203-1160
Phone: 940-565-3154
Fax: 940-369-8978

www.unt.edu
emba@unt.edu

Utah

Brigham Young University
Marriott School of Management
Executive MBA Program

637 TNRB P.O. Box 23012
Provo UT 84602-3012
Photo: (801) 378-3622

emba.byu.edu
emba@byu.edu

University of Utah
David Eccles School of Business
Executive MBA
1645 E. Campus Center Drive
Salt Lake City UT 84112-9301
Phone: (801) 581-5577
Fax: (801) 585-3932

www.business.utah.edu
execbv@business.utah.edu

Virginia

College of William and Mary
The College of William & Mary
Mason School of Business
P.O. Box 8795
Williamsburg, VA 23187-8795
Tel: 757.221.2913
Fax: 757.221.2958

www.mason.wm.edu/EMBA

George Mason University
School of Management
Executive MBA Program
Enterprise Hall, Mail Stop #5F5
4400 University Drive
Fairfax VA 22030
Phone: 703-993-1832
Fax: 703-993-1870

emba@gmu.edu

University of Richmond
Robins School of Business
Corporate MBA
University of Richmond VA 23173
Phone: 804-287-6651
Fax: 804-287-6544

www.richmond.edu
fbell@richmond.edu

Virginia Commonwealth University
Fast Track Executive MBA
1015 Floyd Avenue
Richmond VA 23284-4000
Phone: (804) 828-3939
Fax: (804) 828-6717

www.bus.vcu.edu
fastrack@vcu.edu

The Darden School of Business
The Darden MBA for Executives
Program
Darden Graduate School of
Business Administration
P.O. Box 6550
University of Virginia
Charlottesville, VA 22906
Phone: (434) 243-3622
Fax (434) 243-2332

www.darden.virginia.edu/MBAexec
MBAExec@darden.virginia.edu

Washington

University of Washington
Executive MBA Program
University of Washington Business
School
Box 353220
Seattle, WA 98195-3220
Phone: (206) 685-1333
Fax: (206) 543-6872
Toll Free: 1-888-622-3932

emba@u.washington.edu

Washington DC

George Washington University
The George Washington University
School of Business
Executive MBA Program
Duques Hall, Suite 550
2201 G Street, NW
Washington, DC 20052
Phone: 202-994-1212
http://business.gwu.edu/grad/
emba/index.html
gwmba@gwu.edu

**Georgetown - ESADE Global
Executive MBA
Georgetown University**
McDonough School of Business
Rafik B. Hariri Building, Suite 462
37th and O Streets, NW
Washington DC 20057, USA

www.globalexecmba.com
emba@georgetown.edu

Georgetown Campus Global Executive MBA
McDonough School of Business
Rafik B. Hariri Building, Suite 462
37th and O Streets, NW
Washington, DC 20057

msb.georgetown.edu
emba@georgetown.edu

Executive Master's in Leadership
Georgetown University
McDonough School of Business
Rafik B. Hariri Building, Suite 462
37th and O Streets, NW
Washington, DC 20057

msb.georgetown.edu
emlprogram@georgetown.edu

The Washington Campus
1625 Massachusetts Avenue, NW,
Suite 250
Washington, Washington, D.C.
20036
Phone: 202-234-4446
Fax: 202-234-4505

www.washcampus.edu
mdj@washcampus.edu

Wisconsin

Marquette University
College of Business Administration
executive MBA program
PO Box 1881 Milwaukee WI 53201
Phone: 414-288-7145
Fax: 414-288-1660

www.busadm.mu.edu

University of Wisconsin-Madison
School of Business
Executive MBA Program
975 University Avenue Madison
WI 53706-1323
Phone: 608-265-2034
Fax: 608-262-3607

www.bus.wisc.edu
crieben@bus.wisc.edu

University of Wisconsin-Milwaukee
School of Business Administration
Executive MBA Program
P.O. Box 742
Milwaukee WI 53201
Phone: (414) 229-5738
Fax: 414-229-2372

emba@uwm.edu

West Virginia

University College of Business and Economics
Executive MBA Program
P.O. Box 6025
Morgantown WV 26506-6025
Phone: (304) 293-5408
Fax: (304) 293-2385

www.be.wvu.edu
mba@wvu.edu

International EMBA Program Directory

Argentina

Universidad Austral-IAE
Escuela de Direccion y Negocios de
la Universidad Austral
Executive MBA
Mariano Acosta s/n. Derqui
B1629WWA Pilar
Buenos Aires, Argentina
Phone: 54-2322-481-000
Fax: 54-2322-481-050

www.iae.edu.ar
gacevedo@iae.edu.ar

Australia

Queensland University of Technology
Brisbane Graduate School of Business
Executive MBA Program
Gardens Point Campus
2 George Street
Brisbane, Queensland, Australia 4000
Phone: 07 3138 2653
Fax: 07 3138 5054
GPO Box 2434

www.bus.qut.com
bus@qut.com

University of South Australia
International Graduate School of
Management
International Master of Business
Administration

Way Lee Building, North Terrace
Adelaide
South Australia, Australia 5000
Phone: 61-8-8302-0032
Fax: 61-8-8302-0709

www.unisa.edu.au
igsm.info@unisa.edu.au

Danube-University Krems
MBA Krems
Karl Dorrek StraBe 30
A-3500
Krems Austria
Phone: 43-2732-893-2120
Fax: 43-2732-893-4100

www.mba-krems.at
mba@donau-uni.ac.at

The University of Melbourne

Melbourne Business School
Executive MBA (EMBA)
Tel: 61 3 9349 8413
Fax: 61 3 9349 8271

http://www.mbs.edu/emba
emba@mbs.edu

Brazil

Business School Sao Paulo
Executive MBA Program
Rua Alexander Dumas
2100 15th Floor

Sao Paulo Brazil SP 04717-004
Phone: 55-11-5181-0027
Fax: 55-11-5182-0277

www.bsp.com.br
emba@bsp.com.br

Fundacao Dom Cabral
Executive MBA Program
Rua Bernardo Guimaraes, 3071
30140-083 Belo Horizonte - MG
Brazil
Phone: 55 31 35897434
Fax: 55-31-299-9854

www.domcabral.org.br
pauloresende@fdc.org.br

IBMEC Business School
Executive MBA - General
Management
Rua Maestro Cardim, 1170
Sao Paulo, Brazil
01416-001
Phone: 55-11-3175-2300
Fax: 55-11-287-9076

www.ibmec.br
mbasp@ibmec.br

**Thunderbird, The American
Graduate School of International
Management**
MIM for Executives - Sao Paulo
The American Chamber of
Commerce
Rua da Paz, 1431
Sao Paulo-SP, Brazil
CEP 14713-001
Phone: 55-11-5180-3864

www.t-bird.edu
saopaulo@t-bird.edu

University of Sao Paulo
International Executive MBA
Fundacao Instituto De
Administracao, Faculdade de
Economia, Administracao e
Contabilidade
Av. Prof. Luciano Gualberto, 908
Sao Paulo, Brazil
SP 05508-900
Phone: 55-11-3818-5848
Fax: 55-11-3814-0439

www.fea.usp.br
mbaexec@fia.fea.usp.br

Bulgaria

American University in Bulgaria
Executive MBA Program
1 University Park Street
Elieff Center, Studentski Grad,
Sofia 1700, Bulgaria
359-2- 960-7917

elieffcenter@aubg.bg

Canada

Concordia University
Executive MBA Program
1455 de Maisonneuve Blvd. West,
Suite GM-407
Montreal, Quebec
Canada, H3G-1MB
Phone: (514)848-EMBA
Fax: (514)848-3696

johnmolson.concordia.ca
emba@vax2.concordia.ca

McGill University
Faculty of Management
International Masters Program in
Practicing Management
1001 Sherbrooke Street West
Suite 601
Montreal, Quebec
Canada, H3A 1G5
Phone: (514)398-4017
Fax: (514)398-7443

Queen's University
Queen's School of Business
Queen's Executive MBA - Ottawa
Classroom
350 Albert Street, Suite 220
Ottawa, Ontario
Canada, K1R 1A4
Phone: 613-566-3622
Fax: (613)566-3623

www.business.queensu.ca
ottawa@execmba.com

Queen's University
Queen's School of Business
Queen's Executive MBA National
Videoconference
Mackintosh-Corrty Hall A311
Ontario, Kingston
Canada, K7L3N6
Phone: 613-533-6811
Fax: 613-533-2313

www.business.queensu.ca
national@execmba.com

Saint Mary's University
923 Robie Street
Halifax, Nova Scotia
Canada, B3H 3C3
Phone: 902-420-5175
Fax: 902-420-5175

www.stmarys.ca
bonniekirby@stmarys.ca

Simon Fraser University
Segal Graduate School of Business
Executive MBA Program
500 Granville Street, 3rd Floor
Vancouver, British Columbia
Canada, V6C 1W6
Phone: 778.782.5013
Fax: 778.782.5122

business.sfu.ca/emba
emba_program@sfu.ca

Queen's University
Queen's School of Business
Queen's Executive MBA - Ottawa
Classroom
350 Albert Street, Suite 220
Ottawa, Ontario
Canada, K1R 1A4
Phone: 613-566-3622
Fax: (613)566-3623

www.business.queensu.ca
ottawa@execmba.com

Queen's University
Queen's School of Business
Queen's Executive MBA - Ottawa
Classroom

350 Albert Street, Suite 220
Ottawa, Ontario
Canada, K1R 1A4
Phone: 613-566-3622
Fax: (613)566-3623

www.business.queensu.ca
ottawa@execmba.com

The University of Western Ontario
Richard Ivey School of Business
Executive MBA Program
(Mississauga)
London, Ontario
Canada, N6A 3K7
Phone: 852-2135-2299
Fax: 852-2808-4433

www.ivey.com.hk
emba@ivey.com.hk

The University of Western Ontario
Richard Ivey School of Business
Executive MBA Program (Toronto)
London, Ontario
Canada, N6A 3K7
Phone: 519-661-2172
Fax: 519-850-2341

www.ivey.uwo.ca
execmba@ivey.uwo.ca

The University of Western Ontario
Richard Ivey School of Business
Executive MBA Program (Hong
Kong Campus)
Cheng Yu Tung Management
Institute

5/F Phase One, Hong Kong
Convention &
Exhibition Centre
1 Harbour Road
Wanchai Hong Kong
Phone: 852-2808-4483
Fax: 852-2808-4433

www.ivey.uwo.ca
amelia_chan@ivey.com.hk

University of Calgary
Faculty of Management
The Alberta Calgary Executive
MBA Program
2500 University Drive NW
Calgary
Canada T2N 1N4
Phone: 403-220-8828
Fax: 403-284-7921

www.albertaemba.com

University of Ottawa
Executive MBA Program
Centre for Executive Education
45 O'Connor, Suite 350
Ottawa Ontario
Canada K1P 1A4
Phone: 613-564-9500
Fax: 613-564-9927

www.emba.uottawa.ca
info@emba.uottawa.ca

University of Toronto
Joseph L. Rotman School of
Management
Executive MBA Program

105 St. George Street
Toronto Ontario
Canada M5S 3E6
Phone: 416-978-4441
Fax: 416-978-5549

www.rotman.utoronto.ca
execed@rotman.utoronto.ca

University of Toronto
Joseph L. Rotman School of
Management
Global Executive MBA
105 St. George Street
Toronto Ontario
Canada M5S 3E6
Phone: 416-978-4441
Fax: 416-978-5549

www.rotman.utoronto.ca
execed@rotman.utoronto.ca

Chile

Tulane University
Tulane University
A.B. Freeman School of Business
Chile EMBA Program
Stewart Center for Executive
Education
240 Goldring/Woldenberg
New Orleans LA 70118 -5669
Phone: (504) 865-5481
Fax: (504) 865-6758

www.freeman.tulane.edu

China

The University of Chicago
Graduate School of Business
Executive MBA Program- Asia
101 Penang Road
Singapore, 238 466
Phone: 65-835-64-82
Fax: 65-835-64-83

gsb.uchicago.edu
singapore.inquiries@gsb.uchicago.edu

Tulane University
A.B. Freeman School of Business
Chile EMBA Program
Stewart Center for Executive
Education
240 Goldring/Woldenberg
New Orleans LA 70118 -5669
Phone: (504) 865-5481
Fax: (504) 865-6758

www.freeman.tulane.edu

Denmark

Technical University of Denmark
Center for Technology, Economics
and Management
Master in Management of
Technology
Building 421
DK-2800Lyngby
Denmark
Phone: 45-45-25-61-11
Fax: 45-45-88-43-37

www.tem.dtu.dk
tem@tem.dtu.dk

**The Aarhus School of Business/
University of Southern Denmark**
Executive MBA Program
MBA Program Office
4, Fuglesangs Alle
Aarhus V
Denmark, DK-8210
Phone: 45-89-48-66-88
Fax: 45-86-15-95-77

www.mbachange.dk
mbainfo@asb.dk

Ecuador

**Escuala Superior Politecnica Del
Litoral-ESPOL**
Escuela De Postgrado En
Administracion De Empresas-
ESPAE
Executive MBA
Campus Las Penas
Malecon #100
Guayaquil, Ecuador
Phone: 593-4-530383 or 530057
Fax: 593-4-563044

France

E.M. Lyon
Cesma MBA
23 Avenue Guy de Collongue
BP 174, 69130
Ecully Cedex
France
Phone: 33-4-78-33-78-00
Fax: 33-4-78-33-77-55

www.em-lyon.com
cesmamba@em-lyon.com

ESSEC Business School
CNIT BP 230
Place de la Defense
92053 Paris La Defense
Cedex, France
Phone: 33-1-46-92-49-00
Fax: 33-1-46-92-49-90

Groupe ESC Grenoble
Executive Masters in International
Business
BP 127-12
Rue Pierre Semard
Grenoble
France, 38003
Phone: 33-4-76-70-60-60
Fax: 334-76-70-60-99

www.esc-grenoble.fr
bouvard@esc-grenoble.fir

INSEAD - Fountebleau
Europe Campus
Boulevard de Constance
77305 Fontainebleau
Tel : 33 (0)1 60 72 40 00
Fax : 33 (0)1 60 74 55 00

www.insead.edu/home/
mba.info@insead.edu

Germany

Catholic University of Eichstaett
Graduate School of Business
Auf der Achanz 49
Ingolstadt
Bavaria, Germany
Phone: 49-841-937-1975
Fax: 49-8421-93-1950

Hong-Kong

City University of Hong Kong
Faculty of Business
Executive MBA Program
83 Tat Chee Avenue, Kowloon Tong
Kowloon, Hong Kong
Phone: 852-2788-7888
Fax: 852-2788-7182

www.fb.cityu.edu.hk

**The Hong Kong University of
Science and Technology**
School of Business and Management
Kellogg-HKUST Executive MBA
Program
Clear Water Bay
Kowloon, Hong Kong
Phone: (852)-2358-4180
Fax: (852)2358-1514

www.bm.ust.hk
emba@ust.hk

Ireland

University College, Dublin
Michael Smurfit Graduate School
of Business
Master of Business Administration
Carysfort Avenue
Blackrock County
Dublin, Ireland
Phone: 353-1-706-8860
Fax: 353-1-283-1911

www.ucd.ie
padmin@ucd.ie

Israel

Tel Aviv University
The Leon Recanati Graduate
School of Business Administration
Recanati Executive MBA Program
Faculty of Management
Tel Aviv University
P.O. Box 39010, Ramat Aviv
Tel Aviv
Israel, 69978
Phone: 972-3-640-9955
Fax: 972-3-640-7803

www.recanati.tau.ac.il
remba@tauex.tau.ac.il

Tel Aviv University

**The Leon Recanati
Graduate School of Business
Administration**
Kellogg/Recanati International
Executive MBA Program
Faculty of Management
Tel Aviv University
P.O. Box 39010, Ramat Aviv
Tel Aviv, Israel, 69978
Phone: 972-3-640-9955
Fax: 972-640-7803

www.recanati.tau.ac.il
kremba@tauex.tau.ac.il

Japan

Temple University
Fox School of Business and
Management
Executive MBA Program-Tokyo
2-8-12 Minami Azabu

Minato-ku
Tokyo
Japan, 106-0047
Phone: 81-3-5441-9871
Fax: 81-3-5441-9822

www.tuj.ac.jp/mba/index.html

Mexico

Instituto Panamericano De Alta
Direccion De Empresa (IPADE)
Executive MBA
Floresta #20
Ex-Hacienda De Claveria
Colonia Claveria, Delegacion
Aztcapotzalco
Mexico City, C.P.
Mexico, O2080
Phone: 52-55-5354-1800
Fax: 52-55-5354-1997

www.ipade.mx
raparicio1@ipade.mx

New Zealand

Massey University
Graduate School of Business
11-222 Palmerston North
New Zealand
Phone: 64-6-350-5803
Fax: 64-6-350-5819

mba.massey.ac.nz
MBA@massey.ac.nz

University of Otaga
Advanced Business Program
Executive MBA Program
University of Otago House
P.O. Box 5543

Aukland, New Zealand
Phone: 64-9-373-9720
Fax: 64-9-373-9721

www.otago.ac.nz
emba.admin@stone bow.otago.nz

Romania

**Institute for Business and Public
Administration from Bucharest-
ASEBUSS**
Calea Grivitei nr.8-10
78104 Bucharest
Romania, 78104
Phone: 40-1-211-5940
Fax: 40-1-312-5934

www.asebuss.ro
emba@asebuss.ro

Saudi Arabia

**King Fahd University of
Petroleum & Minerals**
Dr. Aymen Kayal, Assistant Dean
for Graduate Programs
College of Industrial Management
Dhahran - 31261, PO Box: 5074,
Saudi Arabia
Phone # (+9663-8601143)
Fax # (+9663-8603850)

www.kfupm.edu.sa/cim/emba/
emba@kfupm.edu.sa

Slovenia

International Executive
Development Center (IEDC)
Bled School of Management
Executive MBA Program

Presernova cesta 33
4260 Bled
Slovenia
Phone: 386-4-57-92-500
Fax: 386-4-57-92-501

www.iedc.si
emba@iedc.si

Switzerland

International Institute for Management Development-IMD
Executive MBA Program
Chemin de Bellerive 23
PO Box 915
CH1001 Lausanne
Switzerland
Phone: +41 21 618 0342

www.imd.ch

Spain

ESADE Business School
Av. Esplugues, 92-96
08034 Barcelona, Spain

www.globalexecmba.com
globalemba@esade.edu

The University of Chicago
Graduate School of Business
Executive MBA Program - Europe
Carter Arago 271
Barcelona Spain 8007
Phone: 34-93-505-21-50
Fax: 34-93-505-21-55

gsb.uchicago.edu
barcelona.inquires@gsb.uchicago.edu

IE Business School
María de Molina, 11
28006 Madrid Spain
Ph.:+34915689600/+34915689612

www.ie.edu
admissions@ie.edu

University of Navarra
Global Executive MBA
IESE Business School - Barcelona Campus
Avenida Pearson, 21
08034 Barcelona Spain
Tel.: +34 93 253 42 00
Fax: +34 93 253 43 43

IESE Business School—Madrid Campus
Camino del Cerro del Águila, 3
28023 Madrid Spain
Tel.: +34 91 211 30 00
Fax: +34 91 357 29 13

IESE Business School - Munich Office
Pacellistr. 4
80333 Munich Germany
Tel.: +49 89 24 20 97 90
Fax: +49 89 24 20 97 99

IESE Business School - New York Campus
200 W. 57th St. 14th Floor
New York, NY 10019
USA
Tel.: +1 212 956 0400
Fax: +1 212 421 9616

www.iese.edu
globalemba@iese.edu

Taiwan

Tulane University
A.B. Freeman School of Business
Asia Executive MBA Program
Stewart Center for Executive
Education
4112 Goldring/Woldenberg II
New Orleans LA 70118 -5669
Phone: (504) 865-5481
Fax: (504) 865-6758

www.freeman.tulane.edu
executive.ed@tulane.edu

Netherlands

Center for European Studies
Maastricht University at Maastricht
European Executive MBA
Component
European Executive Development
Seminar
P.O. Box 616
6200 MD Maastricht
Witmakersstraat 10
Maastricht
The Netherlands
6211 JB
Phone: 31-43-321-26-27
Fax: 31-43-325-73-24

www.ces.unimaas.nl
excespes@ces.unimaas.nl

Erasmus University Rotterdam
Rotterdam School of Management
International MBA and MBA/MBI
Program

PO Box 1738
Rotterdam 3000 DR
The Netherlands
Phone: 31-10-408-2222
Fax: 31-10-452-9509

www.rsm.nl
info@rsm.nl

Nyenrode Business Universiteit
International (full-time) MBA and
Part-time MBA Program
Straatweg 25
P.O. Box 130
3620 AC Breukelen (just outside
Amsterdam)
The Netherlands
Phone: +31 346 291 291
Fax: +31 346 291 450 1
www.nyenrode.nl
info@nyenrode.nl

United Arab Emirates

University of Sharjah
PO Box 27272 Sharjah
Sharjah
United Arab Emirates
Phone: 971-6-5050091
Fax: 971-6-5050032

www.sharjah.ac.ae
EMBA@sharjah.ac.ae

United Kingdom

Ashridge Business School
MBA Admissions
Berkhamsted

Hertfordshire, United Kingdom
HP4 INS
Phone: 44-1442-84-1143
Fax: 44-1442-84-1144

www.ashridge.com
mba@ashridge.org.uk

Henley Management College
Executive Full Time/Modular MBA
Greenlands, Henley-on-Thomes
Oxfordshire,
United Kingdom
RG9 3AU
Phone: 44-1491-571454
Fax: 44-1491-47887

www.henleymc.ac.uk
mba@henleymc.ac.uk

London Business School
Executive MBA Program
Regent's Park
London
United Kingdom
NW1 4SA
Phone: 44-20-7262-5050
Fax: 44-20-7724-7875

www.london.edu
University of Paisley
Ayrshire Management Center
Executive MBA Program
Craigie House, Craigie Park
Ayr
United Kingdom
KA8 0SS
Phone: 44-1292-886-400
Fax: 44-1292-886-401

www.managementcentre.org.uk
info@managementcentre.org.uk

Saïd Business School
University of Oxford
Park End Street
Oxford
OX1 1HP
United Kingdom
Phone: +44 (0)1865 288 901

www.sbs.oxford.edu/emba
emba-enquiries@sbs.ox.ac.uk

Warwick Business School
University of Warwick
Coventry
CV4 7AL
United Kingdom
Tel: +44 (0) 24 7652 4100
Fax: +44 (0)24 7657 4400

www.warwickmba.com
warwickmba@wbs.ac.uk

Cranfield School of Management
Cranfield University
Cranfield, Bedfordshire
MK43 0AL
United Kingdom
Phone: +44 (0) 1234 754386

www.som.cranfield.ac.uk
MBAenquiries@cranfield.ac.uk

**Nottingham University Business
School**
Jubilee Campus
Nottingham
NG8 1BB
United Kingdom
Tel: +44 (0) 115 951 5500
Fax: +44 (0) 115 951 5503

www.nottingham.ac.uk/business/mba
mba@nottingham.ac.uk

EMBA Program Descriptions

University	Program	Description
Arizona State University	W. P. Carey MBA Executive Program	"Ranked #13 in the world by The Wall Street Journal, the W. P. Carey Executive MBA is the most affordable top 25 EMBA program, making it one of the best values in business education. Small classes of fewer than 50 students allow you to network with peers and alumni. Classes meet twice monthly on Fridays and Saturdays at ASU's Tempe campus, making it convenient for travel from within Arizona and from surrounding states."
Auburn University	Executive MBA Program	Combines five residency weeks at Auburn, one study abroad module and distance-learning courses, over a 21-month period. There are Technology Management and HealthCare Administration concentration options within the regular EMBA, as well as a specialized program for Physicians.
Baruch College/CUNY	Executive MBA Program	The Executive MS at the Zicklin School of Business offers certain unique characteristics that make it especially suitable for the fast track executive. The EMBA offers an innovative structure and instructional methodology. The primary focus and unique characteristic of the program is its contextual orientation which shapes the "decision nexus" of a manager. The program is taught with students belonging to a cohort through a series of integrated modules. The modules focus on different types of decisions and allow the manager to understand the decision making process. As an integral part of the EMBA program students participate in an International Study Tour. Past trips have been to France, Germany, Great Britain, Belgium, Korea, Hong Kong and China.
Baruch College/CUNY	Executive MS in Finance	The Executive MS at the Zicklin School of Business offers certain unique characteristics that make it especially suitable for the fast track executive. The EMS in Finance teaches modern theory, applications, analytic skills, providing the finance professional with tools needed to effectively cope in today
Baylor University	Baylor University (Dallas)	This highly ranked program at the Cooper Aerobics Center focuses on developing executives with integrity and purpose, equipping each one with a strong sense of ethical consideration. Small class sizes facilitates learning in a collaborative and interactive environment.
Binghamton University/ SUNY	Executive MBA Program	Opportunity for general track or health care specialization during the second year of the program.
Birmingham-Southern College	Master of Arts in Public and Private Management (MPPM)	Based on the Yale University model, the MPPM was designed to develop the entrepreneurial, leadership, and managerial skills of engineers, attorneys, physicians and managers from financial, telecommunications, health care and other public, private and social sector organizations.
Boise State University	Executive MBA	"BSU's 21 month program meets 3 to 4 consecutive days each month. Virtual learning and study group participation facilitates learning outside of class. Year 1 begins with a one-week residency at an off-site resort in the the Idaho mountains. The year two international residency brings participants together with EMBA participants from many other cultures. Year 1 courses of Opportunity Assessment, Assessing Competitive Advantage and Fostering Innovation blend functional areas of marketing, finance, operations management, etc. to give a solid foundation. Year 2 depth areas include projects from corporate partners."
Boston University	Executive MBA Program	"The EMBA program's integrated curriculum focuses on Management as a System, a cross-functional understanding of the interdependencies among organizations' components. Through a structured framework of group study, assignments, and classroom teaching, the BU EMBA team learning approach promotes cooperative leadership skills by giving each team member a measurable stake in the success of their colleagues. Students develop a better understanding of how to work more effectively in teams, manage group dynamics, deal with conflict, and effect change. The program also offers a strong global component through a concentrated international module and trip designed to provide an understanding of the many factors that frame the business context in a range of developed and developing economies. The final module, "New Venture Creation and the Capstone Experience", challenges students to work in teams to apply their skills in the development of a comprehensive business plan. Classes meet on alternating weekends (Friday and Saturday), plus 4 residence weeks. Overnight accommodations provided on class nights. Continental breakfast and lunch served on class days. The International trip is 10 days (all expenses paid, ex. International airfare) Periodic family social events and guest speakers on class nights. Dedicated administrative team. Classes meet on alternating weekends (Friday and Saturday), plus 4 residence weeks. Overnight accommodations provided on class nights. Continental breakfast and lunch served on class days. The International trip is 10 days (all expenses paid, ex. International airfare) Periodic family social events and guest speakers on class nights. Dedicated administrative team."
Bowling Green State University	Executive MBA Program	Bowling Green State University offers one of the country's oldest executive MBA programs. Classes in our unique program meet only one weekend per month for 18 months. The program culminates in a study abroad session.
Bradley University	Theresa S. Falcon Executive MBA	Bradley's EMBA program strives to develop leaders who will meet tomorrow's challenges with knowledge and integrity. With an intense focus on leadership and an issues oriented, problem solving approach using an integrated curriculum of various business disciplines, participants will enhance their abilities to face business' most pressing problems. Throughout the program, participants will receive professional coaching on leadership skills. You'll start applying knowledge from the very first day, gain insights into how disciplines interact and leave with a personal development plan that you can follow for the rest of your life.
Brigham Young University	Executive MBA Program	Classes meet from 6:00 p.m. to 9:00 p.m. on Tuesdays and Thursdays. The program begins in late July. Classes are conducted year-round, although there are several breaks throughout each year. Each year of the program begins with a \Residency Week\. Students spend the entirety of this week on BYU campus. Classes are taught on two locations Provo and Salt Lake City."
California State University, Hayward	Transnational Executive MBA Program	TRANSNATIONAL EXECUTIVE MBA PROGRAM The TEMBA Program is a 52 unit global program for high potential mid-career and senior managers with 5-8 years of experience. It involves completing ten residential courses in the United States and three courses overseas on at least two continents. A high-level strategic consulting project for on overseas firm/government is completed by each participant in a team of five or more participants. Specializations in funtional, global regions and product/technology areas can be obtained by completing three additional courses in the follow-up Advanced Executive MBA (AEMBA) Certificate Program.Two cohorts are enrolled currently. Participants complete 520 class contact hours and 260 consulting contact hours and travel to two continents for class residencies and assignments with their consulting companies.

University	Program	Description
California State University, Hayward	Transnational Executive MBA Program, Europe	Transnational Executive MBA Program, Europe TEMBA Europe is a cohort-based global program for mid-career and senior European executives with 5-8 years of work experience. Participants complete ten residential courses in Austria and one course in California. Participants complete a strategic consulting assignment for globally-focused European companies and present their findings to top management. Participants study in-depth the opportunities presented by the enlargement of the European Union. Executives in the program interact with managers in the other global TEMBA programs. One cohort is enrolled currently. Participants have the option to take courses in California, Russia, Singapore and Hong Kong.
Case Western Reserve University	Executive MBA	"The Weatherhead EMBA curriculum is grounded in our experience that great leadership can be taught. For decades, Weatherhead's organizational behavior faculty has built a best-in-class reputation for teaching the art of leadership. We have helped thousands of executives unlock their leadership potential by giving them the tools to carefully examine their leadership strengths and gaps, and to develop a personalized learning plan that ensures they become the best leader they can be. In Weatherhead EMBA, we explore leadership at four levels: self, team, organization and society. Throughout the program, students are taught how to recognize the opportunities for outstanding leadership at each of these levels, and acquire the skills necessary to turn those opportunities into measurable successes throughout their careers."
Case Western Reserve University	Executive MBA Program	Classes are held on alternating Fridays and Saturdays on campus at the Dively Conference Center. The typical daily schedule is from 8:00 a.m. to 4:30 p.m. with a one-hour lunch break. Study Groups of six to eight participants also meet once a week in the evening at a time and place they determine. Typical meetings last three hours. The international study tour experience involves in-depth exposure to cultural and management practices in two different regions or economic centers. An interactive case study between local company leadership and the students is a significant part of the course. The Program fee covers all books, course materials, use of a laptop computer, parking and student fees, plus meals and lodging during the three residency periods, as well as travel, room and selected meal costs for the International Study Tour.
Chapman University	Executive MBA	The Arnold and Mabel Beckman Business and Technology Hall provides students with a state-of-the-art learning environment. The objective of the EMBA program is to develop innovative, proactive leaders. To achieve this, the program offers a broad-based, integrated curriculum through which students build a foundation in all functional areas of business and sharpen their managerial, analytical and decision-making skills. Three in-depth residential seminars enhance the curriculum. Two of the residentials are domestic (San Diego and Washington D.C.) and emphasize regional and national issues while the third is an international trip designed to provide first-hand exposure to managerial practices abroad.
Claremont Graduate University	Executive Management Program	The Executive Management Program at the Drucker School is designed for mid-career executives and professionals who want to make the transition to high-level leadership roles. It is a flexible, non-lockstep program designed to promote interaction between students. We offer the following degrees and certificates: Executive MBA; MA in Management; MS in Advanced Management (post-MBA degree); and Certificates in Strategy, Leadership, and General Management.
Columbia University	Berkeley-Columbia Program	The Berkeley-Columbia Executive MBA Program, launched in June 2002, joins the strengths of Columbia Business School and the Haas School of Business at the University of California, Berkeley. Students complete five terms over 19 months. Classes meet four times per term at Berkeley, Thursday through Saturday, and one time per term at Columbia, Wednesday through Saturday. The program draws faculty members from both schools, and students enjoy a elective options and an international seminar. Berkley-Columbia students obtain two MBA degrees: one from Columbia and one from the Haas School at Berkeley, and enjoy access to each alumni network.
Columbia University	EMBA-Global Americas and Europe	The EMBA-Global Americas & Europe Program was established in 2001 with London Business School. Designed for globally-oriented participants, the 20-month program enrolls approximately 70 students from around the world each May. Students earn MBA degrees from both Schools with full access to two vast networks of faculty and alumni worldwide. The program features an innovative once-a-month alternating schedule between New York City and London with action-based pedagogy.
Columbia University	Executive MBA Friday/ Saturday	Columbia Business School offers a 20-month Executive MBA program which begins in January and September. Students attend on-campus classes on alternating weekends from 8:30 a.m. to 6:45 p.m. on Friday and Saturday. Students complete 21 courses over five consecutive terms, and complete the same number of credits and are awarded the same degree as students in our full-time MBA program. A wide range of elective options are available, including international seminars to Asia, Europe, and Latin America.
Cornell University	Boardroom Executive MBA Program	Classes are held three Saturdays per month, allowing you to complete this 17-month program without disrupting your career or your life. The Cornell Boardroom Executive MBA Program is delivered via a state-of-the-art, real-time, interactive videoconference system that Queen's pioneered and has been using for over a decade with great success.
Cornell University	Executive MBA Program	The Cornell Executive MBA Program meets on alternate weekends (Saturday-Sunday) near New York City over 22 months. The program is taught by Johnson School faculty members, and graduates earn the same MBA degree as full-time Johnson School students. The alternate weekend format and the New York City location draws students from throughout the Eastern U.S. and several foreign countries.
Drexel University	Executive MBA Program	Two formats are offered: an evening EMBA (2 nights per week for 24 months) and a weekend EMBA (1 day per week for 20 months). Both include The GALLUP Leadership Retreat in partnership with THE GALLUP ORGANIZATION
Duke University	The Duke MBA - Cross Continent	The Duke MBA - Cross Continent program allows high-potential managers with 3-9 years experience to earn an internationally focused MBA in less than 2 years, utilizing a format that minimizes the disruption of careers and family life. Following 2 weeks of pre-reading and preparation from home, students cycle through Fuqua's global study locations in China, the UK, Dubai, Russia and India. Over 6 terms, students complete 12 core courses spanning all functional areas of business and 4 elective courses in a chosen discipline. Optional concentrations are offered in energy and environment, entrepreneurship and innovation, strategy, finance, marketing, or health sector management. The balance of the program is delivered via Internet-mediated learning.
Duke University	The Duke MBA - Global Executive	The Duke MBA - Global Executive general management program features a curriculum adjusted to include more global issues and advanced strategies for participants with 10-14+ years of work experience who have or will soon have global responsibilities. The program runs 5 terms over 18 months. Terms begin with 2-3 weeks of pre-reading and preparation, followed by a 2-week face-to-face residential session and 10 weeks of Internet-mediated learning. Residency sites include the UK, Russia, Dubai, India, China, and Durham, North Carolina. An optional concentration in health sector management is available for students seeking specialized training in the business of health care.
Duke University	The Duke MBA - Weekend Executive	The Duke MBA - Weekend Executive program allows high-potential managers with 5-10+ years of work experience to earn their MBA degree in 20 months while continuing in their careers. Classes are held every other weekend (Fri/Sat) with residencies in Durham that include face-to-face classroom interaction followed by 2 weeks of Internet-mediated learning. After a one-week orientation, the program covers 6 terms, during which students take 13 core courses and 4 electives, with an optional 2-course-credit special project to earn a concentration in energy and environment, entrepreneurship and innovation, marketing, strategy, and health sector management.

University	Program	Description
Emory University	Modular Executive MBA Program	The Modular Executive MBA (MEMBA) format allows participants from all over the US and the world to earn an Executive MBA from Emory. This unique format allows students to attend class in nine intensive one-week learning modules, over a period of 21 months (about once a quarter), augmented by distance learning. This is an ideal format for out-of-town or international participants who want to continue working while earning a top ranked MBA. Classes are held in new state-of-the-art building on the Emory campus and students have full access to all campus facilities. The program is focused on general management and leadership development and truly reflects today's business environment: rigorous, diverse and integrated.
Emory University	Modular Executive MBA program	The Modular Executive MBA (MEMBA) format allows participants from all over the US and the world to earn an Executive MBA from Emory. This unique format allows students to attend class in nine intensive one-week learning modules, over a period of 21 months (about once a quarter), augmented by distance learning. This is an ideal format for out-of-town or international participants who want to continue working while earning a top ranked MBA. Classes are held in new state-of-the-art building on the Emory campus and students have full access to all campus facilities. The program is focused on general management and leadership development and truly reflects today's business environment: rigorous, diverse and integrated.
Emory University	Weekend Executive MBA Program	Offered on alternating weekends over a 16-month period, the Weekend Executive MBA course structure includes four terms and one 10-day International Colloquium. Classes are held in new state-of-the-art building on the Emory campus and students have full access to all campus facilities. The program is focused on general management and leadership development and truly reflects today's business environment: rigorous, diverse and integrated. Ranked #1 in Southeast and #7 globally by BusinessWeek '07 and #10 nationally by US News and World Report.
Fairleigh Dickinson University	Executivev MBA in Management	Our Executive MBA program is for talented, high potential senior and mid-level managers. Only a select number of individuals enter this fast paced and intensive Saturday program each year. Our EMBA program is 21 a month, 48 credit program which includes a 2 week International Business Seminar overseas to regions such as Asia and Latin America.
Florida International University	Executive MBA - Miami	Based on FIU's University Park campus, the EMBA Miami Program provides a rigorous MBA curriculum infused with an emphasis on International Business and the strategic use of Information Technology. An 18 month program, this program meets Friday evenings and Saturdays.
Fordham University	Fordhams Accelerated Executive MBA Program	This is a cohort program that meets one weekend per month (Friday through Sunday), for 22 months. The program, which is a full-MBA in Management, meets at the Lincoln Center Campus as well as an off-site conference center. There is also a final residential in China as a capstone pedagogical experience.
George Fox University	EMBA	24 month week-end format cohort program for individuals with five or more years executive experience.
George Mason University	Executive MBA Program	The international residency integrates global perspectives into the curriculum. The program includes one week at Oxford University, where a certificate is earned and one week on continental Europe. The domestic residencies, one in Washington, DC and one in New York City, provide students with business seminars and site visits that leverage our location and focus on how regulation affects business decision making. The program is 21 months long, includes 54 semester credit hours, and has a strong networking with the area business community component.
George Washington University	Executive MBA Program	A program tailored to mid-career executives who want to advance their careers and organizations through technology, entrepreneurial creativity, and global business opportunities. These experienced managers and professionals who are on the fast track to greater leadership responsibilities in their organizations earn a 60 credit hour MBA in 21 months, without career interruption. Our program was the first business school to offer an EMBA program in the region. EMBA faculty are recognized for outstanding research and practice in the business disciplines, and are distinguished for their consulting with top private and public organizations. Class sessions are held once a week on alternating Fridays and Saturdays and in three-week long residencies and a two-week two-country residency held abroad.
Georgetown University	Executive Master's in Leadership (Georgetown University, McDonough School of Business)	The only master's degree program of its kind offered by a prominent business school, Georgetown's Executive Master's in Leadership (EML) is designed to challenge and inspire accomplished executives from business, government, and non-profit organizations. In just 12 months, the program integrates leadership perspectives from business, public policy, psychology, and military science, and it teaches students to become more creative and effective leaders, capable of leading meaningful change in their organizations. The EML program is designed for working executives and meets every other Friday and Saturday on the Georgetown University campus in Washington, D.C. Students are required to participate in two intensive, D.C.-based workshops, as well as a global leadership project that will challenge them to integrate and apply their experience and learning to a real leadership problem.
Georgetown University	Georgetown Campus Global Executive MBA (Georgetown University, McDonough School of Business)	The Georgetown Campus Global Executive MBA Program has been ranked among the top MBA programs worldwide for more than a decade. It augments core MBA business disciplines with specialized courses in global business, individual leadership coaching, and the practical experience of two global consulting projects, delivered in locations as diverse as Mexico, Turkey, Dubai, China, Vietnam, and India. This accelerated, 18-month program is designed for accomplished professionals with a minimum of eight years post-baccalaureate experience. Classes are arranged in cohorts that meet Fridays and Saturdays on alternate weekends on Georgetown's Washington, D.C., campus.
Georgetown University	Georgetown-ESADE Global Executive MBA	Georgetown University offers the Georgetown-ESADE Global Executive MBA for highly mobile, accomplished professionals who take their study of global management beyond the classroom through a series of intensive modules in locations such as New York City, Moscow, Bangalore, and Buenos Aires. Two of Georgetown
Georgia Institute of Technology	Executive Masters in Management of Technology	The Executive Master's Program in Management of Technology equips professionals with the skills necessary to succeed in today's rapidly changing technology-driven business world. The Friday and Saturday, every-other- week format allows the participant to attend the program without career interruption.
Georgia State University	Executive MBA Program	An 18 month program designed for busy professionals who want to earn an MBA from a top ranked school without interrupting their career. Classes are held alternating Fridays and Saturdays which allows students to better meet professional commitments. The Robinson EMBA program ranked among the top 25 in the world by BusinessWeek. Learning methodologies include case studies, simulations, class discussions, and company specific projects.
Golden Gate University	Executive MBA Program	The EMBA program is for committed executives professionals and entrepreneurs with five or more years of managerial experience. It begins with classic MBA skills--economics, finance, accounting, operations, marketing, international management, leadership and the public environment--and adds unique year-long projects in strategic planning and personal career development. Courses are taught by senior faculty who bring superb academic preparation and corporate experience to the program.
Golden Gate University	Golden Gate University	The EMBA program is for committed executives, professionals, and entrepreneurs with five or more years of managerial experience. It begins with classic MBA skills, economics, finance, accounting, operations, marketing, international management, leadership and public environment--and ads unique year long projects in strategic planning and personal career development. Courses are taught by senior faculty who bring superb academic pepration and corporate experiences to the program.
Grand Canyon University	Ken Blanchard Executive MBA Program at Grand Canyon University	If you are a seasoned leader, manager, business owner, administrator, or board member desiring to achieve unprecedented success as you take on increasing responsibilities, then the time may be right to consider the Ken Blanchard Executive MBA Program. This highly innovative program has been designed to combine Ken Blanchard

University	Program	Description
Hawaii Pacific University	Weekend MBA for Business Professionals	An 18-month program for business professionals that proivdes an exceptional blend of innovative instructions and professional experience. The primary goal is for students to become more effective managers and leaders in a global economy marked by uncertainty and change.
Hofstra University	Executive MBA Program	General MBA geared toward executives and focused on global dimensions of business.
Kennesaw State University	BellSouth/Cingular Corporate In-House MBA (CIMBA)	The BellSouth Corporate MBA (CIMBA) program is designed to equip the middle manager in BellSouth Corporation with the business knowledge, personal skills and leadership skills that are necessary to compete in the highly competitive and volatile telecommunications industry. The program is taught on site at BellSouth locations to BellSouth employees.
Kennesaw State University	MBA for Experienced Professionals	The MBA for Experienced Professionals is a team-taught, team-processed executive format program with a cross-functional, integrated curriculum. This 18-month program meets one weekend per month. This convenient schedule maximizes benefits with the use of a distance learning platform to support learning between associates and faculty when not meeting face-to-face.
Kent State University	Executive MBA Program	This EMBA program is a 19-month graduate program that offers business students the convenience of Saturday on-site business classes combined with optional online classes.
Louisiana State University	James C. and Cherie H. Flores Executive MBA Program	The Flores Executive MBA Program is intended for the working professional with a minimum of five years of business experience. The program constitutes 17 months of study over two academic years with classes held on alternate Fridays and Saturdays. Two one-week periods of concentrated study are also included. The 42-hour core curriculum consists of 14 core courses covering all major business fields. The curriculum includes three elective courses, which cover special topics of interest.
Loyola College in Maryland	Executive MBA Program	"The 21-month curriculum includes a thematic structure to each of the six modules (Business Foundations, The Firm & Its Environments, Global Challenge, Process of Value Creation, Strategy of Innovation, and The Integrated Challenge), residencies at the start of each academic year, an international field study, and a final retreat focusing on leadership and corporate social responsibility. Student average age is 40. Average number of years of work experience is 20 years with 8-10 years of managerial experience.
Loyola College in Maryland	MBA Fellows Program	The MBA Fellows Program is a 2.5 year, Saturday-only cohort program designed for fast-track, emerging leaders seeking to advance their careers. Contemporary issues of today's managers are addressed using a program that builds content around integrating themes within and across course modules. It is primarily delivered over ten, 10-week modules during which students take the equivalent of two courses per module (summers off). Classes are held on Saturdays only, ending in early afternoon.
Loyola Marymount University	Executive MBA	Produces principled leaders who have confidence in their ability to shape the direction of, and achieve results in, the organizations they lead. Promotes self-awareness and the ability to see the broader impact of management decisions. Provides personalized education with individual attention; integrating experiential projects with academics, so knowledge can be immediately applied; addressing total performance (business knowledge, execution, managerial competencies and leadership); and focusing on personal development and professional growth, with individual guidance from executive career coaches. Includes both domestic and international case study trips.
Loyola University Maryland	Executive MBA Program	The 21 month curriculum includes a thematic structure to each of the six modules (Business Foundations, The Firm & Its Environments, Global Challenge, Process of Value Creation, Strategy of Innovation, and the Integrated Challenge), residencies at the start of each academic year, an international field study, and a final retreat focusing on leadership and corporate responsibility. Student average age is 40. Average number of years of work experience is 20 years with 8-10 years of managerial experience. Please delete the above paragraph and change to the following: The 21-month curriculum emphasizes leadership development, executive coaching, and strategic integration of concepts. It is delivered over six modules, during which students take the equivalent of three courses per module (students have two months with no classes scheduled during the summer). Class days occur one eight hour day each week, alternating between Fridays and Saturdays.Integration is a main theme of the program. A program capstone project completes each module in which students reflect on the concepts introduced in each of the classes throughout the term.
Marquette University	Executive MBA Program	This is a 17 month, cohort program. The classes meet every other weekend, all day Friday and Saturday. The class is limited to 30 students and has an international orientation. Tuition is $38,000 for the Class of 2005 and is all inclusive (i.e., tuition, texts and materials, international trip, including travel to and from, single occupancy hotel, two meals a day; also includes all meals on campus, a laptop computer which you keep, parking and all fees.
Mercer University	Executive MBA Program	The Executive MBA Program at Mercer University is a 21-month, lock-step program. Classes are held on Mercer
Michigan State University	The Executive MBA	For over 40 years, the MSU EMBA program has educated managers for executive leadership responsibilities. The 21-month, team-based evening program includes a one-week academic residency on the MSU campus and an international business seminar. Classes are held at MSU's Management Education Center in Troy, Michigan.
Michigan University	Executive MBA	Michigan's Executive MBA combines personalized leadership development with a sophisticated focus on a strategic perspective. The world class curriculum is tailored specifically to the needs of high potential executives and combines onsite and remote features in a way that mirrors the collaborative work style that defines today's global business environment. The monthly format provides flexibility to manage professional and personal obligations while completing the degree. Customized leadership development is integrated throughout the program and complements the analytical and strategic content of the curriculum to develop the skills necessary to lead and drive change in your organization. Residency Requirements: Two 10 day extended residencies and 2-3 day residencies each month. A variety of technologies are used to deliver curriculum and facilitate ongoing collaboration during off campus weeks, keeping faculty, students and teams engaged and connected.
Naval Postgraduate School	Executive MBA	Part-time program which is aimed at mid-grade active duty Naval officers to prepare them for senior leadership positions. The Defense-focused curriculum, taught by resident NPS faculty, includes courses in organizational management, finance, acquisition and public policy to develop critical analysis and decision making skills. Residency Requirements: One week immersion session is required at the beginning of the program conducted at the NPS campus in Monterey, CA
New Jersey Institute of Technology	Executive Program - MS/ Management	The NJIT Master of Business Administration (MBA) in Management Technology program is fully accredited by the American Association of Collegiate Schools of Business (AACSB). The program is designed to prepare and develop business leaders who can meet the needs and issues of a technology-driven, global business environment. Students receive a grounding in traditional management theory that is integrated with applied knowledge of new and emerging technologies. The curriculum emphasizes the use of information systems and technology, strategic planning, and the integration of business functions, focusing on areas of management that support executive decision-making. Topics covered include information systems, strategic planning, marketing, finance, accounting, human resources, the global economy, technology management, the environment and legal and ethical issues.
New York University	Executive MBA Program	Two concentrations, Management and Finance, are offered in the August start date; only Management is offered in January. A global study tour is an integral, required portion of each year for both start dates. Students help to choose electives that are offered in the second year to EMBA cohort only.

University	Program	Description
New York University	TRIUM Global Executive MBA Program	The TRIUM Global EMBA is a joint degree program offered by New York University, Leonard N. Stern School of Business, HEC Paris, School of Management and the London School of Economics and Political Science. The program offers over 500 hours of live classroom instruction plus 500 hours of distance learning. Includes, four 2-week modules at the three partner schools and two 1-week modules at internationally significant locations.
Northeastern University	Executive MBA Program	Leading Innovation and Growth in the Global Economy is the theme of our innovative EMBA program. The curriculum features a long weekend in Washington D.C. to examine business/government issues, plus two international residencies, one in Mexico and one in Europe, to foster cultural sensitivity and knowledge of global business.
Northern Illinois University	Executive MBA	An 18-month, Saturday-only program. The program offers face-to-face instruction and real-world educational opportunities through the Year 1 business consulting project and year 2 Capstone Project. Both courses work with actual Chicago-area companies. The Executive MBA Program at NIU is consistently ranked as one of the best MBA programs within the Chicago market by Crain's Chicago Business.
Northwestern University	Executive MBA Programs - North American	A two-year general management program which runs on a traditional academic calendar, with the summer off. Classes meet every other weekend at the Allen Center on the Evanston campus of Northwestern University. The North American Program has two start dates, beginning in September and January annually.
Northwestern University	Executive MBA Programs - Regional	A two-year general management program which runs on a traditional academic calendar, with the summer off. Classes meet one day a week, on alternating Fridays and Saturdays. Classes are held at the Allen Center on the Evanston campus of Northwestern University. The Regional Program has one start date in September.
Northwestern University	Kellogg Executive MBA Program, The Kellogg School of Management at Northwestern University	A two-year general management program which runs on a traditional academic calendar, with the summer off. Twice-Monthly Programs meet every other weekend at the Allen Center on the Evanston campus of Northwestern University, with intakes in both September and January annually. Our Miami Program meets monthly on our Miami Campus, with an intake in January annually.
Ohio State University	Executive MBA Program	The program is a blend of distance learning and on-site instruction. Managers meet on campus three consecutive days (Thursday, Friday and Saturday) once each month. There is a one-week residency session at the beginning of the program and a week long international experience. Program has full use of the college's new state-of-the-art campus and distance delivery of assignments when not on campus. Delivery modes include web based course delivery of up to 30% of the program, interactive case and problem-solving discussion groups, instructor online help sessions and other distance tools and resources. An interactive global capstone course is combined with an international experience. Newly developed integrated electives prepare students for 21st century business challenges.
Pace University	Executive MBA Program	The e.MBA@PACE is a web-assisted\\ Executive MBA designed for experienced\\ managers and professionals who cannot\\ attend weekly classes. This innovative program \\ combines the convenience of online learning with ten residencies (a total of 35 days) over two years. The curriculum focuses on nine large scale cross-disciplinary projects team-taught by six senior faculty.
Pepperdine University	Executive MBA Program	Fifty-unit program. One-on-one tutorials in addition to regular classes. Program begins with Effective Executive Workshop held at Villa Graziadio Executive Center on our Malibu campus.
Purdue University	Executive Master of Business Administration Program (EMB)	Distance learning and computer application to business problem solving are key features. Six two-week residencies spread over 22 months, following a four day orientation, draws participants from around the world. Internet-supported off-campus assignments and discussion forums for each course allow learning and interaction to continue between residencies. International trip at end.
Purdue University	International Masters in Management (IMM) Program	Dual-degree program with three European Business School partners: Tias in the Netherlands, CEU in Budapest, Hungary, and GISMA in Hannover, Germany. Graduates receive an MBA from Purdue, and a second MBA from Tias. Six two-week residencies over a 22-month period rotate among the four schools, using faculty from each.
Queens University of Charlotte	McColl Executive MBA	The McColl Executive MBA is a two-year program delivered on alternating Fridays and Saturdays. The program admits one class in August of each year. The unique curriculum is topically integrated to stress practical application of business fundamentals. Emphasis is placed on leadership development through coursework, workshops and access to professional management coaches and senior executives. Summer activities are international study tours and management consulting projects for non-profit agencies.
Rice University	The MBA Program for Executives	The program is divided into 11 mini-semesters consisting of four course modules and an extended learning lab for course module integration, team building, career management, and math and computer training. An international trip and Washington Campus program are among the 14 credit hours of electives offered. A laptop computer, all books, materials, breakfast and lunch on class days,and parking are provided.
Rochester Institute of Technology	Executive MBA Program	The RIT Executive MBA is an integrated, two-year cohort program designed to develop senior executives and experienced managers in organizations serious about improving customer satisfaction, product quality, and organizational success. Using practical approaches to improving business results and increasing personal productivity, participants in the program strengthen their leadership skills by collaborating with teams of professional peers and faculty and by applying cross-functional approaches to enhancing their analytical and decision-making capabilities. The first-year curriculum focuses on core business concepts and provides fundamental skills, knowledge, and perspectives in accounting, statistics, leadership, finance, and economics. The second year extends that foundation and develops cross-functional analysis with an emphasis on strategy, marketing, technology, and international business. Interdisciplinary examples, case analysis, and applied orientation are key components of the program. The EMBA program also includes practical experience obtained through capstone projects conducted for local companies; ongoing support for career-oriented skills such as career development planning, communications, and team building; the application of a cross-functional business simulation model; and an international business trip to Prague.
Rockhurst University	The Executive Fellows Program	The Executive Fellows MBA is Kansas City's oldest and most prestigious executive MBA, designed to assist regional firms develop executive capability in promising upper-level managers. Sponsoring firms nominate candidates who undergo a highly competitive selection process. The Executive Fellow learns from lectures, case studies, projects and interaction with peers, guests and experienced faculty. The carefully designed program of study allows an executive to step beyond his or her current position to explore personal capabilities for greater growth and responsibility.
Rollins College	Executive MBA Program	The EMBA program is an intensive 21-month program designed to provide a strong foundation in critical business and organizational skills. Application of business concepts is central to the program's mission. Applicants average thirteen years of work experience at the management level with solid experience managing people and budgets.
Saint Joseph's University	Executive MBA Program	Our accelerated 20-Month Executive MBA Program is a lock-step, cohort model. Beginning with orientation at the end of each August, you will progress together through five consecutive semesters, one class per week on alternating Fridays and Saturdays. Once you cover the requisite accounting and financial concepts, you will immerse yourself in our innovative curriculum.
Saint Louis University	Executive Master of International Business	The Boeing Institute of International Business at Saint Louis University
Saint Mary's College of California	Executive MBA Program	The Saint Mary's EMBA Program is the oldest and largest EMBA program in the Bay Area. Offering a thoughtful mix of theory and practice, the Program provides a high quality educational experience in a variety of convenient formats (Saturday only, Alternate Weekends, Evenings and Hybrid) and locations in the Bay Area (Moraga, Santa Clara and San Ramon)and Sacramento.

University	Program	Description
San Diego State University	MBA for Executives Program	The goals of the MBA for Executives program are to enhance your leadership performance and prepare you for positions of greater management responsibility. Attend classes on an alternating Friday/Saturday schedule. Earn an AACSB and WASC accredited MBA in less than two years.
Santa Clara University	Executive MBA Program	Tailored to meet the needs of Silicon Valley executives. Designed to help executives refine current skills and acquire new knowledge. 2 off site residential leadership weekends. 3 day trip to a local/coastal resort. These are the opening and closing of the program.
Southern Methodist University	Cox School of Business Executive MBA	"The SMU Cox EMBA is a broad-based, fast-paced, in-depth global leadership experience praised by participants, sponsors, and those in the business world for the preparation it offers those ready for the unique challenges of the executive suite. Consistently ranked one of the best in the world, the curriculum is forward-thinking and taught by some of the most notable professors in academia.
		Cox EMBA students represent the top minds in business from a varying array of industries and disciplines. SMU Cox brings nationally recognized faculty together with experienced students in a small, private-school setting. This intimate, collaborative environment allows for close interaction in the classroom as well as in study groups and other activities outside of class.
		This high-quality interaction is augmented with innovative programs, an international study trip, and a global network of professionals and alumni-all bolstered by a longstanding commitment to working professionals. The James M. Collins Executive Education Center, home for our EMBA program, epitomizes this commitment-shared by the Cox School, SMU, and the business community."
Stetson University	EMBA	"The EMBA Program at Celebration offers professionals from any academic background a way to earn an MBA degree in less than two years while still working. Our program brings together high-potential managers with a faculty consisting of experienced business leaders and leaders in their academic fields. Our EMBA Program is tailored to the fast-paced schedule of today's executives and managers with a flexible alternating Friday and Saturday schedule. The select group of EMBA participants ranges from managers of large corporations to entrepreneurs and officers in small companies."
Suffolk University	Executive MBA Program	Saturday-only, cohort-based program can be completed in 18 months. Eighteen course curriculum plus program experiential. Emphasis on leadership and practical application in global environment. International seminar and Washing Campus are required. First Executive MBA program in New England. Participants average 12 years of professional work experience, minimum requirement is seven years demonstrated leadership experience. GMAT is optional.
Syracuse University	MBA & MS Programs	The central strength of the Syracuse Executive MBA Program is the carefully crafted curriculum, designed to furnish the knowledge, skills and context to successfully execute strategies and lead an organization through change. A comprehensive program expressly for middle-and-senior-level professionals, that will quickly translate into value for participant and sponsor.
Temple University	Executive MBA Program	The Temple University Executive MBA program is designed so that participants learn as much from their peers, as well as from faculty. These professionals, entrepreneurs and mid- to upper-level managers with 10 to 15 years of experience bring with them the commitment and experience that helps create a dynamic learning community. Our more than 300 loyal alumni in disciplines from medicine to engineering are also a valuable resource. They hold high-level positions throughout the Greater Philadelphia region and around the world, and their participation in our program is high. Our EMBA faculty are selected not only for their considerable expertise but also for their extraordinary ability to communicate with executives and encourage them to share ideas and experience. They are adept at using information technology and a variety of teaching methods - lectures, discussions, case analysis, computer assignments, business projects - to facilitate team building and to help connect theory and practice. Our EMBA curriculum, refined over 17 years, takes into account our student
Temple University	Executive MBA Program - Tokyo	The EMBA program in Tokyo, like its counterpart in Philadelphia, is composed of sixteen graduate courses that have been specifically designed for experienced managers. Drawing all the functional areas within business, these courses lead participants to develop their abilities as problem solvers, strategic thinkers, and decision makers. Professors who teach in the program are selected for their academic expertise, awareness of current business trends and ability to communicate with executives. Because the Fox School is committed to academic excellence, most of the professors come from Temple
Texas A & M University	Mays Executive MBA Program	Team oriented with modular curriculum and peer-learning environment. Classes meet at The University Center in The Woodlands, Texas. International trip is optional. Residency week required prior to start of first class.
Texas Christian University	Executive MBA Program	International trip: Required 3-hour international business class; May of first year. Residence Requirements: Four day seminar at the onset of program. Personal computer provided by Texas Christian University.
The College of William and Mary	Executive MBA Program	Our Executive MBA Program is a 20-month experience designed for busy and hard-working mid-career professionals who do not want to interrupt their careers while earning their MBA degrees.
Tulane University	Asia Executive MBA Program	This 13-month, 48-credit hour program includes two three-week intensive seminars held at Tulane
Tulane University	Chile Executive MBA Program	This 21-month, 48 credit hour program begins in Santiago each August and includes an international seminar on Tulane
Tulane University	Houston EMBA Option II	Designed for students with three to five years of work experience to earn an MBA in an accelerated format without job interference. The 23-month program offers a lock-step curriculum and students attend classes on Friday evenings, Saturdays, and Sunday afternoons every other weekend. Graduates earn an MBA with concentrations in finance and general management.
Tulane University	Houston Executive MBA Program	This 19-month, 48-credit hour program begins each November and includes one intensive week and an international seminar. Classes meet primarily on alternate Friday/Saturday weekends. Prep courses in accounting and quantitative skills are offered.
Tulane University	New Orleans Executive MBA Program	This 19-month, 48-credit hour program begins each January and includes one intensive week and an international seminar. Classes meet primarily on alternate Friday/Saturday weekends. Prep courses in accounting and quantitative skills are offered.
University at Buffalo	Executive MBA Program	The Executive MBA at the School of Management is designed for high-potential managers. They develop relationships with other executives and learn from internationally recognized faculty. The cutting-edge management practices articulated throughout the program will strategically impact your organization. The EMBA also includes a program-long personal development course on emotional intelligence.
University of Alabama	Executive MBA Program	Rated as one of the most outstanding Return on Investments by Forbes Magazine, this weekend Executive Program will enable you to enhance your skills as you interact with other seasoned executives. Our faculty are among some of the most innovative in their field and have many years
University of Arkansas at Little Rock	Executive MBA	The refocused, applications-oriented Executive MBA (EMBA) includes experiential learning integrating all functional fields of business and features leadership development, professional coaching, and an international field study. Team-based courses are enhanced by executive panels and live case studies and projects. Only EMBA program in Arkansas.
University of California Irvine	Executive MBA Program	The Executive MBA prepares managers and executives for an ever-changing, globally competitive business environment. For nearly 20 years, this EMBA program for working professionals has served executives, managers, professionals, entrepreneurs and technical experts throughout the West Coast region. UCI faculty is ranked 5th in the nation in Intellectual Capital.

University	Program	Description
University of California Irvine	Health Care Executive MBA Program	The Health Care Executive MBA is a comprehensive academic experience exclusively for individuals working in the health care industry. The program is for professionals in the pharmaceutical, biotechnology and medical device industries, and the full range of medical professionals. Participants have significant relevant work experience, demonstrate leadership abilities and a proven track record of success.
University of California, Berkeley	Berkeley-Columbia Executive MBA Program	The Berkeley-Columbia Executive MBA Program combines the curricular, research, and professional strengths of two of the world
University of California, Los Angeles	UCLA Anderson School of Management Executive MBA Program	The UCLA Anderson School of Management Executive MBA Program allows you to earn a top-tier MBA in just two weekends a month, while you continue to progress in your current profession. The EMBA Program allows senior executives to help shape the operations and ambitions of their organization by connecting with likeminded executives, enhancing their leadership skills and broadening their knowledge of global cultures and markets. A UCLA Anderson MBA degree is a powerful tool in the face of new business and career challenges. For more information, please visit our website at: http://www.anderson.ucla.edu/x24273.xml
University of Central Florida	Executive MBA	The program is designed to prepare executives and managers for the challenges they will face as they progress to positions of top leadership. The skills they develop and refine during this program help each graduate to achieve his or her fullest career potential and become an increasingly valuable organizational member. The EMBA program is comprised of 13 courses that mirror the program's quantitative strengths. The format includes a three-day kick-off and a one-week international trip. Innovative teaching methodologies such as team-based, action-learning projects, interdisciplinary case studies, simulations, debating-the-issues activities and self-assessment exercises enhance the learning experience.
University of Chicago	Executive MBA Program - Asia	Classes are held in one-week modules over 20 months; students spend 2 weeks in Chicago and 1 week in Barcelona taking classes with students from the North America and Europe programs.
University of Chicago	Executive MBA Program - Europe	Classes are held in one-week modules over 20 months; students spend 2 weeks in Chicago and 1 week in Singapore taking classes with students from the North America and Europe programs.
University of Chicago	Executive MBA Program - North America	Program includes 4 one-week sessions (1 at the beginning of the program, 3 in the second summer). Students from the Chicago program are inter-mixed with students in the Barcelona and Singapore programs during these sessions. Two weeks take place in Chicago, one week in Barcelona, and one week in Singapore.
University of Colorado	Executive MBA in Health Administration	Offers a business degree decision-makers who are health care professionals (physicians, nurses, administrators).
University of Colorado	Executive MBA Program	Emphasis on leadership and financial decision-making skills. International trip is required. Program is offered by the University of Colorado's three graduate business schools -- The Leeds School at CU Boulder, the Business School at CU Denver, and the graduate school of business at Colorado Springs.
University of Connecticut	Executive Master of Business Administration	The Executive MBA at the University of Connecticut is a twenty-month (48-credit) program. The program begins with an In-Residence Week, held at UConn's main campus during which students get acquainted with the program, faculty, classmates, and prepare for their upcoming projects. After In-Residence Week, classes meet every other weekend from September to June. An International Study Trip takes place in June when students travel to a foreign country, studying foreign business practices, management styles and norms, operations and the culture. The trip lasts one week. During the summer students work on their Executive Management Projects which incorporates their experience from the trip with the knowledge and skills gained from the first half of the program. The normal class schedule resumes in August and the program ends in April with a commencement ceremony.
University of Delaware	Executive MBA Program	Residency Required: International Residency & Opening Residence Week.
University of Denver	Executive MBA	As the eighth oldest business school in the US, the Daniels College of Business has combined business relevance with academic excellence for nearly 100 years. With the longest running Executive MBA program in the region - 30 years strong - our alumni are testament to the fact that a Daniels EMBA is not just an adjunct reaction to a market opportunity; it
University of Florida	Executive MBA	Program curriculum is 48 credit hours and requires 8 years of professional work experience. The curriculum reflects the College
University of Georgia	Executive MBA Program	Program content emphasizes leadership development, and includes personal leadership coaching. Content delivery provides an approximate 50/50 mix of face-to-face sessions and distance learning. International Trip: There is a two-week residency at the end of the Program. Solicit input from participants in determining destination and schedule.
University of Houston	Executive MBA Program	Program 1 - 22 months; Program 2 - 18 months; Laptop computer and International Business Residency provided.
University of Illinois at Urbana-Champaign	The Executive MBA	MBA program with a general management focus targeted to executives and working professionals. Classes are held alternating weekends in downtown Chicago.
University of Iowa	Executive MBA Program	A 21-month cohort program meeting on alternate Fridays and Saturdays on campus in Iowa City. Includes two 5-day Residency Periods (August just prior to be beginning of fall semester) and a second year 10-day international business seminar (Typically in March).
University of Maryland	Executive MBA Program	An 18 month program, based on a systemic approach to management that focuses on managing the interation of the functional business areas. The program emphasizes leadership skill development and foundational business knowledge. The program is applied, practical and unique. In addition to the foundation courses, students are engaged in leadership skill development throughout the duration of the program (Leadership Mastery curriculum). Students also engage in Action Learning Projects throughout the curriculum. These are projects undertaken on behalf of the students' employers. Teams of three students do three consulting engagements for their respective employers, guided by experience faculty advisors. Residency Requirements: Every other weekend format (all day Friday and all day Saturday) with one full week at the beginning and end of the program. Accomodations are at the the University of Maryland, University College Inn and Conference Center by Marriott.
University of Maryland University College	Executive MBA Program	The 43-credit Executive Master of Business Administration is an accelerated 21-month program designed for managers with at least five years of business or management experience. Developed with business leaders on an Advisory Board, and delivered by a faculty experienced in business and knowledgeable in academic content, the EMBA is designed to equip today's managers for success in the global marketplace. Special features of the EMBA program include: Cohort based program; Global and cross-cultural perspective on all management issues; Online interaction among program participants; International study trip to meet with business leaders on other continents; Internet technology to support the management of teams and projects; Leadership and team development provided by the National Leadership Institute; Speakers with expertise in business and government; A capstone project in which each teams is assigned to a sponsoring corporation to complete a strategic business plan for global market expansion.
University of Memphis	Executive MBA Program	The Fogelman College offers the only business degree program in the Memphis community that meets the stringent requirements for accreditation by the American Assembly of Collegiate Schools of Business (AACSB). Because of the program

University	Program	Description
University of Miami	Executive MBA Program	The University of Miami offers an intense and challenging career-centered curriculum, world-class faculty and one of the largest alumni networks of any business school. Students may pursue special areas of interest by choosing from a broad range of elective courses. The UM School of Business Administration offers four distinct EMBA programs: Executive MBA, Executive MBA in Health Sector Management and Policy, Master of Science in Professional Management/Executive MBA (taught entirely in Spanish), and a joint Executive MBA/Master of Science in Industrial Engineering program. The program is offered at the School of Business main campus in Coral Gables, Fla., and off-site in Palm Beach, Fla. and San Juan, Puerto Rico. The EMBA programs are completed in 23 months; the MSPM/EMBA program is completed in 22 months.
University of Michigan	Executive MBA Program	Michigan's Executive MBA offers a unique emphasis on leadership development, a results-oriented curriculum created specifically for high-potential executives, and a combination of on-campus and on-line learning that gives participants great flexibility in balancing commitments. Parallel to courses is a Professional Development Program in which students go through a guided assessment process and identification of goals. Using workshops and interactive lectures the program provides the next-level skills required to be successful at the highest levels of leadership. Residency Requirements: Two 10-day residencies at beginning and midpoints. During weeks when not in residence, distance learning technologies are used to augment in-class teaching.
University of Minnesota	Carlson Executive MBA (CEMBA)	Pre-Program Workshops in Accounting,statistics, and math prep. Live-in residencies kick-off each fall semester for first and second year students. The 18 month program includes a luncheon Leadership Speaker Series and an Executive Negotiations Workshop. An Executive Career Coach and Study Group Coach assist students throughout the year. The final program experience is a two-week residency delivered abroad. The 2004-2005 international residency sites are Stockholm and St.Petersburg.
University of Missouri-Kansas City	Executive MBA Program	Executive, international and Washington, D.C. residencies; four integrated curriculum modules. Skill application projects: innovation study, organizational assessment project and public service application project. An emphasis on entrepreneurship and leadership skill development.
University of Nevada, Las Vegas	Executive MBA	The Executive MBA program is designed to meet the educational needs of executives. The EMBA program of study will target mid- to senior-level executives. The program offers an integrated blend of theory and practice and provides a general management emphasis suited to the needs of executives in leadership positions. The program provides opportunities for integrating professional experiences with academic management education. It familiarizes students with cutting-edge issues of disciplines that encompass management science. It helps experienced professionals to clearly formulate their management philosophy and capabilities and thus, fosters their professional growth. The program combines the ability that comes from experience with high-quality educational knowledge that challenges, inspires, and adds value.
University of New Hampshire	Executive MBA Program	The Executive MBA program is an accelerated 19-month program geared for professionals with seven or more years of work exprience. Classes meet alternating Fridays/Saturdays and are held at the New England Conference Center, a residential facility located on the Durham campus. Additionally, students participate in three residencies. The first of which is held at the beginning of the program for a week on campus. In the second year, students spend three days in New York City for the finance course. And the program culminates with ten days abroad as part of the International Management course.
University of New Mexico	Executive MBA Program	Our EMBA represents one of the best educational values in the world; with a total program price of just under $26,000, we cost less than half the national average for comparable, AACSB-accredited programs. Recently updated, the curriculum consists of 48 credit hours including two electives and an optional international study trip. On average, participants have 8 years of management experience, 25% hold advanced degrees, 35% are female, 20% are minorities, and 15% reside outside of Albuquerque.
University of New Orleans	Executive MBA	The goal of the University of New Orleans Executive MBA program is to provide experienced managers, successful entrepreneurs and professionals with the highest quality master
University of North Carolina-Chapel Hill	Executive MBA Evening Program	Two-year program includes common core curriculum, plus 20 elective hours. The International Trip and Executive MBA Project are optional. There are two required immersion weekends.
University of North Carolina-Chapel Hill	Executive MBA Weekend Program	Twenty-month program includes common core curriculum, plus 20 elective hours and two one-week residencies. The International Trip and Executive MBA Project are optional.
University of North Carolina-Chapel Hill	OneMBA® Global Executive MBA Program	OneMBA® is offered by a collaborative partnership of The Chinese University of Hong Kong (CUHK), Fundacao Getulio Vargas (FGV-EAESP), Monterrey Tech Graduate School of Business Administration and Leadership (EGADE-ITESM), Erasmus University Rotterdam, Rotterdam School of Management (RSM) and The University of North Carolina at Chapel Hill (UNC). The twenty-one month program is designed for achievement-oriented professionals living and working in each of the school's regions. Executives study at their home business schools for two-thirds of the program and spend one-third of their time in residential modules in Asia, Europe and North and South America. Each home university offers globally coordinated courses with global virtual teams and specific courses relevant to its region. Residency Requirement: 4 week-long residencies, 3 are overseas.
University of Notre Dame	University of Notre Dame Executive MBA Program	The University of Notre Dame established the Executive MBA (EMBA) program in South Bend in 1982. This 21-month program begins each August and includes once-per-month sessions (Thursday afternoon through Saturday afternoon) at Notre Dame, three one-week immersions on campus and a seven-to-ten-day project-based international immersion. The first campus-based immersion highlights Notre Dame's signature Executive Integral Leadership experience. This multidimensional and holistic learning experience focuses on your development as an authentic leader and incorporates both powerful evaluation tools such as 360 assessments and executive coaching as well as highly interactive classroom and group experiences. The final immersion is an intensive week of electives, taken with students from the Chicago-based Notre Dame EMBA program. Between the second and third terms you will participate in the international immersion, a project-based experience in which you and 4-5 teammates consult with a global corporation or NGO to take on one of 12 to 15 real-time strategic challenges or opportunities. The full curriculum takes a balanced approach to your education, recognizing the need to growth for both your business competence through a rigorous study of analytics and general management skills; and growth for you personally through the exploration of principles-based leadership development. Students engage the program individually and in collaborative study teams. These teams share their intellectual capital, complementary skills and work experiences.
University of Notre Dame	University of Notre Dame Executive MBA Program	The University of Notre Dame established its Chicago-based Executive MBA (EMBA) program in January 2002. The program is held in the Notre Dame Chicago Commons in the Santa Fe Building at Michigan and Jackson in downtown Chicago. The 17-month program begins each January and meets Friday and Saturday biweekly. The program includes four one-week residencies on the main Notre Dame campus. The second campus-based immersion is Notre Dame's signature Executive Integral Leadership week. This multidimensional and holistic learning experience focuses on your development as an authentic leader and incorporates both powerful evaluation tools such as 360 assessments and executive coaching as well as highly interactive classroom and group experiences. The final immersion is an intensive week of electives, taken with students from the South Bend-based Notre Dame EMBA program. As a Chicago-based Notre Dame student you will also have the option to participate in one of two international immersion residencies in Asia or South America. The full curriculum takes a balanced approach to your education, recognizing the need to growth for both your business competence through a rigorous study of analytics and general management skills; and growth for you personally through the exploration of principles-based leadership development. Students engage the program individually and in collaborative study teams. These teams share their intellectual capital, complementary skills and work experiences.

University	Program	Description
University of Oregon	EMBA	Since 1985 the business schools at Oregon's three largest public universities (University of Oregon, which grants the degree, Oregon State University, and Portland State University) have offered one of the highest quality Executive MBA programs in the country. OEMBA Mission: to educate high potential managers and executives in business theory and practice for strategic decision-making in a competitive, global economy. Top faculty are selected from the three universities to teach. Courses are delivered on alternating Fridays and Saturdays in downtown Portland. First and second year Residencies are delivered at the UO in Eugene. All fees are included in the tuition. One cohort begins each fall. The program is 18 months with a summer break, 72 credits, and includes a capstone Business Project and global study trip.
University of Pennsylvania	The Wharton School - Philadelphia Campus	Wharton offers one MBA degree with two program formats to earn it. MBA Exec applicants must meet the same admissions criteria and undergo the same academic requirements to graduate as their full-time counterparts. One cohort of students is admitted every year in both Philadelphia and San Francisco. The Wharton MBA program for Executives offers the equivalent education as Wharton's full-time MBA program by structuring a required residential experience which enables students to immerse themselves completely in their studies every other weekend. Students complete 11.25 credit units of core coursework and 8 credit units of elective courses. Each MBA Exec class chooses a set of electives to be offered during the second year. Typically, over 30 electives are offered. A one-week required overseas experience following the required Global Competitive Strategy course occurs in the second year.
University of Pennsylvania	The Wharton School - San Francisco Campus	Wharton offers one MBA degree with two program formats to earn it. MBA Exec applicants must meet the same admissions criteria and undergo the same academic requirements to graduate as their full-time counterparts. One cohort of students is admitted every year in both Philadelphia and San Francisco. The Wharton MBA program for Executives offers the equivalent education as Wharton's full-time MBA program by structuring a required residential experience which enables students to immerse themselves completely in their studies every other weekend. Students complete 11.25 credit units of core coursework and 8 credit units of elective courses. Each MBA Exec class chooses a set of electives to be offered during the second year. Typically, over 30 electives are offered. A one-week required overseas experience following the required Global Competitive Strategy course occurs in the second year.
University of Pittsburgh	Executive MBA	The Executive MBA (EMBA) Worldwide program at the University of Pittsburgh Katz Graduate School of Business offers a high-quality MBA that is recognized both locally and globally. The cohort-base of the EMBA program provides a unique opportunity to learn, not only from our distinguished faculty, but from classmates as well, and enables professionals to build their network. That network extends across the globe, with our EMBA Program being offered in South America and Central Europe. We provide the broad business acumen needed to have an understanding of business, the ability to make strategic decisions and lead effectively.
University of Rochester	Executive MBA Program	Weekend team-building workshop for students and partners as part of orientation. Study teams are an integral part of the program. EMBA programs offered in Rochester, the Netherlands and in Switzerland. International guest speaker seminar (in Europe). International students have nine-week residency in Rochester.
University of San Francisco	MBA for Executives	Few professionals can take 15 months of their schedule in your life to study. The Professional MBA for Executives class schedule maximizes your classroom experience by linking traditional classroom time with professional work responsibilities. You will attend classes one evening a week and alternate Saturdays. You will be part of a small group of highly qualified students all participating in the same course of study to promote relationship building and team learning.
University of South Florida	Executive MBA Program	Over 800 executives and physicians have completed the USF EMBA since 1981. The curriculum, as taught by the highly experienced faculty, is practical and immediately applicable to business world situations. Classes meet on one Friday and two Saturdays per month over four semesters. The international trip component is optional.
University of Southern California	Executive MBA	"The USC Marshall Executive MBA (EMBA) Program is designed for senior managers and seasoned professionals who wish to remain fully employed as they pursue their graduate studies. This 21-month program incorporates a successful thematic MBA curriculum that gets to the heart of issues that senior managers and seasoned professionals encounter on a daily basis. We concentrate learning objectives on the 'interrelatedness' of business functions as opposed to the teaching of individual disciplines as unrelated functional entities. This approach has resulted in a program that consists of ten 'themes,' two domestic off-site sessions, and one international off-site session. Two Outstanding Locations Choose the setting most convenient for you. We offer our EMBA Program on USC's historic University Park Campus in Los Angeles and our new EMBA San Diego Program at the La Costa Executive Learning Center in Carlsbad, California. Classes in Los Angeles and San Diego meet bi-weekly on Fridays and Saturdays (from 8:45am to 4:30pm). All participants attend an off-site international session that provides an insightful global perspective."
University of St. Thomas	Executive MBA Program	An accelerated degree program designed to improve the performance of experienced managers and leaders. Integrative course assignments require students to apply classroom learning to their own jobs in their own organizations. Coursework and assignments emphasize the interrelationships among customers, products, people and processes. This cross-functional approach develops a comprehensive, integrated view of organizational leadership.
University of Tennessee	Aerospace & Defense MBA Program	The Aerospace MBA focuses exclusively on the aerospace industry. The program provides indepth managerial assessment and personlized development plan. Instead of a Master's thesis, students complete three projects in real-time application of program tools and concepts. Structure provides one integrated program instead of numerous stand-alone courses.
University of Tennessee	Executive MBA Program	The Executive MBA (EMBA) is an integrated program for high potential executives who want to earn an accredited degree in 12 months. Offered by the College of Business Administration at the University of Tennessee, the program is designed for experienced executives (10 years preferred) who desire skills that will enable them to transform their companies and advance their careers. The 12-month modular format is comprised of four residency periods, including one required international residency, and periodic interactive, live distance learning sessions on Wednesday nights. The program emphasizes strategic thinking and leadership development and has a stated goal of transforming the way that students think, lead, and learn. UT's Executive MBA program offers the following benefits to students: All assignments are applied to the participant's organization. Global seminars are conducted in September within developing economies. Courses are taught by top faculty in the College of Business who work closely with each individual. One year completion, with classes beginning in January and ending in December. Active alumni network.
University of Tennessee	Physician Executive MBA Program	The Physician Executive Masters in Business Administration (PEMBA) program is an advanced educational degree offered by The University of Tennessee, College of Business Administration suited for physicians seeking high quality management and business operation skills. The program is conveniently available nationwide, requiring only 4 one-week on-site periods during the 12-month program; all other course hours are available at your computer desktop via the Internet. Classes start in early January; graduation is in December of each year. UT's Physician Executive MBA incorporates these unique features: Short residency periods and advanced distance education technology allows you to continue your full time professional career. Fast completion - only one year long. Classes are composed of physicians only, affording valuable personal networking opportunities. Continuing Medical Education (CME) credits available. Personalized leadership assessment and development program. Extensive computer skills development. Active Physician Leader Alumni Network.

University	Program	Description
University of Tennessee	Professional MBA Program	The Professional MBA is primarily a 16-month weekend program for working professionals with five years of experience who want to earn an accredited degree while continuing to work full-time. The integrated curriculum and three management projects allow for real-time application of program tools and concepts which are designed to add value for both the student and his or her organization. The 16-month format is comprised of approximately three Saturdays per month, periodic Tuesday evening distance classes, and two and one-half weeks of residency periods. An optional international trip is available.
University of Tennessee	Senior Executive MBA Program	The Senior Executive MBA (SEMBA) is an integrated program for high potential executives who want to earn an accredited degree in 12 months. Offered by the College of Business Administration at the University of Tennessee, the program is designed for experienced executives (10 years minimum) who desire skills that will enable them to transform their companies and advance their careers. The 12-month modular format is comprised of six residency periods, including one required international residency, and periodic interactive, live distance learning sessions on Wednesday nights. The program emphasizes strategic thinking and leadership development and has a stated goal of transforming the way that students think, lead, and learn. UT's Senior Executive MBA program offers the following benefits to students: All assignments are applied to the participant's organization. Global seminars are conducted in May within developing economies. Courses are taught by top faculty in the College of Business who work closely with each individual. One year completion, with classes beginning in January and ending in December. Active alumni network.
University of Tennessee at Chattanooga	Executive MBA Program, Dept. 6056	The program features innovative and exciting curriculum designed by UTC faculty and business leaders in the community. Courses are taught by world-class faculty who are excited about working with executives. UTC's College of Business offers the only AACSB accredited programs in the area. EMBA students have many opportunities to network with other local professionals Classes are held conveniently on campus in downtown Chattanooga.
University of Texas - Dallas	Global Leadership Executive MBA Program	The Global Leadership Executive MBA (GLEMBA), cited by Forbes magazine as one of the \Best on the Web for three consecutive years is a blended on-campus and online EMBA program with a specialization in international business management In addition to MBA core courses
University of Texas at Austin	Executive MBA in Mexico City	There are seven weekend class sessions in the fall, eight in the spring, and five in the summer. In addition, three one-week seminars are held over the two-year period: two in Austin and one International Seminar.
University of Texas at Austin	Executive MBA Program	The Texas Executive MBA is a 21-month program designed for academically qualified mid-career professionals who want to pursue an MBA degree without having to carry the full responsibilities of their current jobs. Classes are held at the new AT&T Executive Education and Conference Center on Fridays and Saturdays of alternating weekends. With rigorous coursework and innovative curriculum, the Texas Executive MBA ranks among the finest educational experiences in the country. The program requires a serious commitment from both the individual and the employer. Students earn the same MBA degree earned as the full-time MBA program at The University of Texas at Austin.
University of Texas at Dallas	Alliance Medical Management Education	The growing complexity of healthcare requires physician and administrative leaders with well-developed business skills. The Alliance offers these leaders a unique, customized opportunity to develop and refine their practical knowledge of: negotiation and conflict management medical cost and performance management healthcare financial management service quality and patient satisfaction medical information systems and data management healthcare strategic management federal healthcare policy and regulation Led by nationally recognized business and medical school faculties, physicians and senior administrators have the opportunity to learn from real-world case studies and share insights and experiences with their peers. Classes are eligible for graduate academic credit, Category 1 CME credit toward the AMA Physician's Recognition Award and CEU credit for healthcare administrators. This unique program is available only to licensed MDs and DOs and senior healthcare administrators. Class size is limited to thirty-five and acceptance into the program is competitive.
University of Texas at Dallas	Executive MBA Program	Integrated program has focus of managing for change. Recent changes to program include: 4 credit hours of class-determined electives; more emphasis on project management skills in the field project and field project happens during the second year.
University of Texas at Dallas	Project Management MBA Program	This innovative program has a project management focus. It also has 3 completion options. A certificate after the first 21 hours. A Master of Science after the next 19 hours. A Master of Business Administration after the next 13 hours. The certificate phase is taught using an intergrated curriculum. The program is offered both on campus and online. On campus meets Thursday, Friday and Saturday once per month. The on campus program takes 28 months to complete the MBA. The online program is designed with weekly lessons and takes 32 months to complete the MBA. Degree options include a 2 week International study tour.
University of Toledo	Executive MBA Program	The curriculum is designed to enhance students ability to effectively lead change and growth in todays ultra-competitive environment. Participants take 16 dynamic courses built around three major themes designed to create a competitive advantage: Entrepreneurship/Intrapreneurship & Integration of Business Functions, E-business Competitive Challenge, and Competition in the Global Marketplace. The program is lock-stepped and lasts 15 months.
University of Utah	Executive MBA	Designed exclusively for high-potential professionals, the Executive MBA Program prepares experienced executives for even higher levels of leadership, analysis, interpersonal, and strategic planning skills. Students attend classes alternating Fridays and Saturdays for 21 months, allowing them to enrich their career and life, without putting either on hold.
University of Washington	Regional Program Executive MBA Program	The Regional EMBA Program has been in operation for over 20 years. It continues to draw students from Seattle metropolitan area companies, and has an alumni base of over 1000 individuals located around the world.
University of Wisconsin-Madison	Executive MBA Program	A small (30-40 student), innovative program taught bi-monthly in a Friday/Saturday format for two academic years. Primary instructors are award winning, full-time faculty selected for their extensive business experience, relevant research, and teaching excellence. Students are actively involved in the learning experience through a series of projects that address current issues in their own and team members and organizations. The highly rated program is delivered in a state-of the art facility that takes advantage of a wide range of traditional and emerging learning technologies. Entering students are at or near executive level and graduates include leading executives at a wide range of top organizations. A second year international trip, included in program tuition, is integrated with the curriculum to address many of the business, economic, and cultural issues that are critical to operating in a global environment. Student surveys reveal a high level of student satisfaction as well as excellent career progress and salary growth after graduation.
University of Wisconsin-Milwaukee	Executive MBA Program	Celebrating 30 years of delivering results-oriented management skills to mid-career executives, the University of Wisconsin-Milwaukee EMBA is a four semester program in which students attend classes one full day a week on alternating Fridays and Saturdays. The 22 month program duration includes a 3 month summer break between the first and second year. All students attend a week-long international residency at the end of the first year (cost is included in the tuition) -- the most recent trip included company visits in Shanghai and Beijing.
Vanderbilt University	Executive MBA Program	Designed for seasoned professionals, this program offers a rigorous, world-class 60-credit-hour hour MBA that meets on alternate Saturdays over a 24-month period. The experience is enhanced by the "C-Team Experience", in which students work and study in cross-functional teams to gain critical perspectives and executive decision-making skills.

University	Program	Description
Villanova University	Executive MBA Program	Module based non-traditional integrated curriculum focusing on targeted themes determined, developed and delivered in partnership between core academics and key business leaders. Constant review and development of our curriculum is the premise for an evolving, relevant and integrated learning experience for busy fast-track executives. Class meets alternating Friday/Saturday (two-day cycle) with residential overnight accommodations plus a weeklong orientation and a weeklong international experience. Each of five modules contains eight 2-day weekends.
Wake Forest University	Fast Track Executive MBA Program	The curriculum is taught in a unique, team-oriented, integrative way using \just-in-time\" principles
Washington University in St. Louis	Monthly Executive MBA Program	The Monthly Executive MBA, offered in St. Louis and Kansas City, is a general management program designed especially for senior or senior-track executives with eight years managerial experience. It meets once a month for three days and includes International residency in Shanghai, China.
Washington University in St. Louis	Weekend Executive MBA Program	The Weekend Executive MBA is a general management program designed especially for senior or senior-track executives with eight years professional experience. It meets on alternating weekends and includes an Orientation residency as well as an International residency in Shanghai, China.
West Virginia University	Executive MBA Program	Program offered via interactive distance learning. Interactive West Virginia sites include: Beckley, Bluefield, Charleston, Lewisburg, Morgantown, New Martinsville, Parkersburg, Shepherdstown and Wheeling. Pennsylvania site is in the Pittsburgh suburb of Bridgeville, PA.
West Virginia University	Online Executive MBA Program	West Virginia University's online Executive MBA program prepares you for leadership positions in the corporate world. Whether your interest is finance, marketing, management, entrepreneurial, or non-profit management, you will master these skills in a team environment, equipping you to assume a new role within your existing company or enhancing your previous skill set for a new opportunity. The online format enables working professionals to take advantage of an Executive MBA education without taking a leave of absence from work or being confined to evening or weekend classroom commitments. While WVU is embracing the online instructional delivery, we are also committed to experiential learning so four 3-4 day residencies are required. These residencies will enhance your educational experience by exposing you to the business/ government intersection in our nation's capital and participating in a venture capital fair.
Winthrop University	Executive MBA Program	Provides an opportunity for the experienced professional to obtain an MBA with an academic approach that minimizes disruption of either work or personal pursuits. The program combines diverse learning with real-world experience, resulting in a challenging, stimulating learning environment that provides for maximum return on time and resources invested. The program attracts mid-and-senior level managers with 6-10 years of work experience.
Wisconsin University	Executive MBA Program	A small (30-40 student), innovative program taught bi-monthly in a Friday/Saturday format for two academic years. Primary instructors are award winning, full-time faculty selected for their extensive business experience, relevant research, and teaching excellence. Students are actively involved in the learning experience through a series of projects that address current issues in their own and team members and organizations. The highly rated program is delivered in a state-of-the art facility that takes advantage of a wide range of traditional and emerging learning technologies. Entering students are at or near executive level and graduates include leading executives at a wide range of top organizations. A second year international trip, included in program tuition, is integrated with the curriculum to address many of the business, economic, and cultural issues that are critical to operating in a global environment. Student surveys reveal a high level of student satisfaction as well as excellent career progress and salary growth after graduation.
Xavier University	Xavier University Executive MBA Program	Xavier's Executive MBA (XMBA) program educates today's leaders so that they can make better business decisions tomorrow. The XMBA program is an intense, fast-paced, and highly selective program for the experienced business professional on track for a top leadership role. If you're looking for a Masters in Business Administration from a nationally ranked and accredited university, AND you want to be among an elite group of students and alumni destined for leadership positions throughout the world, apply today for the XMBA program.
Yale University	Yale MBA for Executives: Leadership in Healthcare	The MBA for Executives at Yale School of Management is designed for experienced professionals from organizations spanning the healthcare world, including hospitals and clinics, managed care, public agencies and regulatory bodies, insurance, pharmaceuticals, healthcare finance and consulting, non profit healthcare services, and medical devices. This diversity makes our classroom a true cross-section of the healthcare sector, and a place where students can learn about the managerial challenges facing other sector participants, as well as acquire the skills they need to tackle their own challenges. The program format consists of a concentrated every-other-weekend (Friday/Saturday) class schedule, which offers executives the opportunity to earn a Yale MBA in 22 months, without career disruption.
Youngstown State University	Executive MBA Program	The program begins with a required 5-day residency at an off-campus site, which lays the groundwork for the entire academic program. Study teams are an integral part of this interactive program. Participants meet on Saturdays for the 18 month program. Additional features include a required international trip, which is included in the cost of the program.
University of Minnesota	Carlson Executive MBA (CEMBA)	Pre-Program Workshops in accounting, statistics, executive communication, and Case Analysis Workshop. Live-in residencies kick-off each fall semester for first and second year students. The 4-semester program includes a Leadership Speaker Series and an Executive Negotiations Workshop. An Executive Career Coach and Study Group Consultant assist students throughout the year. Cross cultural projects are completed with students from the Carlson Global Executive MBA Programs in Austria, Poland and China. The final program experience is a two-week residency delivered abroad. The 2007-2008 international residency sites are Hong Kong, Guangzhou, China,and Shanhai, China.
Wesleyan College	Executive EMBA	To accommodate the working professional, this program can be completed over 19 months of weekend coursework. Teaching is centered on case studies, simulations, and other techniques to utilize fully the experience of the students and the expertise of the faculty members.
University of New Haven	Executive Master of Business Administration	The Executive MBA Program at the University of New Haven is the second oldest program in New England - founded in 1976 - with over 1200 graduates to date. It is designed for experienced, full time managers who want to prepare themselves for general management. Emphasis is placed on instilling the concepts and tools of management rather than developing proficiency in specific business specialties. The program runs for just under two years, beginning in either September or February.
Benedictine College	Executive MBA	This accelerated one-year program is designed for managers, business owners, military officers and executives in non-profit organizations. Tailored to the working professional, the program emphasizes global business, technology, and entrepreneurship. Weekend cohort model stimulates learning, team building and networking.
Thunderbird, the Garvin School of International Management	Executive MBA in International Management	Three-part curriculum of world business, international studies and second language. All-inclusive fee except for airfare on second trip. Cohort structure with separate classes for language study. Week-long language immersion camp during program. Two international trips: first to Mexico and second to either Europe or Asia.
Thunderbird, the Garvin School of International Management	Executive MBA in International Management - Central & Eastern Europe	This is a 10-module program which lasts 14 months. Typical of the Thunderbird offshore EMBA program, there are 64 in-class instruction days plus web-based learning. Fee includes tuition and all course materials only. International Trip: (2) trips to the Thunderbird Archamps campus in Geneva, and (1) trip to the Thunderbird Campus in Glendale, Arizona.

University	Program	Description
Baldwin-Wallace College	Executive MBA Program	At Baldwin-Wallace, we provide personal attention to our Executive MBA students from a faculty with broad academic and practical business experience who are dedicated teachers. Our focus is on meeting the needs of the working executive and preparing them for leadership roles.
Cleveland State University	Executive MBA Program	Cleveland State University's Executive MBA program provides a unique learning opportunity for highly motivated business executives, managers and professionals to earn an MBA degree in less than two years without interrupting their careers. The program curriculum emphasizes general management skills and provides balanced coverage of the major Business disciplines. Students take two classes concurrently, completing 56 credit hours of course work. Classes meet on a three-Saturday, one-Friday per month cycle. The 22-month program includes a study-travel program in international business including travel abroad and a special topics seminar. Program fees including the travel program, a notebook computer, all textbooks and materials, a distinguished speaker series and meals.
Jacksonville University	Executive MBA Program	Grounded in a compelling holistic leadership framework, the program recognizes that sustainable high performance today requires attention to mind, body and spirit. Leader knowledge is critical, of course, but we also know that attention to a leader's physical, emotional and psychological well-being is equally critical in today's dynamic business environments. We collaborate with the world-renown Mayo Clinic in providing an executive health assessment and seminars to achieve this goal. Program is 16 months/47 credit hours.
Lake Forest Graduate School of Management	Executive MBA Program	At Lake Forest Graduate School of Management, students Learn from Experience -- the extensive business experience of our 100% practitioner faculty, fellow students who average 12+ years professional experience, the experience of immediately applying new learning to current workplace challenges, and LFGSM
Ohio University	Executive MBA Program	Offered at the Ohio University Lancaster Regional Campus since 1977, the EMBA will offer classes exclusively at the Ohio University Pickerington Center beginning with the fall 2004 term, making the EMBA more convenient and accessible for participants in the Central Ohio area. Course work in the program emphasizes strategic management and leadership.
Rensselaer Polytechnic Institute	Executive MBA Program	For experienced managers with six or more years of management experience. Takes place Fridays and Saturdays of alternate weeks during two academic years with summer off between year one and year two. Generalized MBA that takes advantage of Rensselaer's Lally School excellence in innovation and technology.
Rutgers - The State University of New Jersey	Executive MBA Program	This program is strongly focused on the applied and practical aspects of doing business. The faculty is definitely cutting-edge, with very significant corporate experience. Student quality is extremely high. Executives average 14 to 16 years of experience. At least 35 percent have graduate degrees and approximately 15 percent of the class have Ph.D. or MD degrees. Over 70 percent enroll thanks to very positive feedback from colleagues at work who are former Rutgers EMBA students. The curriculum changes constantly and rapidly to meet the changing needs of this technology-driven, globalized economy. Some recent additions to the curriculum include financial statement analysis, forensic accounting, maximizing global team effectiveness in an internet-driven economy, negotiations, executive leadership during economic downturns, and global supply chain management.
University of Nebraska at Omaha	Executive MBA Program	The UNOmaha Executive MBA program provides experienced managers and professionals with an applied and integrative business management education that develops and furthers their critical thinking and leadership abilities so that they can better manage resources, leverage information technology, understand diverse cultures, and effectively address strategic issues in a dynamic global economy. As a capstone for the program, all students complete a sponsored \real world\" business consulting project that includes two weeks of overseas on-site research."
Baylor University	Executive MBA Program (Austin-Waco)	A 21 month program with two travel residencies focusing on International Business policy and strategy. The AWEMBA model has been modified to incorporate a 25% online delivery of content to help meet the schedule needs of today
Virginia Commonwealth University	Fast Track Executive MBA	The Fast Track MBA is an intensive program with classes scheduled to meet every other weekend. It is designed to function as a real business environment through a thematic approach of seven different interdisciplinary modules. This unique approach promotes a more detailed analysis of business topics and themes using methods such as special projects, case studies, computer simulations, team teaching and team learning.
University of Oregon	Oregon Executive MBA Program	Classes meet alternating Fridays and Saturdays, for 18 months, in our state-of-the-art executive classroom suite in downtown Portland. The convenient schedule and location are designed for busy professionals from throughout the region. Tuition includes registration, books, materials, parking and class-day meals.
University of Virginia	The Darden School MBA for Executives Program	This innovative degree program combines the compelling strengths of our highly regarded executive education and traditional MBA programs
The University of Indianapolis	The University of Indianapolis Executive MBA	"The University of Indianapolis Executive MBA allows high potential managers to earn their MBA in 20 months while continuing their careers. Classes are held on Saturdays. There are two courses each Saturday. The program consists of 42 credit hours and 14 courses. Classes are held on campus and at company locations. "
Colorado State University	Colorado State University Executive MBA Program	Students in this program include high-performing managers, executives, and entrepreneurs who seek an engaging learning experience while maintaining an active career. The program replicates a corporate environment with twice-weekly evening classes in the downtown Denver Executive MBA Center. The classes draw on the expertise of a diverse mix of professionals with 8 or more years of substantive work experience, representing organizations from Colorado as well as national and multinational corporations and public-sector entities. This generalist MBA program prepares students for success in operations management positions with significant leadership and strategic aspects.
University of Chicago	Chicago Booth Executive MBA Europe	"Founded in 1898, The University of Chicago Booth School of Business is the second oldest business school in the US and one of the most distinguished in the world. Our programs consistently rank among the top 6 schools in surveys worldwide. Our Executive MBA program was the first of its kind in the world, and our innovations in business education and leading edge research have produced ideas and leaders that shape the world of business. We proudly claim 6 Nobel Prizes among our current and former faculty Chicago Booth has three permanent campuses in Chicago, Singapore and London. No matter which campus you attend, the Executive MBA program is 'pure Chicago'. Each campus has the same curriculum, and one Chicago Booth faculty teaches all our programmes - full time, part time, worldwide – through the same distinctive 'Chicago Approach'. Our Executive MBA Program is a rigorous, part-time general management curriculum utilising a modular format of 16 one-week sessions spread over 21 months (ie, 1 week of classes – from Monday to Saturday- approximately every 4-6 weeks). Students from all three campuses begin the program together in late June at the Chicago campus, and go on to spend 25% of their study time with students from the other campuses throughout the programme. As the only top tiered business school with permanent campuses on three continents, Chicago Booth is able to offer a world class education to executives from all over the globe. Contact us to continue the conversation to find out how you can advance your knowledge, transform your impact, and become a business force."

University	Program	Description
University of Sharjah	Executive MBA Program	The program is designed to deliver world-class business education with an express emphasis on the Gulf business environment. It consists mainly of 42 credit hours including a final project. Up to 18 credits of foundation courses may be added for some candidates. The program is being undertaken in cooperation with the University of Arizona-Tucson and The American University of Beirut.
London Business School	EMBA - Global Americas and Europe	This 20-month Executive MBA programme, run jointly by London and Columbia Business Schools, is designed for highly ambitious mid-career professionals who have, or aspire to have, transnational responsibilities. Core courses are taught in monthly class weeks in London and New York. Students choose electives from the portfolios of Columbia, London and The University of Hong Kong (HKU) Business Schools. The programme has one intake each May.
London Business School	EMBA - Global Asia	A ground-breaking Executive MBA programme run jointly by London, Columbia and HKU Business Schools, studied over 16-20 months. EMBA-Global Asia is designed for high-potential, globally-focused executives and managers who are seeking to deepen their understanding of both Western and Eastern business theory and practice, without interrupting their careers.
London Business School	Executive MBA	This rigorous, 20-month programme is designed to transform ambitious mid-career managers into senior business people, without the need for students to interrupt their career. Core courses are taught on Fridays and Saturdays of alternate weeks. Students then undertake electives, an international assignment and management report. The EMBA has start dates in January and September and awards an MBA.
London Business School	Dubai-London Executive MBA	A 20 month dual-campus programme for employed professionals who are passionate about business in the Gulf region. It transforms mid-career managers into influential business people with the skills, knowledge and networks for career success. Starting in January and September, core courses are taught in monthly block weeks at the Dubai International Financial Centre, followed by electives at London Business School.
Nyenrode Business Universiteit	International MBA and Part-time MBA	"Nyenrode offers the International MBA as one of its core programs. Founded in 1982, it nowadays appeals to an international community of students, attracting candidates from over 20 countries each year and making the Nyenrode network more multicultural than ever before. The Nyenrode MBA has strong ties with the Kellogg School of Management (USA), one of the leading business schools in the world and the University of Stellenbosch (South Africa). The International MBA students have the opportunity to follow a module at Kellogg in the United States as part of the program. The program, taught in English, is full-time and only takes 13 months to complete. The International is geared towards developing globally-minded business leaders and managers who possess specific competencies essential for the success of 21st century organizations. The Part-time MBA takes 21 months to complete and aims to accelerate your professional growth, enabling you to excel as an entrepreneurial manager in any environment."
IMD University	EMBA	The IMD Executive MBA takes you beyond the basics to a true understanding of the forces that will shape business in the future. It prepares you for senior management challenges and responsibilities - a rigorous modular MBA for fast-rising global business leaders. The Executive MBA program is a rigorous, action-oriented degree program that thrives on diversity and gives both you and your company what you're looking for. Its major themes are: business fundamentals, globalization, leadership, strategy and execution.
IE Business School	IE Brown Executive MBA	The IE Brown Executive MBA is a highly innovative program designed to provide senior managers with the opportunity to develop and broaden their management and leadership skills in an intensive, international environment. The program brings together faculty from two world class academic institutions, integrating leading management thinking with wider perspectives from the humanities, engineering and life sciences. The program contains unique inter-disciplinary approaches and content developed by IE and Brown that prepares participants for an ever more complex and more challenging global economy.
IESE Business School	Global Executive MBA	The International Executive MBA Program at IE Business School provides all the ingredients for professional success in international business management and entrepreneurship. Aimed at experienced professionals who are driven towards career objectives and multicultural learning interaction, the International Executive MBA provides practical knowledge and innovative management tools needed to maximize professional potential and success.
ESADE	Executive MBA Program	The Executive MBA is designed to achieve three main goals: 1) Develop the participants
Escuela Superior Politecnica del Litoral - ESPOL	Executive MBA Program	Students move through the program in cohort. Program taught by local and foreign faculty. Students are required to develop a Business plan as a Final Project requirement. International Trip is optional.
IE University	IE Brown Executive MBA	The IE Brown Executive MBA is a highly innovative program designed to provide senior managers with the opportunity to develop and broaden their management and leadership skills in an intensive, international environment. The program brings together faculty from two world class academic institutions, integrating leading management thinking with wider perspectives from the humanities, engineering and life sciences. The program contains unique inter-disciplinary approaches and content developed by IE and Brown that prepares participants for an ever more complex and more challenging global economy.
IE University	International Executive MBA	The International Executive MBA Program at IE Business School provides all the ingredients for professional success in international business management and entrepreneurship. Aimed at experienced professionals who are driven towards career objectives and multicultural learning interaction, the International Executive MBA provides practical knowledge and innovative management tools needed to maximize professional potential and success.
Universidad de Navarra	Executive MBA - IESE - Universidad de Navarra	MBA program compatible with your job. For people who have an university degree and more than five years work experience t The EMBA is a part-time program with a clear international focus, offered at IESE's Madrid and Barcelona campus.General management perspective: All topics are covered from the position of a top executive. International focus. Excellent faculty. Bilingual program: Spanish and English. Intensive use of case method. International week at the China Europe International Business School (CEIBS) in Shanghai (China) and New York Team work: Students from each year are divided into heterogeneous teams comprised of students with differing experiences and professional backgrounds.
EADA	Executive MBA	EADA prepares participants to successfully take on executive positions placing an emphasis on the development of analytical capacities, making decisions and strategy implementation skills, and leadership. We provide executives with an inter-functional and global general perspective of the company, covering all the concepts, models and tools that are applied to business management in today's world. What you will accomplish:
University of South Africa (UNISA)	The Masters in Business Leadership Program	Purpose of the MBL degree: Multifunctional leaders and managers that contribute to society. 1st Year: Fundamentals of functional management and the interface between the economic environment of organisations. Human Resource Management; Marketing Management; Financial management Accounting; Operational management; Economics and the global business enviroment; Strategic management. 2nd Year: Core managerial competencies for contemporary and contextual management in Africa. Leadership and organisational dynamics; Strategic financial management; Strategy dynamics and international business; Information resource management; Business research; Business ethics. 3rd Year: A critical reflective mindset and develop research based contributions to society. Research report; Executive project management; Research based elective. Contact hours per student: 120 hours per year and examinations centres spread accross the globe.

University	Program	Description
IEDC - Bled School of Management	1-year Executive MBA Program	The IEDC - Bled School of Management International Executive MBA is a professional degree program for managers. It attracts a strong international group of high-potential individuals who possess relevant business experience. Its innovative curriculum, focused on general management in an international environment, is taught by world-class faculty from the best European and North American business schools. The one-year International Executive MBA consists of 17 residential weeks divided into three 5-week and one 2-week modules in one year, and includes an international field visit. The modular approach enables participants, coming from all over the world, to join the International Executive MBA without leaving their jobs, and allows them to implement their new knowledge and skills in their companies between modules. The program begins in January of each year and participants graduate the following December.
IEDC, Bled School of Management	Executive MBA Program (www.iedc.si/programs/mba)	"TRANSFORMING YOUR LEADERSHIP POTENTIAL INTO LEADERSHIP PERFORMANCE. At IEDC, we bring together the best teachers in the world with the most promising managers of the region to create a learning process that stretches the mind, expands your leadership repertoire, and changes the quality of decision making for better results. Building on the strengths of people in the program, IEDC uses innovative methods and tools throughout the entire EMBA program. So, whether it is Arts and Leadership Series or CEO Masterclasses, you are guaranteed a cutting-edge curriculum celebrated internationally for its innovation and impact. Spending 17 intense weeks in company of accomplished managers and leading scholars marks only the beginning of relationships that last a lifetime. An alumni network of over 40,000 executives from more than 60 countries is waiting for your graduation."
University of Chicago	Executive MBA	Founded in 1898, the University of Chicago Graduate School of Business - a Nobel Prize winning powerhouse - created the world's first executive MBA program in 1943 to provide senior managers and executives with the most up-to-date management education. The same EMBA program is now available in our Asia Campus in Singapore as well as in our European Campus in London and our North American Campus in Chicago.
University of Chicago	Executive MBA	Founded in 1898, the University of Chicago Graduate School of Business - a Nobel Prize winning powerhouse - created the world's first executive MBA program in 1943 to provide senior managers and executives with the most up-to-date management education. The same EMBA program is now available in our Asia Campus in Singapore as well as in our European Campus in London and our North American Campus in Chicago.
University of Paisley	Executive MBA Program - online learning	This innovative 2-year part-time program has recently been redesigned and new electronic learning materials developed. It is a highly flexible program featuring the Virtual Campus, an interactive web-based learning environment, with full student resources and support offered online. Three levels of awards exist within the program - Certificate in Resource Management, Diploma in Strategic Management and Executive MBA.
King Fahd University of Petroleum & Minerals	Executive MBA Program	Program length is 16 months (four semesters). Students move through the program as a cohort group. Ongoing classes meet on a five star hotel. The tuition fee of 32,500 Saudi Riyals (around $8,667.00) is due at the beginning of each semester.
IBS Moscow	Executive MBA	The mission of the program is enlarging the knowledge of the business world, improving analytical skills, enhancing decision-making and sharpening the strategic vision. The Executive MBA Program comprises: core course, specialization and selection of electives, which are all based on global business issues and complemented with the specifics of the Russian market.
Institute for Business and Public Administration from Bucharest-	Executive MBA Program	Students are taught in English by American professors from top U.S. business schools (Kennesaw State University - Atlanta) and by Romanian professors trained at Harvard, MIT, Stanford, Wharton and Northwestern. The program includes three Residence weeks per academic year: two in Romania and one in Atlanta-USA when Romanian and American executives have joint presentations in front of the Kennesaw State University professors.
University of Minnesota	Warsaw Executive MBA	Joint Faculty Council oversees curriculum of Warsaw executive MBA degree program. Warsaw EMBA program includes final semester field study in area of professional interest. New curriculum implemented Fall 2002 Partner University: Warsaw School of Economics. wemba.sgh.waw.pl Program Language: English & Polish
Massey University	Executive (2 Year) MBA Programme	The Massey University MBA is a national and international programme offered in four main centres in New Zealand. There are three modes of delivery: full time (15 months), executive (25 months) and modular (42 months). The modes start throughout the year with inter-modal transfer possible. The Executive (2 Year) MBA Programme is offered in two main centres in New Zealand, ie Wellington and Auckland.
Erasmus University - Rotterdam, The Netherlands	Global Executive MBA - OneMBA	Five top business schools from Asia, Europe and North and South America have formed a partnership to design and deliver OneMBA, a premier global executive MBA program that is radically different from the global programs offered by other leading business schools. OneMBA is distinguished by its span of five business cultures in Asia, Europe and North and South America. It connects a globally diverse network of executives living and working on four continents. The OneMBA curriculum was developed jointly and will be taught by leading faculty from each of the partner schools.
Tilburg University	Executive MBA - International Masters in Management (IMM)	The EMBA Program offering an International Masters in Management
Instituto Panamericano De Alta Dirección De Empresa (IPADE)	Executive MBA	Two years, six (four-month terms), 600 sessions, case methodology.
Bocconi University	MBA Part Time	A modular programme MBA for middle managers or professional with an average of 8 years of working experience
Politecnico di Milano	Executive Master of Business Administration	The Executive MBA at MIP-Politecnico di Milano is a modular, two years programme for people and companies that want to develop their managerial competence. Classes take place in evening hours and Saturdays. All the Courses of the Programme are taught in Italian. Every year MIP starts two editions of the Executive MBA (November and March). Admission is limited to 50 people each edition.
Tel Aviv University	Kellogg-Recanati International Executive MBA Program	Classes are conducted in English. Classes are taught by Kellogg and Recanati faculty. All regular modules take place on the campus of Tel Aviv University. Some intensive modules are conducted abroad.
Tel Aviv University	Recanati Executive MBA Program	The program is located in Tel Aviv. All classes are conducted in Hebrew.
City University of Hong Kong	Executive MBA Program	The main themes of the Program are on China Business, Service Management and Leadership. The Program is designed around three interlinked components including 7 foundation courses, 6 electives from China business and service management focus and 4 integration courses. Executive Consultancy Mission(Residential Trip normally held in China), CEO Forum, EMBA Project, Leadership and Strategic Management are highlights of the program. Indigenous materials are used such as recent and relevant Asian case studies mainly drawn from the Business Faculty's Office for Chinese Managment Development.
Hong Kong University of Science and Technology	Kellogg-HKUST Executive MBA Program	The Best of Both Worlds. As a partnership between two leading universities, the Kellogg

University	Program	Description
The University of Western Ontario	Executive MBA	The Ivey Executive MBA program is an integrated management development experience that you will share in its entirety with your classmates. The program is structured to give you both the critical elements of business leadership and an ability to deal with the complex cross-enterprise challenges facing organizations at home and abroad. Our approach is practical, provides you immediate value, and is suited to experienced managers or professionals. Throughout the program, we challenge you to solve real problems faced by real managers.
WHU - Otto Beisheim	Kellogg-WHU Executive MBA Program	The Kellogg-WHU Executive MBA Program develops the skills of the current global manager. The program is taught by senior faculty members of the Kellogg School and the WHU and integrates all of the managerial disciplines, focusing on a synthesis of American and European management styles. The content of the program is tailored to the needs of the participants and their companies and institutions. Emphasis is on three specific areas of management skills: behaviour in learning organizations, international management and managing groups of cooperating firms for international competitiveness.
Grenoble Ecole de Management	Executive MBA	International business for managers working in the global business environment. Students must live in Grenoble during study.
INSEAD	Executive MBA	The INSEAD Executive MBA brings together the best of both worlds: the international reputation of our INSEAD MBA programme and our leading experience in Executive Education. It combines the analytical rigor in management with the art of executive leadership.
Helsinki School of Economics	Executive MBA - Helsinki	The Helsinki School of Economics (HSE) Executive MBA Program is designed for experienced managers who need to deepen their knowledge of complex international business principles while at the same time further develop practical management skills and tools which are readily applicable to their present challenges. HSE Executive MBA program participants develop internationally transportable skills that empower them to become outstanding business leaders with the competence, confidence and networks vital to make appropriate executive level decisions. The HSE Executive MBA program focuses upon key management issues in the fields of finance, marketing, leadership and strategy. The modular structure of the HSE Executive MBA program is designed so that participants can realistically balance their studies with their work- and home-life. Dynamic group interaction, take-home exams, readings and assignments complement and complete the learning experience. The entire program may be completed within 20 months. The program is currently delivered in Helsinki, Poznan, Seoul, Singapore and Beijing. Participants may take modules at different locations. Experienced professors representing renowned business schools worldwide deliver the HSE Executive MBA program modules.
Henley Management College	Executive Full Time MBA	Executive MBA - International - aimed at people with about 10 years or more experience, from UK and non UK backgrounds. As well as core MBA topics, emphasis on Personal Development and teamwork International trip: 1 yr Program has 12 weeks in UK, 1 week in Spain or South Africa, 1 weeks in US, 2 weeks Asia Pacific
Ashridge Business School	The Ashridge Full Time MBA	The Ashridge full time MBA has been redesigned to offer an integrated, leadership-based curriculum, based on thematic modules addressing issues such as leading change, business in society and organisational life-cycle.
University of Warwick	Executive MBA Program (Modular)	"The Warwick Executive MBA participants visit campus for a week at a time at regular intervals to explore a particular subject in depth. This route combines the flexibility of part-time study with the benefits of interactive learning and is perfect if you want to plan well ahead. It"
Aalborg University	Masters Programme in Management of Technology	The Masters Programme in Management of Technology is a 2-year, part-time post-experience education primarily for engineers from industry and public institutions who want to understand the complex interplay of modern organizations and to develop innovative solutions for their company's business development. Individual projects are carried out in each semester in own organization.
Technical University of Denmark	Master in Management of Technology	Project and consulting work for participant companies are integrated in the program. Key Words: Innovation, Business Development, Change Management, Leadership Skills.
Aarhus School of Business	Executive MBA Program	Executive MBA programme with a focus on change management.
Copenhagen Business School	Executive MBA Program	The Executive MBA Program at CBS offers well educated, highly experienced business managers and their companies great value by transforming functional management thinking and enhancing general management practices into general management competencies in the increasingly competitive global business environment. The program offers a very strong focus on leadership and personal development. The faculty members who teach in the EMBA Program hail from all corners of the globe, and have been carefully selected for their experience in business and effectiveness in classroom, not to mention the quality of their research in international business. These professors all build on their experience as current and past faculty members of world-class institutions including IMD, the University of Virginia, IESE, Harvard, MIT and CBS. International Trip(s): 3
University of Minnesota	China Executive MBA	Joint Faculty Council oversees curriculum of China offshore executive MBA program. China EMBA program includes a residency in Minneapolis, MN. All other coursework occurs at Lingnan (University) College in Guangzhou, China. Partner University: Lingnan (University) College, Zhongshan University www.chemba.com Program Language: English.
Washington University in St. Louis	Shanghai Executive MBA Program	The Executive MBA Shanghai Program is a general management program designed for middle and senior management executives with at least five years of managerial experience. It meets monthly for a Friday-Monday class session and includes an Orientation and an International Residency in St. Louis.
Washington University in St. Louis	Shanghai Executive MBA Program	The Executive MBA Shanghai Program is a general management program designed for middle and senior management executives with at least five years of managerial experience. It meets monthly for a Friday-Monday class session and includes an Orientation residency and an International residency in St. Louis.
Tsinghua University	Executive EMBA	With outstanding tradition and prominent academic resources, Tsinghua Executive MBA Program is one of the best senior-level executive education programs that train China's business leaders with Chinese and global perspectives for business management.
Cornell University	Cornell - Queen's Execuitve MBA	Cornell - Queen's Executive MBA is an 18-month program that enable you to earn both a Queen's MBA and a Cornell MBA while you continue to work. Residential sessions are held at both Queen's and Cornell. Class sessions are shared with your US counterparts, and led by professors from both schools.
Queen's University	Cornell - Queen's Execuitve MBA	Cornell - Queen's Execuitve MBA is an 18-month program that enable you to earn both a Queen's MBA and a Cornell MBA while you continue to work. Residential sessions are held at both Queen's and Cornell. Class sessions are shared with your US counterparts, and led by professors from both schools.
Concordia University	Executive MBA Program	The Executive MBA at the AACSB-accredited John Molson School of Business, the second-oldest program of its kind in Canada, is located in the bilingual, cosmopolitan city of Montreal. The multi-ethnic background of many of our students brings an international flavour and perspective to classes that are held on alternate Fridays and Saturdays, over a 20-month period. We offer a comprehensive curriculum designed to prepare graduates to become CEOs and general managers, delivered via small classes and a very personalized, high-service approach to our students. We pride ourselves on an outstanding international study trip, organized by the Director of the Program.

University	Program	Description
McGill University	International Masters Program in Practicing Management	Five top business schools from around the world (Canada, England, France, India and Japan) have joined forces to develop what may be the next generation program in management education. The intent is to break the mold of conventional university-based MBA teaching, as well as in-house management development to offer significant education to practicing managers in the context of their own jobs and the needs of their own organizations. The program runs with a limited number of companies each sending several participants to a given class, people in mid-career who are considered likely candidates for senior management positions. The classroom activity takes place in five modules; four of two weeks and a final one of three weeks, spread over a year and a half. The content is designed not around the functional silos of traditional management education (marketing finance operations etc.) but in terms of managerial "mindsets" one of each module: the practice of managing - the reflective mindset; managing organizations - the analytic mindset; managing context - the worldly mindset; managing people - the collaborative mindset; and managing change - the catalytic mindset. Each school hosts one of the modules and recruits the companies from its region. Thus with the class not only going to but also coming from these five areas the IMPM becomes an authentic international experience.
Queen's University	Queens Executive MBA - Ottawa Classroom	Queen's Executive MBA is a 15 month program that enables you to earn a Queen's MBA in 15 months while you continue to work. It is offered everywhere in Canada. The program inlcudes one-on-one Personal Coaching, startegic electives, an optional international study trip, a global business project, Career Coaching and an optional Fit to Lead(TM) program.
Queen's University	Queens Executive MBA National Videoconference	Queen's Executive MBA is a 15 month program that enables you to earn a Queen's MBA in 15 months while you continue to work. It is offered everywhere in Canada. The program inlcudes one-on-one Personal Coaching, startegic electives, an optional international study trip, a global business project, Career Coaching and an optional Fit to Lead(TM) program.
Queens University	Queen's Accelerated MBA for Business Graduates	Queen's Acceleraqted MBA for Business Graduates is an MBA program designed specifically for people with an undergraduate degree in business from a recognized business school. The program enables students to earn a Queen's MBA in 12 months while they contiue to work. The curriculum is designed to build on your undergraduate learning.
Queens University	Queen's Execuitve MBA	Queen's Executive MBA is a 15 month program that enables you to earn a Queen's MBA in 15 months while you continue to work. It is offered everywhere in Canada. The program inlcudes one-on-one Personal Coaching, startegic electives, an optional international study trip, a global business project, Career Coaching and an optional Fit to Lead(TM) program.
Saint Mary's University	Executive MBA Program	Designed to develop skills required for senior management. A global perspective is emphasized with an international trip being a required part of the course work. Participants complete a work related major research project over the two years of the program.
Simon Fraser University	Executive MBA Program	The SFU EMBA program is designed for experienced, mid-career managers & professionals seeking to improve their capacity to lead, strategize and manage change. Students come together every other weekend to interact with faculty and fellow students in the classroom and in study groups. Our team-based environment stimulates discussion, debate and decision-making.
University of Calgary	The Alberta/Haskayne Executive MBA Program	Our Executive MBA Program is designed to build the capabilities you need to be successful. Our goal is to equip our graduates to meet the entrepreneurial, administrative and leadership demands of executive management. You will be immersed in an action learning environment that will engage you in intense, team-oriented experiences that will address the immediate strategic needs of your organization. You will be exposed to the latest management theory and research in a curriculum designed to give you a broader, more global perspective. You will connect with a powerful network on mentors and coaches who will help you unlock your potential.
University of Ottawa	University of Ottawa Executive MBA	The University of Ottawa Executive MBA Program is 21 intensive months of rigorous academic learning, hands-on projects, and major consulting assignments delivered in a technologically advanced and highly professional setting. Experienced executives and professionals benefit from the one-day-per-week class schedule that supports continued career progression and offers the opportunity to rapidly integrate newly learned concepts on the job. While Ottawa
University of Toronto	Global Executive MBA OMNIUM	The OMNIUM Global Executive MBA participants learn through strategic immersion in the four main economic regions of the world
University of Toronto	MBA for Executives	The One-year MBA for Executives at the Rotman School is an integrated program that combines innovation with the added advantage of swift completion. The curriculum is built around classes held every two weeks on Fridays and Saturdays, and four, one-week residential modules.
University of Western Ontario	Executive MBA Program (Continental Section)	Case-based teaching method which leverages students' work experience in all aspects of business management. Individual course projects plus two major program projects. Ten-day international trip to student-chosen location at conclusion of Program. Optional one-week study trip to Mexico City in October.
University of Western Ontario	Executive MBA Program (Hong Kong Campus)	Case-based teaching method which leverages the work experience of participants with diverse nationalities, industry sectors and functional specialties. Individual course projects plus three major program projects. A one-week residence period in London, jointly with the Continental EMBA section at the beginning of second year. Ivey offers students the flexibility to move within its EMBA sections in case of geographic relocations.
University of Western Ontario	Executive MBA Program (Mississauga Campus)	Case-based teaching method which leverages students' work experience in all aspects of business management. Individual course projects plus two major program projects. Ten-day international trip to student-chosen location at conclusion of Program. Optional one-week study trip to Mexico City in October. Ivey offers students the flexibility to move within its EMBA sections if transferred by their company.
York University	The Joint Kellogg-Schulich Executive MBA	Joint EMBA Program between Kellogg School of Management (Northwestern University) and the Schulich School of Business (York University). 2 residence weeks required
Sobey School of Business	Sobey School of Business Executive MBA	The Executive MBA is designed for mature managers and professionals who are able to earn a Master of Business Administration degree in two years without leaving full time employment. Classes take place on Fridays and Saturdays on alternate weekends, with assignments to be completed between classes. The 30
Faculdades Integradas de Sao Paulo	Global Executive MBA	The only Executive MBA program, in Brazil, with strong academic and professional connections with major European MBA programs, and with both Brazilian and European faculty. Our humanistic-cum-managerial approach offers unique, highly-effective tools to improve the skills and entrepreneurial capabilities our students need to create shareholder's value in the corporations they manage. Our program pay special attention to such paramount disciplines as Business Ethics, Corporate Social Responsibility and Environmental Management, along with such fundamental ones as Strategic Management, Entrepreneurship, Leadership, Corporate Finance, etc.
Instituto Veris - IBMEC Sao Paulo	Executive MBA - Finance	Dedicated to executives with managerial experience willing to develop a career path to top management positions and need a strong finance background, together with a broad view of managerial functions, a strategic perspective, decision-making skills and ability to manage people and processes. International Trip: Two week - University of Illinois at Urbana Champaign - College of Commerce and Business Administration.
University of Sau Paolo	International Executive MBA	480 class hours per year; dissertation required, 18 month duration. Two international trips included to the United States, Europe or China. Focus on strategic management for senior managers.

University	Program	Description
BSP - Brazil	Executive MBA Program	The only MBA in Brazil to be taught entirely in English by a Brazilian business school. BSP utilizes the case study method, focusing on national and multinational companies operating within the Brazilian and Latin America economic reality. Near the end of the program, students travel to the Rotman School of Management at the University of Toronto, Canada for a two-week international business program, also conducted in English.
Brazilian Business School	Executive MBA Program	There are eight core disciplines (marketing, human resources, business math, business history, macroeconomics, corporate finance, business communications and accounting). Upon completion, the student can choose among three fields: entrepreneurship, marketing and finance.
Fundacao Dom Cabral	MBA Empresarial	Classes meet five times per year for seven-day sessions, plus 460 hours of distance education. There is a total of 570 class hours per year. Individual dissertation is required. Program conducted in Portuguese and English. Optional international module at Kellogg School of Management.
Fundacao Dom Cabral	MBA Executivo	The program is modular including two one week long module, one two weeks module in Canada and 12 weekend modules (Friday and Saturday). In additional to the presential module it also includes 460 hours of distance education. There is a total of 570 class hours per year. Individual dissertation is required. Program conducted in Portuguese and English. The international module is conducted by the Sauder School of Business at the University of British Columbia.
Vlerick Leuven Gent Management School	Executive EMBA	The Vlerick Executive MBA is an intensive two-year management programme delivered in the heart of Europe. Participants have a large variety of degrees, are active in various professional domains and work for different firms and organisations. An essential part of the programme is the final project that is carried out in the participant's company.
University of Minnesota	Vienna Executive MBA	Joint Faculty Council oversees curriculum of Vienna offshore executive MBA degree program. Vienna EMBA program includes a residency in Warsaw, Poland and Minneapolis, MN. Partner University: Vienna University of Business and Economics. www.emba.at Program Language: English
Danube-University Krems	Executive MBA	Executive MBA Program of the Business School of Danube University Krems: General Management Education for Managers with professional and managerial experience with special european focus. Study trips to China & USA are part of the program. Danube University Krems is the only stately run university for postgraduate studies in Austria. The EMBA Program was established in 1991 by the Scientific Academy of Lower Austria. The aim of the Danube University Krems is to provide qualified post-graduate programs in many different fields including Economics & Managerial Studies, European Law, Medical Sciences, Information Technology and Construction Sciences. The Business School of Danube Uniersity Krems cooperates with many universities and institutions, such as the University of British Columbia in Vancouver, the Weatherhead School of Management at the Case Western Reserve University in Cleveland, Hong Kong Univesity of Science and Technology.
Queensland University of Technology	Executive MBA Program	Our Executive MBA (EMBA) is a tailored program for more experienced managers offered in an intensive, flexibly delivered format. The Executive delivery format provides managers with a convenient and accessible study option to obtain an MBA. Classes are scheduled once a month over a Friday to Sunday weekend session, with 20 hours of classes each weekend session each month of the program, plus two intensive sessions of 10-14 days in January of each year. The course is 20 months in duration, including an international study tour to China with site visits, lectures and cultural experiences.
University of Melbourne	Executive MBA	The Melbourne Business School Executive MBA program (EMBA) is an innovative international experience designed for senior managers.
Queensland University of Technology	Executive MBA Program	QUT'S Executive MBA program is designed for senior executives and is tailored to fit the working life of the busy professional. Intensive weekend sessions allow participants to balance study with minimal interference to business commitments and assists participants to maintain career momentum. Classes are scheduled one weekend per month (Friday to Sunday) for 22 months and includes an optional international tour to China. The program provides quality networking opportunities as its only open to those with a minimum of five years management experience.
IAE	Executive MBA	The Program develops the conceptual and analytical skills required for management,decision making and successful implementation through updated tools and practices used in the international market Optional: A two-week international trip to the US taking classes at Darden, Wharton and Harvard, including company visits on the East Coast.
Ivey Business School	The Cheng Yu Tung Management Institute	The first bschool established its presence in Hong Kong in 1998. It is one of the four true case-teaching business schools in the world and is the only one within this group with a permanent campus in Hong Kong. At its permanent campus

EMBA Program Comparisons

University	School	Country	State	Type	First Year Created	Degree Offered	Start Dates	Class Times	Int'l Trip	Residency	Program Length
Arizona State University	College of Business	USA	Arizona	EMBA	1979	MBA/EMBA	Aug	One day a week alternating Fridays and Saturdays.	Trip Required	No Residency Required	22
Auburn University	College of Business	USA	Alabama	EMBA	1998	MBA	Jan, Aug	1 Week residencies balanced with distance learning modules	Trip Required	Residency Required	21
Baruch College/ CUNY	Zicklin School of Business	USA	New York	EMBA	1983	MBA	Sep	One day per week, Primarily Saturdays and approx. One Friday per month(8:30 a.m. - 5:30 p.m.)	Trip Required	No Residency Required	22
Baruch College/ CUNY	Zicklin School of Business	USA	New York	EMBA	1997	MSF	Sep	Two days per week, one evening per week (6:00 p.m. - 9:00 p.m.) and Saturday (8:30 a.m. - 5:30 p.m.)	Trip Required	No Residency Required	10
Baylor University		USA	Texas	EMBA	1993	EMBA	Aug	Classes meet on alternating weekends, on Friday afternoons from 2:30 to 6:30 p.m. and Saturdays from 8:00 a.m. to 5:00 p.m.	Trip Required	Residency Required	21
Binghamton University/ SUNY	School of Management	USA	New York	EMBA	1996	MBA	Aug	Friday and Saturday generally once per month - exeption twice per month during the first month of each semester.	No Trip	Residency Required	21
Birmingham-Southern College	Division of Business and Graduate Programs	USA	Alabama	EMBA	1982	MBA	Feb, Jun, Sep	Monday through Thursday evenings from 6 p.m. to 9 p.m.	Trip Optional	No Residency Required	24
Boise State University		USA	Idaho	EMBA	2006	MBA	Sept.	Once ea. Mo. (Th to Sat or W to Sat)	Yes	Yes	21
Boston University	School of Management	USA	Massachusetts	MBA	1988	MBA	January	Every two weeks on Friday and Saturday, and four week-long residencies	Trip Required	Residency Required	18
Bowling Green State University	College of Business Administration	USA	Ohio	EMBA	1976	MBA	Jan	One weekend per month, Friday, Saturday and Sunday (8:00 am - 5:00 pm)	Trip Required	No Residency Required	18
Bradley University	Foster College of Business	USA	Illinois		2001	MBA	Aug, Jan	8AM to 5 PM Friday and Saturday, every other weekend.	Yes-Mandatory	No	15
Brigham Young University	Marriott School	USA	Utah	EMBA	1983	MBA	Aug	Tuesday and Thursday evenings (6 p.m. to 9 p.m.), occasional Saturdays	Trip Required	Residency Required	24
California State University, Hayward	School of Business and Economics	USA	California	EMBA	2001	EMBA	Feb, Sep	Thursday-Sunday, one weekend per month for both programs.	Trip Required	Residency Required	13
California State University, Hayward	School of Business and Economics	USA	California	EMBA	2004	EMBA	Jun, Nov	Thursday-Sunday, one weekend per month.	Trip Required	Residency Required	12

For the latest school information visit www.EMBAWorld.com

Distance Learning	Denomination	Application Fee	Deposit	Total Program Cost	Accreditation	Jointly Offered	Class Size	Undergrad Degree Req'd	Interview Req'd	Min Management Req'd	Min Work Experience Req'd
Not Distance Learning	US$		0	62500	AACSB		47	Yes	Yes	7	10
Not Distance Learning	US$		1000	39600	AACSB, SACS		40	Yes	Yes, except	8	8
Not Distance Learning	US$		3000	57800	AACSB		23	Yes	Yes	5	5
Not Distance Learning	US$		3000	32500	AACSB		26	Yes	Yes	5	3
Not Distance Learning	US$		2000	63500	AACSB		36	Yes	Yes	5	5
Not Distance Learning	US$		100	34800	AACSB		26	Yes	Yes	2	5
Not Distance Learning	US$		25	26950	AACSB		20	Yes	Yes	2	3
10%	USA	USD55	USD1,900	USD41,000	AACSB	No	28	Yes	Yes	6	8
No distance learning	USD	USD125	USD1,500	USD84,000	AACSB		45	Yes, except	Yes	5	10
Not Distance Learning	US$		500	42000	AACSB		21	Yes	Yes, except	3	5
No		USD40	USD500	USD49,600	AACSB	No	25-30	Yes with exceptions	Yes	5	7 years
Not Distance Learning	US$		500	31000	AACSB		70	Yes	Yes	4	4
Not Distance Learning	US$		75	42000	AACSB, WASC		30	Yes	Yes	3	5
Not Distance Learning	US$		75	37000	AACSB, WASC	International Business School Stryia	15	Yes	Yes	3	5

For the latest school information visit www.EMBAWorld.com

University	School	Country	State	Type	First Year Created	Degree Offered	Start Dates	Class Times	Int'l Trip	Residency	Program Length
Case Western Reserve University	Weatherhead School of Management	USA	Ohio	EMBA	1970	MBA	Aug	Fall & Spring Semesters are comprised of a 1 week visit and 2-3 day visits. A total of 12 visits to campus. Class days run 8:00am - 5:30pm	Takes place in June (Third Semster of the program)	Fall & Spring Semesters are comprised of a 1 week visit and 2-3 day visits. A total of 12 visits to campus. Class days run 8:00am - 5:30pm	21
Case Western Reserve University	Weatherhead School of Management	USA	Ohio	EMBA	1979	MBA	Aug	Once a week, alternating Fridays and Saturdays	Trip Required	No Residency Required	21
Chapman University	George L. Argyros School of Business and Economics	USA	California	EMBA	1995	MBA	Aug	Thursday (7:00 p.m. - 10:00 p.m.); Saturday (9:00 a.m. - 12:00 p.m.)	Trip Required	Residency Required	21
Claremont Graduate University	Peter F. Drucker and Masatoshi Ito Graduate School of Management	USA	California	EMBA	1971	EMBA, Master's in Management. Master's of Science in Advanced Management.	Jan, March, May, July, Sept., Oct.	Various choices offered (not a lockstep program): weekday evenings, Saturdays, weekend intensives.	YES- Oxford (Optional)	Residency Required	24
Columbia University	Graduate School of Business	USA	New York	EMBA	2002	MBA MBA from Berkeley also	May	Classes meet four sessions per term at Berkeley (Thursday - Saturday) and one session per term in New York (Wednesday-Saturday)	Trip Required	Residency Required	19
Columbia University	Graduate School of Business	USA & UK	New York & London	EMBA	2001	MBA MBA from London Business School also	May	Classes meet four times per term, Wednesday-Saturday, alternating between NY and London during the first year. Students can take Friday/Saturday electives during the second year.	Trip Required	Residency Required	20
Columbia University	Graduate School of Business	USA	New York	EMBA	1968	MBA	May & Jan	Classes meet every other Friday and Saturday	Trip Required	Occasional residency weeks required, including the International Seminar	20
Cornell University	Johnson Graduate School of Management	USA	New York	EMBA	2005	MBA	Jun		Trip Required	Residency Required	16
Cornell University	Johnson Graduate School of Management	USA	New York	EMBA	1999	MBA	Jul	Alternate weekends (Saturday-Sunday): Saturday 8:00 a.m. - 5:00 p.m.; Sunday, 8:00 a.m. - 1:00 p.m. One week in residence on the Cornell Campus begins each of the four terms.	Trip Required	Residency Required	22

For the latest school information visit www.EMBAWorld.com

Distance Learning	Denomination	Application Fee	Deposit	Total Program Cost	Accreditation	Jointly Offered	Class Size	Undergrad Degree Req'd	Interview Req'd	Min Management Req'd	Min Work Experience Req'd
	US$	USD100	USD750	USD92,000	AACSB	no	AVG 30	Yes with exceptions	Yes	5	10 years
Not Distance Learning	US$		750	80000	AACSB		28	Yes with exceptions	Yes	5	10
Not Distance Learning	US$		500	52000	AACSB		16	Yes	Yes	2	7
Not Distance Learning	US$	USD60	Not Required	$1,683 per unit - $80,784	WASC, AACSB		15	YES	YES	5	5 years
Not Distance Learning	US$	$200	$2,500	$150,000	AACSB	Haas School of Business at the University of California, Berekley	70	Yes	Yes	5	5
Not Distance Learning	US$	$200	$4,000	$145,000	AACSB	London Business School	70	Yes	Yes		5
Not Distance Learning	US$	$250	$2,000	$149,000	AACSB		120	Yes	Yes		5
Distance Learning	US$		0	0	AACSB	Queen's School of Business	0	Yes	Yes	0	0
Not Distance Learning	US$		2000	107600	AACSB		58	Yes	Yes	0	7

For the latest school information visit www.EMBAWorld.com

University	School	Country	State	Type	First Year Created	Degree Offered	Start Dates	Class Times	Int'l Trip	Residency	Program Length
Drexel University	Bennett S. LeBow College of Business	USA	Pennsylvania	EMBA	1997	EMBA	Sep	Once per week, alternating Fridays and Saturdays from 8 am to 5 pm; three days at the beginning of the first year. Evening Program: Monday & Thursday evenings from 6:00 - 9:00 pm with three full days in first year.	Trip Required	No Residency Required	21
Duke University	Fuqua School of Business	USA	North Carolina	EMBA	2000	MBA	August	1 week of residential classroom requirement every 9-10 weeks	Trip Required	Residency Required	16
Duke University	Fuqua School of Business	USA	North Carolina	EMBA	1996	MBA	May	2 weeks of residential classroom requirements every 12-14 weeks	Trip Required	Residency Required	18
Duke University	Fuqua School of Business	USA	North Carolina	EMBA	1984	MBA	June	Friday and Saturday every other weekend	Trip Optional	Residency Required	19
Emory University	Goizueta Business School	USA	Georgia	EMBA	2002	MBA	August	8 one-week residencies at Emory; 1 international residency; Approx. 1 residency per quarter over 21 months	Yes- required	Residency required for out-of-town participants	21
Emory University	Goizueta Business School	USA	Georgia	EMBA	1978	MBA	Aug	8 one-week residencies at Emory; 1 international residency; Approx. 1 residency per quarter over 21 months	Yes - Required	Residency required for out-of-town participants	21
Emory University	Goizueta Business School	USA	Georgia	EMBA	1978	MBA	December	Alternating Weekends Friday & Saturday; some Thursdays	Yes - Required	No Residency Required	16
Fairleigh Dickinson University	Samuel J. Silberman College of Business	USA	New Jersey	EMBA	1974	EMBA	Feb, Sep	Each course is conducted over 5 weeks meeting each Saturday from 8:50am to 4:30pm. Occasional Friday for seminars or outside speakers.	Trip Required	No Residency Required	21
Florida International University	College of Business Administration	USA	Florida	EMBA	1995	MBA	Sep	Friday evenings (4:30-9 p.m.) and Saturdays (8:30-5:30).	Trip Required	Residency Required	18
Fordham University	Graduate School of Business	USA	New York	EMBA	1998	MBA	Aug	The Program predominately meets one weekend per month (Friday-Sunday) from 9:00 am to 5:00 pm on each meeting date.	Trip Required	Residency Required	22
George Fox University	School of Management	USA	Oregon	EMBA	2005	MBA	Jan,Sep	Weekend format	Trip Required	No Residency Required	24
George Mason University	School of Management	USA	Virginia	EMBA	1991	MBA	Aug	alternating Fridays and Saturdays from 8:00 a.m. - 4:30 p.m.	Trip Required	Residency Required	21

For the latest school information visit www.EMBAWorld.com

Distance Learning	Denomination	Application Fee	Deposit	Total Program Cost	Accreditation	Jointly Offered	Class Size	Undergrad Degree Req'd	Interview Req'd	Min Management Req'd	Min Work Experience Req'd
Not Distance Learning	US$		1000	65000	AACSB		42	Yes	Yes	5	8
Not Distance Learning	US$	USD200	USD5,000	USD120,100	AACSB		118	Yes	Yes	0	3
Not Distance Learning	US$	USD200	USD7,500	USD140,900	AACSB		60	Yes	Yes	0	10
Not Distance Learning	US$	USD200	USD2,000	USD102,900	AACSB		71	Yes	Yes	0	5
30% distance learning; 70% in-class	US$	USD150	USD1,000	Residency tuition-$98,500; non-residency-$90,200	AACSB	No	35-40	Yes- Required	Yes- required	5	7 years
30% distance learning; 70% in-class	US$	150	1000	98500 Residency tuition; (90200 non-residency)	AACSB		35-40	Yes	Yes	5	5
not distance learning	US $	USD150	USD1,000	USD94,000	AACSB	No	83 (2 cohorts)	Yes - Required	Yes - Required	5	7 years
Not Distance Learning	US$		40	45450	AACSB		21	Yes	Yes	5	5
Not Distance Learning	US$		2000	42000	AACSB		28	Yes	Yes	5	8
Not Distance Learning	US$		500	70500	AACSB		25	Yes	Yes	5	7
Not Distance Learning	US$		40	0	NWCCU		15	Yes	Yes	5	10
Not Distance Learning	US$		5000	55 000	AACSB		26	Yes with exceptions	Yes	7	7

For the latest school information visit www.EMBAWorld.com

University	School	Country	State	Type	First Year Created	Degree Offered	Start Dates	Class Times	Int'l Trip	Residency	Program Length
George Washington University	School of Business and Public Management	USA	Washington DC	EMBA	1991	MBA	Aug	Once a week, alternating Fridays and Saturdays from 8:30am-5:30pm	Trip Required	Residency Required	21
Georgetown University	McDonough School of Business	USA	Washington, DC	EMBA	2005	Executive Master's Degree	March	Alternate weekends, Fridays and Saturdays	One week-long international residency	Two domestic and one international	13
Georgetown University	McDonough School of Business	USA	Washington, DC	EMBA	1994	MBA	August	Alternate Weekends, Fridays and Saturdays	Two global consulting projects	Four residencies; two global and two domestic	18
Georgetown University	School of Business	USA	Four Continents	EMBA	2008	MBA	June	Six 12-day modules covering four continents	Six 12-day modules covering four continents	Six 12-day modules covering four continents	15
Georgia Institute of Technology	College of Management	USA	Georgia	EMBA	1995	MBA MSMOT	May	All day Friday & Saturday every other week	Trip Required	Residency Required	19
Georgia State University	J. Mack Robinson College of Business	USA	Georgia	EMBA	1980	MBA	Aug	Once a week, alternating Fridays and Saturdays (8:00 a.m. - 5:30 p.m.)	Trip Required	Residency Required	18
Golden Gate University	School of Business	USA	San Francisco	EMBA	1978	MBA	Jan Sep	every other weekend on Saturday and Sunday, 8:00am to 6:00pm	Trip Required	No Residency Required	12
Golden Gate University	Golden Gate University	USA	California	EMBA		MBA Management	January	8:00 to 6:00	Yes		12
Grand Canyon University		USA	Arizona	EMBA	2007	EMBA	Two starts a year	24/7 Online access blended with three residency sessions	No Trip	Three four day sessions in Southern California and Phoenix, Arizona	12
Hawaii Pacific University	College of Business Administration	USA	Hawaii	EMBA	1996	MBA	Sep	Fridays (5:15 - 8:10 pm) and Saturdays (8:00 am - 4:00 pm)	No Trip	No Residency Required	18
Hofstra University	Frank G. Zarb School of Business	USA	New York	EMBA	2000	MBA	Sep	Alternating Fridays and Saturdays 8:00 a.m. - 6:00 p.m.	Trip Required	Residency Required	20
Kennesaw State University	Michael J. Coles College of Business	USA	Georgia	EMBA	1997	EMBA	Aug	One weekend per month, Friday (12:00 p.m. - 6:00 p.m.); Saturday (8:00 a.m. - 5:00 p.m.); Sunday (8:00 a.m. - 5:00 p.m.)	No Trip	Residency Required	28
Kennesaw State University	Michael J. Coles College of Business	USA	Georgia	EMBA	1993	EMBA	Nov	One weekend per month, Friday (8:00 a.m. - 5:00 p.m.); Saturday (8:00 a.m. - 5:00 p.m.); Sunday (8:00 a.m. - 5:00 p.m.)	Trip Required	Residency Required	18
Kent State University	Graduate School of Management	USA	Ohio	EMBA	1978	MBA	Aug	Saturdays	Trip Required	Residency Required	19
Louisiana State University	E.J. Ourso College of Business Administration	USA	Louisiana	EMBA	1991	MBA	Aug	Alternate Friday, Saturdays 8:00 am - 5:00 pm	Trip Required	No Residency Required	17
Loyola College in Maryland	Joseph A. Sellinger, S. J. School of Business and Management	USA	Maryland	EMBA	1973	M.B.A.	Sep	8:00 a.m. to 4:50 p.m., one day per week, alternating Fridays and Saturdays (September-May) for two academic years	Trip Required	Residency Required	21

For the latest school information visit www.EMBAWorld.com

Distance Learning	Denomination	Application Fee	Deposit	Total Program Cost	Accreditation	Jointly Offered	Class Size	Undergrad Degree Req'd	Interview Req'd	Min Management Req'd	Min Work Experience Req'd
Not Distance Learning	US$		60	2000	AACSB		17	Yes	Yes, except	10	5
No	USD	USD175	USD5,000	USD63,000	AACSB	No	30-40	Yes	Yes	8	8 years
No	USD	USD175	USD5,000	USD105,000	AACSB	No	50-60	Yes	Yes	8	8 years
No	US$ (or Euro)	$175	10000	130000		Georgetown University and ESADE Business School	30-40	Yes	Yes	8	8
Not Distance Learning	US$		1000	56000	AACSB		42	Yes	Yes	0	5
Not Distance Learning	US$		500	50500	AACSB		34	Yes	Yes	5	7
Not Distance Learning	US$		55	40000	WASC		21	Yes	Yes	5	8
No	US$	USD55	0	USD57,600	WASC	No		Yes	Yes	8	8 years
Online format	US$	None	None	$45,000 - tuition and texts included	Higher Learning Commission of North Central Association	N/A	15 - 25	Yes, from a regionally accredited institution	Yes	5	5
Not Distance Learning	US$		500	21900	WASC		34	Yes	Yes, except	5	5
Not Distance Learning	US$		5000	62000	AACSB		15	Yes	Yes	7	7
Not Distance Learning	US$		0	0	AACSB SACS		27	Yes	Yes	5	5
Not Distance Learning	US$		500	55000	AACSB SACS	The Institute for Business and Public Administration (ASEBUSS) Bucharest, Romania	59	Yes	Yes	5	5
Not Distance Learning	US$		1000	28000	AACSB		22	Yes	Yes	5	5
Not Distance Learning	US$		500	54506	AACSB		16	Yes	Yes	0	5
Not Distance Learning	US$		1000	$58,500 for all 2 years for the EMBA Class of '10	AACSB		25	Yes with exceptions	Yes	8	8

University	School	Country	State	Type	First Year Created	Degree Offered	Start Dates	Class Times	Int'l Trip	Residency	Program Length
Loyola College in Maryland	Joseph A. Sellinger, S. J. School of Business and Management	USA	Maryland	EMBA	1985	M.B.A.	Sep	one day per week for a half-day on Saturdays only for two and one-half academic years	Trip Required	Residency Required	27
Loyola Marymount University	College of Business Administration	USA	California	EMBA	2000	MBA	mid-August	All day Friday and Saturday every other weekend	Trip Required	3-1/2 day Residency required	21
Loyola University Maryland	Loyola University Maryland	USA	Maryland	EMBA	1973	MBA	Sep	8:00 a.m. to 4:50 p.m., one day per week, alternating Fridays and Saturdays (September-May) for two academic years.	Trip Required	Residency Required	21
Marquette University	College of Business Administration	USA	Wisconsin	EMBA	1996	MBA	Aug	Friday and Saturday, 8:00 am - 5:00 pm, on alternate weekends	Trip Required	Residency Required	17
Mercer University	Stetson School of Business and Economics	USA	Georgia	EMBA	1995	MBA	Aug	Fridays and Saturdays every other week	Trip Required	No Residency Required	21
Michigan State University	Eli Broad Graduate School of Management	USA	Michigan	EMBA	1964	MBA	Aug	Monday and Thursday evening sessions from 6:30 to 10:00 p.m., one residency week, and international business seminar (8-10 days).	Trip Required	Residency Required	21
Michigan University	Ross School of Business	USA	Michigan	EMBA	2001	MBA	August & January	Once per month, Friday & Saturday (8:00 am - 5:30 pm)	Optional	Mandatory	20
Naval Postgraduate School	Graduate School of Business and Public Policy	USA	California	EMBA	2002	MBA EMBA MSCM, MSPM	Apr, Oct	Cohorts meet once a week (same day each week) at a designated sight from 8:00 - 4:00 p.m.	No Trip	No Residency Required	24
New Jersey Institute of Technology	School of Management	USA	New Jersey	EMBA	1992	MBA	Sep	Friday and Saturday on alternating weekends	Trip Required	Residency Required	18
New York University	Leonard N. Stern School of Business	USA	New York	EMBA	1982	MBA	Jan, Aug	Once a week, alternating Fridays and Saturdays (Aug); Friday - Saturday every 2 weeks (Jan)	Trip Required	Residency Required	22
New York University	Leonard N. Stern School of Business	USA	New York	EMBA	2001	MBA	September	6 modules over 16 months in 5 international locations	Trip Required	Residency Required	16
Northeastern University	Graduate School of Business Administration	USA	Massachusetts	EMBA	1978	MBA	Jan	once a week, on alternating Fridays and Saturdays. Program length is 14 months	Trip Required	No Residency Required	16
Northern Illinois University	College of Business	USA	Illinois	EMBA	1982	MBA	August	8 a.m. - 5 p.m., Saturdays	Mandatory	Mandatory	18
Northwestern University	Kellogg Graduate School of Management	USA	Illinois	EMBA	1994	MBA	Jan Sep	Sept. start: Friday afternoon, all day Saturday & Sunday morning on alternate weekends. Jan. start: Friday afternoon & all day Saturday on alternate weekends.	Trip Optional	Residency Required	22

For the latest school information visit www.EMBAWorld.com

Distance Learning	Denomination	Application Fee	Deposit	Total Program Cost	Accreditation	Jointly Offered	Class Size	Undergrad Degree Req'd	Interview Req'd	Min Management Req'd	Min Work Experience Req'd
Not Distance Learning	US$		1000	$56,000 for all 2 1/2 years for the Fellows MBA Class of '11	AACSB		40	Yes with exceptions	Yes	4	4
Not distance learning	US$	USD100	USD1,000	USD83,000	AACSB	No	20	Yes	Yes	6	0
Not Distance Learning	US$		USD1,000	$62,500 for all 2 years for the EMBA Class of '11	AACSB		25	Yes	Yes	8	8
Not Distance Learning	US$		1000	38000	AACSB		23	Yes	Yes	5	5
Not Distance Learning	US$		50	36000	AACSB Southern Association of Colleges & Schools		26	Yes	Yes	1	7
Not Distance Learning	US$		1000	65500	AACSB		58	Yes	Yes	4	7
Some	U.S.		USD1,500	$120,000 in state; $125,000 out of state	AACSB		40 to 60	Yes	Yes	5	10
Distance Learning	US$		0	0	AACSB		25	Yes	Yes, except	8	12
Distance Learning	US$		100	1000	AACSB		25	Yes	Yes	5	7
Not Distance Learning	US$		2000	111300	AACSB EQUIS		61	Yes with exceptions	Yes	3	10
Yes	USD	USD 180.00	USD 13,000	USD 129,500	AACSB EQUIS AMBA	HEC, Paris and London School of Economics and Political Science	65	Yes	Yes	5	10
Not Distance Learning	US$		1500	64380	AACSB		25	Yes with exceptions	Yes	5	8
N/A	U.S.	USD40	2000, due upon acceptance	USD40,500	AACSB-International		35	Yes	Yes		5 years
Not Distance Learning	US$		5000	113600	AACSB		73	Yes with exceptions	Yes	8	8

For the latest school information visit www.EMBAWorld.com

University	School	Country	State	Type	First Year Created	Degree Offered	Start Dates	Class Times	Int'l Trip	Residency	Program Length
Northwestern University	Kellogg Graduate School of Management	USA	Illinois	EMBA	1976	MBA	Sep	Once a week, alternating Fridays and Saturdays	Trip Optional	Residency Required	22
Northwestern University	The Kellogg School of Management at Northwestern University	USA	Illinois	EMBA	1976	EMBA	September or January annually	Friday-Sunday (September in Evanston) on alternate weekends; Friday-Saturday (January in Evanston) on alternate weekends; Thursday-Sunday (January in Miami) monthly	Trip Optional	Residency Required	22
Ohio State University	Max M. Fisher College of Business	USA	Ohio	EMBA	2001	MBA	Dec	Thursday, Friday, Saturday (three consecutive days once a month).	Trip Required	No Residency Required	18
Pace University	Lubin School of Business	USA	New York	EMBA	1969	MBA EMBA	Jan	Internet-supported with 10 residencies	No Trip	Residency Required	23
Pepperdine University	Graziadio School of Business and Management	USA	California	EMBA	1985	MBA	Jan, Apr, Sept	every third weekend, Friday (2:30 p.m.-10:00 p.m.) and all day Saturday 8am-5pm.	Trip Required	Residency Required	20
Purdue University	Krannert Graduate School of Management	USA	Indiana	EMBA	1983	MBA	Jul	Six residencies of two weeks each over 22 months.	Trip Required	Residency Required	22
Purdue University	Krannert Graduate School of Management	USA	Indiana	EMBA	1995	MBA	Feb	Six residencies of two weeks each over 22 months.	No Trip	Residency Required	22
Queens University of Charlotte	McColl Graduate School of Business	USA	North Carolina	EMBA	1990	MBA	August	Alternating Fridays and Saturdays, 8:30 a.m. to 5:00 p.m.	Required	No Residency Required	20
Rice University	Jones Graduate School of Management	USA	Texas	EMBA	1998	MBA	Jul	On the Rice University campus, Friday and Saturday every other week, 8 a.m. - 6 p.m.	Trip Optional	No Residency Required	22
Rochester Institute of Technology	College of Business	USA	New York	EMBA	1993	EMBA	Aug	Friday and Saturday on alternating weekends	Trip Required	Residency Required	22
Rockhurst University	Helzberg School of Management	USA	Missouri	EMBA	1978	EMBA	Aug	Once a week, alternating Fridays and Saturdays, 8 a.m. - 5 p.m.	Trip Required	No Residency Required	22
Rollins College	Roy E. Crummer Graduate School of Business	USA	Florida	EMBA	1982	MBA	Jul	Classes meet once a week on alternating Fridays and Saturdays, all day from 8:00 a.m. to 5:00 p.m.	Trip Required	No Residency Required	21
Saint Joseph's University	Erivan K. Haub School of Business	USA	Pennsylvania	EMBA	1990	MBA	May, Aug	One full day a week, alternating Fridays and Saturdays, 8 a.m. - 5 p.m.	Trip Required	Residency Required	21
Saint Louis University	John Cook School of Business	USA	Missouri	EMBA	1990	EMBA Executive Master of International Business	Aug	Friday afternoon and Saturday for nine class sessions plus final examination session	Trip Required	No Residency Required	21

For the latest school information visit www.EMBAWorld.com

Distance Learning	Denomination	Application Fee	Deposit	Total Program Cost	Accreditation	Jointly Offered	Class Size	Undergrad Degree Req'd	Interview Req'd	Min Management Req'd	Min Work Experience Req'd
Not Distance Learning	US$		5000	103600	AACSB		69	Yes with exceptions	Yes	8	8
None	US$	USD150	$5K	$148 for two years, new program cost to be annouced in late spring	AACSB		75	Yes with exceptions	Yes	8	8
Not Distance Learning	US$		200	58000	AACSB		56	Yes	Yes	7	7
Distance Learning	US$		1000	66 500	AACSB		25	Yes	Yes	5	5
Not Distance Learning	US$		100	1000	AACSB		25	Yes	Yes	2	7
Not Distance Learning	US$		55	54055	AACSB		32	Yes	No	0	5
Not Distance Learning	US$		55	54055	AACSB	Tias Business School at Tilburg University German International Graduate School of Management and Education Central European University	61	Yes	Yes, except	0	5
Not Distance Learning	US$	75	1000	59000	AACSB, ACBSP	No	28	Yes (Can be waived)	Yes	5 to 7	5 - 7
Not Distance Learning	US$		5000	77000	AACSB		84	Yes	Yes	2	10
Not Distance Learning	US$		100	52900	AACSB		14	Yes	Yes	0	8
Not Distance Learning	US$		0	43900	AACSB in candidancy		23	Yes with exceptions	Yes	15	9
Not Distance Learning	US$		50	49600	AACSB		42	Yes with exceptions	Yes	6	8
Not Distance Learning	US$		4000	50000	AACSB		30	Yes	Yes	5	5
Not Distance Learning	US$		50	500	AACSB		25	Yes	Yes	5	5

University	School	Country	State	Type	First Year Created	Degree Offered	Start Dates	Class Times	Int'l Trip	Residency	Program Length
Saint Mary's College of California	Graduate Business Programs	USA	California	EMBA	1975	MBA EMBA MS in Financial Analysis and Investment Management)	Jan, Apr, Oct	Two weeknight evenings; all day Saturday; every other weekend (Friday evening through Saturday afternoon); or hybrid (alternate Saturdays and web-based)	No Trip	Residency Required	18
San Diego State University	College of Business Administration	USA	California	EMBA	1991	MBA	Aug	Friday and Saturday alternating weeks	Trip Required	No Residency Required	24
Santa Clara University	Leavey School of Business	USA	California	EMBA	1999	MBA	Aug	every other Friday (12:30 - 6:30 pm) and Saturday (8:30 am - 2:30 pm)	No Trip	No Residency Required	17
Southern Methodist University	Cox School of Business	USA	Texas	EMBA	1976	MBA	Aug	Alternating Fridays and Saturdays - 8:00 a.m. - 5:00 p.m.	Trip Required	No Residency Required	21
Stetson University	School of Business Administration	USA	Florida	EMBA	2003	MBA	August	Every other Friday & Saturday 8:30- 4:30 p.m.	Trip required	U.S. Citizens & International Students welcome	19
Suffolk University	Frank Sawyer School of Management	USA	Massachusetts	EMBA	1975	EMBA	Mar, Oct	Saturdays (8:30 a.m. - 5:00 p.m.)	Trip Required	No Residency Required	18
Syracuse University	School of Management	USA	New York	EMBA	1985	MBA		on Fridays and/ or Saturdays four or five times per month (usually one full weekend in session and one full weekend free per month). No classes during July and August.	Trip Required	Residency Required	22
Temple University	Fox School of Business and Management	USA	Pennsylvania	EMBA	1985	EMBA	Aug	One consecutive Friday/Saturday, one additional Saturday with online material in asynchronous meetings throughout the program.	Trip Required	No Residency Required	22
Temple University	Fox School of Business and Management	USA	Pennsylvania	EMBA	1996	EMBA	May	Once a week - Saturday only. (40 Saturdays per year)	Trip Optional	No Residency Required	24
Texas A & M University	Mays Business School	USA	Texas	EMBA	1999	MBA	Aug	Friday and Saturday alternate weekends (9:00 a.m. - 4:30 p.m.)	No Trip	Residency Required	21
Texas Christian University	MJ Neeley School of Business	USA	Texas	EMBA	2001	MBA	Aug	Alternating weekends, Friday & Saturday (8:00 a.m. - 5:00 p.m.) excluding summer.	Trip Required	No Residency Required	21
The College of William and Mary	Mason School of Business	USA	Virginia	EMBA		MBA	Jan	once day a week; alternating Fridays and Saturdays	yes	3 domestic; 1 international	20
Tulane University	A. B. Freeman School of Business	USA	Louisiana	EMBA	1993	MBA	Jan	Two three-week seminars at Tulane's New Orleans campus, combined with two Saturdays and two Sundays each month in Asia.	Trip Required	No Residency Required	13

For the latest school information visit www.EMBAWorld.com

Distance Learning	Denomination	Application Fee	Deposit	Total Program Cost	Accreditation	Jointly Offered	Class Size	Undergrad Degree Req'd	Interview Req'd	Min Management Req'd	Min Work Experience Req'd
Not Distance Learning	US$		50	0	WASC		17	Yes	Yes	5	5
Not Distance Learning	US$		500	34800	AACSB WASC		38	Yes	Yes	10	5
Not Distance Learning	US$		1000	68000	AACSB WASC		24	Yes	Yes	5	10
Not Distance Learning	US$	100	2800	99300	AACSB		90	No - Exceptional cases with substantial business experience/success	Yes	5	8
No residency required	US$	none	USD2,000	USD55,000.00	AACSB International	No	20-25	Yes	Yes	5 to 7	
Not Distance Learning	US$		400	51000	AACSB		25	Yes with exceptions	Yes	7	10
Distance Learning			50	0	AACSB		50				
Not Distance Learning	US$		1000	55280	AACSB		25	Yes	Yes	5	10
Not Distance Learning	US$		0	58400	AACSB		21	Yes	Yes	5	5
Not Distance Learning	US$		500	43000	AACSB		49	Yes	Yes	7	10
Not Distance Learning	US$		2000	57200	AACSB		50	Yes, except	Yes	5	8
No		$100	USD4,500	$69,500 *subject to change	AACSB		30-35		yes	5	10
Not Distance Learning	US$		2000	27000	AACSB SACS	NTU, NCCU, NTUST, NCTU, Fudan, Tsinghua, Zhongshan, Shanghai Jiaotong	39	Yes	Yes	5	8

University	School	Country	State	Type	First Year Created	Degree Offered	Start Dates	Class Times	Int'l Trip	Residency	Program Length
Tulane University	A. B. Freeman School of Business	USA	Louisiana	EMBA	1997	MBA	Aug	Thursday, Friday, and Saturday every third weekend, plus an international seminar.	Trip Required	No Residency Required	21
Tulane University	A. B. Freeman School of Business	USA	Louisiana	EMBA	2003	MBA	May	Friday evenings, Saturdays, and Sunday afternoons every other weekend.	Trip Required	No Residency Required	23
Tulane University	A. B. Freeman School of Business	USA	Louisiana	EMBA	2002	MBA	Dec	Friday and Saturday of alternating weekends, plus an intensive week and an international seminar.	Trip Required	No Residency Required	19
Tulane University	A. B. Freeman School of Business	USA	Louisiana	EMBA	1982	MBA	Jan	Friday and Saturday of alternating weekends, plus an intensive week and an international seminar.	Trip Required	No Residency Required	19
University at Buffalo	School of Management	USA	New York	EMBA	1994	MBA	Aug	One week each August; followed by once a week, alternating weekends (Fridays and Saturdays) for remainder of each school year.	Trip Required	No Residency Required	22
University of Alabama	Manderson Graduate School of Business	USA	Alabama	EMBA	1985	MBA	Dec	Friday/Saturday alternating weekends	Trip Required	No Residency Required	17
University of Arkansas at Little Rock	College of Business Administration	USA	Arkansas	EMBA	1997	MBA	Jul	Friday 8:15 a.m. to 6:30 p.m.; Saturday 8:30 a.m. to 6:00 p.m., alternating weekends	Trip Required	Residency Required	18
University of California Irvine	Graduate School of Management	USA	California	EMBA	1985	MBA	Sep	All day Friday and Saturday every other week.	Trip Required	No Residency Required	21
University of California Irvine	Graduate School of Management	USA	California	EMBA	1996	MBA	Sep	One extended weekend per month.	No Trip	No Residency Required	24
University of California, Berkeley	Haas School of Business	USA	California	EMBA	2002	MBA	May	Thursday through Saturday approximately every three weeks (with a few Wed-Sat blocks).	Trip Required	Residency Required	19
University of California, Los Angeles	Anderson School of Management	USA	California	EMBA	1981	Masters in Business Administration	Fall start (September)	All day Friday and Saturday, every other weekend	Yes. China Residential required		22
University of Central Florida	College of Business Administration	USA	Florida	EMBA	1992	MBA EMBA	Aug	Friday and Saturday on alternating weekends	Trip Required	No Residency Required	20
University of Chicago	Graduate School of Business	USA	Illinois	EMBA	2000	MBA	Jun	16 one-week modules spread over 20 months (Monday - Saturday)	Trip Required	No Residency Required	20
University of Chicago	Graduate School of Business	USA	Illinois	EMBA	1994	MBA	Jun	16 one-week modules spread over 20 months (Monday - Saturday)	Trip Required	No Residency Required	20
University of Chicago	Graduate School of Business	USA	Illinois	EMBA	1943	MBA	Jun	Fridays and Saturdays every other week, plus four residential weeks	Trip Required	No Residency Required	20
University of Colorado	Three Campus Consortium	USA	Colorado	EMBA	1985	EMBA	Jul	approx. 8 days in July, 6 days in January each year	No Trip	Residency Required	24

For the latest school information visit www.EMBAWorld.com

Distance Learning	Denomination	Application Fee	Deposit	Total Program Cost	Accreditation	Jointly Offered	Class Size	Undergrad Degree Req'd	Interview Req'd	Min Management Req'd	Min Work Experience Req'd
Not Distance Learning	US$		1000	25000	AACSB SACS, AMBA	Universidad de Chile	30	Yes	Yes	5	5
Not Distance Learning	US$		1000	62000	AACSB SACS		43	Yes	Yes	0	3
Not Distance Learning	US$		1000	65000	AACSB SACS		20	Yes	Yes	5	7
Not Distance Learning	US$		1000	53000	AACSB SACS		19	Yes	Yes	5	7
Not Distance Learning	US$		250	36000	AACSB		25	Yes with exceptions	Yes	5	5
Not Distance Learning	US$		500	39000	AACSB		32	Yes	Yes	3	5
Not Distance Learning	US$		1500	29500	AACSB		23	Yes	Yes	5	5
Not Distance Learning	US$		1000	62500	AACSB		61	Yes	Yes	4	8
Not Distance Learning	US$		1000	62500	AACSB		45	Yes	Yes	1	5
Not Distance Learning	US$		1700	118750	AACSB	University of California, Berkeley – Haas School of Business Columbia Business School	68	Yes	Yes, except	5	5
No	USD	$200	USD2,500	For the Class of 2012, $57,000 per year for a 2 year total of $114,000	AACSB	No but have 6 exchange partner universities	72	Yes	Yes	8	10
Not Distance Learning	US$		1000	33500	AACSB		15	Yes	Yes	3	5
Not Distance Learning	US$		5000	84000	AACSB		88	Yes	Yes	5	10
Not Distance Learning	US$		5000	93000	AACSB		80	Yes	Yes	5	10
Not Distance Learning	US$		5000	102000	AACSB		85	Yes	Yes	5	10
Distance Learning	US$		1000	43000	AACSB ACEHSA		24	Yes	Yes	5	8

For the latest school information visit www.EMBAWorld.com

University	School	Country	State	Type	First Year Created	Degree Offered	Start Dates	Class Times	Int'l Trip	Residency	Program Length
University of Colorado	Three Campus Consortium	USA	Colorado	EMBA	1981	EMBA dual EMBA/MS	Sep	alternating Fridays and Saturdays	Trip Required	Residency Required	21
University of Connecticut	School of Business Administration	USA	Connecticut	EMBA	1991	MBA	September	Friday and Saturday, alternating weeks	Required	No Residency Required	20
University of Delaware	Alfred Lerner College of Business & Economics	USA	Delaware	EMBA	1994	MBA	Aug	Friday evenings from 4-9:00 p.m. and Saturdays from 8:00 am - 5:00 p.m.	Trip Required	Residency Required	19
University of Denver	Daniels College of Business	USA	Denver	EMBA	1973	MBA EMBA Graduate Business Certificates; Management Essentials Program; Corporate Custom Programs	Mar, Sept	Alternating Fridays and Saturdays, 8 a.m. to 5 p.m.	Trip Required	No Residency Required	18
University of Florida	Warrington College of Business Administration	USA	Florida	EMBA	1993	MBA EMBA	Aug	One extended weekend per month, Friday through Sunday, at the University of Florida campus in Gainesville, Florida	No Trip	Residency Required	20
University of Georgia	Terry College of Business	USA	Georgia	EMBA	2001	MBA	Sep	Friday & Saturday (8:30 a.m. - 5:00 p.m.) approx once per month	Trip Required	Residency Required	18
University of Houston	C.T. Bauer College of Business	USA	Texas	EMBA	1978	MBA	Aug	2 Programs, Program 1: Monday & Thursday evenings, Program 2: Alternating weekends (Fri./Sat.),	Trip Required	Residency Required	18
University of Illinois at Urbana-Champaign	College of Commerce and Business Administration	USA	Illinois	EMBA	1975	MBA	Aug	Alternating weekends (typically two weekends per month). Fridays 8:30am-8:00pm, Saturdays 8:00am-5:00pm.	Trip Required	Residency Required	15
University of Iowa	Henry B. Tippie School of Management	USA	Iowa	EMBA	1978	MBA	Aug	once a week, alternating Fridays or Saturdays (8:30 a.m. - 4:30 p.m.)	Trip Required	Residency Required	21
University of Maryland	Robert H. Smith School of Business	USA	Maryland	EMBA	2003	EMBA	Mar, Sept	Every other weekend. Friday (8:00 am - 9:30 pm), and Saturday (8:00 am - 6:00 pm).	Trip Optional	Residency Required	18
University of Maryland	Robert H. Smith School of Business	USA	Maryland	EMBA							
University of Maryland University College	Graduate School	USA	Maryland	EMBA	1998	MBA	Apr, Oct	Every other Saturday (8:30 am - 5:00 pm) with alternating Saturdays for submission of online assignments	Trip Required	No Residency Required	21
University of Memphis	Fogelman College of Business and Economics	USA	Tennessee	EMBA	1981	EMBA	Aug	every week, alternating Fridays and Saturdays	Trip Required	Residency Required	21

For the latest school information visit www.EMBAWorld.com

Distance Learning	Denomination	Application Fee	Deposit	Total Program Cost	Accreditation	Jointly Offered	Class Size	Undergrad Degree Req'd	Interview Req'd	Min Management Req'd	Min Work Experience Req'd
Not Distance Learning	US$		1000	48000	AACSB		44	No	Yes	5	8
Not distance learning	US$		0	58000	AACSB		25	Yes	Yes	2	5
Not Distance Learning	US$		500	65000	AACSB		18	Yes	Yes	5	5
Not Distance Learning	US$		50	50000	AACSB		23	Yes	Yes	8	10
Not Distance Learning	US$		1500	32000	AACSB EQUIS		26	Yes	No	5	8
Not Distance Learning	US$		75	54 000	AACSB		40	Yes with exceptions	Yes	0	5
Not Distance Learning	US$		75	46500	AACSB		61	Yes	Yes	5	5
Not Distance Learning	US$		2000	72000	AACSB		35	Yes	Yes	5	7
Not Distance Learning	US$		2000	43000	AACSB		38	Yes with exceptions	Yes	5	7
Not Distance Learning	US$		500	79500	AACSB		27	Yes	Yes	8	8
Not Distance Learning	US$		500	37842	AACSB Commission on Higher Education of the Middle States Association of Colleges and Schools; and International Association of Colleges of Business Education		31	Yes	Yes	5	5
Not Distance Learning	US$		1500	39270	AACSB SACS		20	Yes	Yes	5	5

University	School	Country	State	Type	First Year Created	Degree Offered	Start Dates	Class Times	Int'l Trip	Residency	Program Length
University of Miami	School of Business Administration	USA	Florida	EMBA	1973	MBA	January	The Executive EMBA programs (both on and off-campus) meet on Saturdays. The Executive MBA in Health Sector Management and Policy meets one weekend per month (Fri., Sat., Sun.). The MSPM/EMBA program meets for seven two-week sessions over 22 months. The joint Executive MBA/Master of Science in Industrial Engineering program meets on Saturdays. Complete your degree without interrupting your career. Seven two-week sessions over 15 months	No	Not required	23
University of Michigan	University of Michigan Business School	USA	Michigan	EMBA	2001	MBA	Aug	Once per month, Friday & Saturday (8:00 am - 5:30 pm)	No Trip	Residency Required	20
University of Minnesota	Curtis L. Carlson School of Management	USA	Minnesota	EMBA	1981	EMBA	Sep	Friday and Saturday every other week for four semesters (summer off)	Trip Required	Residency Required	18
University of Missouri-Kansas City	Henry W. Bloch School of Business and Public Administration	USA	Missouri	EMBA	1995	EMBA	Aug	Friday and Saturday, alternating weeks, 8:00 AM to 4:30 PM	Trip Optional	Residency Required	21
University of Nevada, Las Vegas	College of Business	USA	Nevada	EMBA	2002	MBA	Jul	Friday and Saturdays, every other weekend (8:30 am - 5:30 pm)	Trip Required	No Residency Required	18
University of New Hampshire	Whittemore School of Business and Economics	USA	New Hampshire	EMBA	1977	MBA	Sep	Friday and Saturday alternating weeks	Trip Required	Residency Required	19
University of New Mexico	Robert O. Anderson School and Graduate School of Management	USA	New Mexico	EMBA	1971	MBA	Jun	Every other Friday and Saturday (alternate weekends) Fridays, 1 - 6 p.m. and Saturdays, 8 a.m. - 1 p.m.	Trip Optional	No Residency Required	25
University of New Orleans	College of Business Administration	USA	Louisiana	EMBA	1996	MBA	Jul	Every other week, Friday & Saturday (8:00 am - 6:00 pm)	Trip Optional	No Residency Required	17
University of North Carolina-Chapel Hill	Kenan-Flagler Business School	USA	North Carolina	EMBA	1986	MBA	Aug	Monday and Thursday evenings, 6:00 p.m. - 9:15 p.m. plus one three-day weekend and one two-day weekend	Trip Optional	Residency Required	24
University of North Carolina-Chapel Hill	Kenan-Flagler Business School	USA	North Carolina	EMBA	1999	MBA	Jan	Weekends, every other Friday and Saturday, plus two residency weeks	Trip Optional	Residency Required	20

For the latest school information visit www.EMBAWorld.com

Distance Learning	Denomination	Application Fee	Deposit	Total Program Cost	Accreditation	Jointly Offered	Class Size	Undergrad Degree Req'd	Interview Req'd	Min Management Req'd	Min Work Experience Req'd
None	US$	USD100	USD1,000	USD68,352	AACSB, SCAS, and CAHME (for EMBA in Health Sector Management and Policy)	Yes	114	Yes, an undergraduate degree is required	Yes, with exceptions		6
Not Distance Learning	US$		750	100000	AACSB		65	Yes	Yes	5	10
Not Distance Learning	US$		750	68250	AACSB		60	Yes	Yes	5	8
Not Distance Learning	US$		100	37500	AACSB		51	Yes	Yes, except	5	7
Not Distance Learning	US$		100	37000	AACSB		14	Yes with exceptions	Yes	5	7
Not Distance Learning	US$		500	45800	AACSB neasac		21	Yes	Yes	5	7
Not Distance Learning	US$		540	25920	AACSB		62	Yes	Yes	5	5
Not Distance Learning	US$		500	26000	AACSB		42	Yes	Yes	5	5
Not Distance Learning	US$		USD1,500	USD71,000	AACSB		69	Yes with exceptions	Yes	0	5
Not Distance Learning	US$		USD1,500	USD87,000	AACSB		60	Yes with exceptions	Yes	0	5

University	School	Country	State	Type	First Year Created	Degree Offered	Start Dates	Class Times	Int'l Trip	Residency	Program Length
University of North Carolina-Chapel Hill	Kenan-Flagler Business School	USA	North Carolina	EMBA	2002	MBA	Sep	One 3 day weekend (Friday, Saturday & Sunday) per month plus residencies	Trip Required	Residency Required	21
University of Notre Dame		USA	Indiana	EMBA	1982	EMBA	August	Four week-long residencies and monthly sessions from Thursday afternoon to Saturday afternoon	Trip is required and project-based	Residency required	22
University of Notre Dame		USA	Illinois	EMBA	2002	EMBA	January	Four week-long residencies and alternating weekends during semesters	Trip is optional	Residency required	18
University of Oregon	University of Oregon	USA	Oregon	EMBA	1995	MBA	Sept	Once a week, alternating Fridays and Saturdays	Yes	both first and second year	18
University of Pennsylvania	Wharton School	USA	Pennsylvania	EMBA	1975	MBA	May	Alternating Friday and Saturdays, with a few exceptions	Yes	Yes	24
University of Pennsylvania	Wharton School	USA	California	EMBA	2001	MBA	May	Alternating Friday and Saturdays, with a few exceptions	Yes	Yes	24
University of Pittsburgh	Katz Graduate School of Business	USA	Pennsylvania	EMBA		MBA	Program begins each January	Friday 8am-6pm; Saturday 9am-5pm; alternating weekends	Prague, Czech Republic & Sao Paulo, Brazil	None	19
University of Rochester	William E. Simon Graduate School of Business	USA	New York	EMBA	1966	MBA	Sep	Fridays	Trip Required	Residency Required	22
University of San Francisco	School of Business / Graduate School of Management	USA	California	EMBA	1991	MBA EMBA	Jan, Sept	alternate Wednesdays and Fridays (5:00 - 9:00pm), every other Saturday (8:00am - 5:00pm).	No Trip	Residency Required	15
University of South Florida	College of Business Administration	USA	Florida	EMBA	1981	MBA	Aug	One Friday and two Saturdays a month for four semesters; over a twenty month period.	Trip Optional	No Residency Required	20
University of Southern California	Marshall School of Business	USA	California	EMBA		MBA	Fall	8:50 am - 4:30 pm	Yes (required)		21
University of St. Thomas	College of Business	USA	Minnesota	EMBA	1984	MBA	Mar, Oct	Once a month, Friday and Saturday, 8:30 a.m. - 5:00 p.m	No Trip	No Residency Required	30
University of Tennessee	College of Business Administration	USA	Tennessee	EMBA	2004	MBA	Jan	Six, week-long residence periods and 20 Internet-based, interactive, distance-learning sessions.	Trip Required	Residency Required	12
University of Tennessee	College of Business Administration	USA	Tennessee	EMBA	1998	MBA	Aug	Four residence periods, 2 weeks each quarter, throughout the year including one international residence period. Internet-based classes on Wednesday nights between residence periods.	Trip Optional	Residency Required	16

For the latest school information visit www.EMBAWorld.com

Distance Learning	Denomination	Application Fee	Deposit	Total Program Cost	Accreditation	Jointly Offered	Class Size	Undergrad Degree Req'd	Interview Req'd	Min Management Req'd	Min Work Experience Req'd
Not Distance Learning	US$		USD1,500	USD96,500	AACSB	The Chinese University of Hong Kong Fundacao Getulio Vargas Erasmus University Rotterdam, Rotterdam School of Management EGADE-ITESM	35	Yes with exceptions	Yes	0	7
No	US$	USD100	USD2,500	USD86,000	AACSB		60	Yes	Yes	5	5
No	US$	USD100	USD2,500	USD90,000	AACSB	No	60	Yes	Yes	5	5
No	US$		USD1,000	USD52,000	AACSB	University of Oregon, Oregon State University, Portland State University	45	Yes	Yes	3	5
No	US$	USD180	USD2,500	USD162,300	AACSB Middle States	No	115	Yes with exceptions	Yes	3	5
No	US$	USD180	USD2,500	USD172,200	AACSB Middle States	No	95	Yes with exceptions	Yes	3	5
none	USD	None	None	$65,000 for Program beginning January 2010	AACSB		30-45 students	Yes	Yes	3 to 8	5
Not Distance Learning	US$		2000	78500	AACSB	Universitat Bern	35	Yes with exceptions	Yes	6	10
Not Distance Learning	US$		1000	56000	AACSB		24	Yes	Yes	5	8
Not Distance Learning	US$		1000	32000	AACSB		48	Yes	Yes	5	5
n/a	USD	USD150.00	2500	112000	Yes		Los Angeles 75 San Diego 55	Yes	Yes		8
Not Distance Learning	US$		75	38920	NCACS		46	Yes	Yes	5	5
Not Distance Learning	US$		1000	52000	AACSB		26	Yes	Yes, except	3	10
Not Distance Learning	US$		1000	64000	AACSB		25	Yes	Yes	10	7

For the latest school information visit www.EMBAWorld.com

University	School	Country	State	Type	First Year Created	Degree Offered	Start Dates	Class Times	Int'l Trip	Residency	Program Length
University of Tennessee	College of Business Administration	USA	Tennessee	EMBA	1998	MBA	Jan	Four one-week residential periods evenly distributed throughout the year. Forty weekly interactive Internet-based cyber classes held on Saturday mornings, 9 a.m. - Noon	No Trip	Residency Required	12
University of Tennessee	College of Business Administration	USA	Tennessee	EMBA	1998	MBA	Aug	Two one-week residence periods, approximately three Saturdays per month (on campus) and Tuesday evenings via distance learning.	Trip Optional	Residency Required	16
University of Tennessee	College of Business Administration	USA	Tennessee	EMBA	1994	MBA	Jan	Four, two-week residence periods and 15 distance learning sessions.	Trip Required	Residency Required	12
University of Tennessee at Chattanooga	College of Business Administration	USA	Tennessee	EMBA	1992	MBA EMBA Macc	Jan, Aug	Friday afternoons (1:00 - 5:30 pm) and all day Saturday (8:00 am - 5:00 pm)	Trip Required	No Residency Required	24
University of Texas - Dallas	School of Management	USA	Texas	EMBA	1995	MBA	Jan, April, and Aug	Blended format that is primarily online with on campus delivery during five weekend retreats.	Trip Required	Residency Required	23
University of Texas at Austin	McCombs School of Business	USA	Texas	EMBA	1996	EMBA	Aug	Friday and Saturday 8:00 am - 5:30 pm classes every 2 weeks for two years on ITESM's Tlalpan campus in Mexico City. Attendance at two 1 week Austin Seminars and one 1 week international seminar	Trip Required	No Residency Required	22
University of Texas at Austin	McCombs School of Business	USA	Texas	EMBA		MBA	August each year	Classes are scheduled on alternate weekends, meeting on both Friday and Saturday from 8:00am-5:30pm	Varies but has been in Beijing, China for the past couple of years.	Not included in Tuition. Separate package offered.	21
University of Texas at Dallas	School of Management	USA	Texas	EMBA	1998	EMBA	Feb, Apr, Jun, Aug, Oct, Sep	4 1/2 days, every two months - on site	No Trip	Residency Required	16
University of Texas at Dallas	School of Management	USA	Texas	EMBA	1992	EMBA	Sep	every other week on Friday and Saturday	Trip Required	Residency Required	21
University of Texas at Dallas	School of Management	USA	Texas	EMBA	2001	EMBA	Jan, Sep	Online weekly lessons. On campus meets once per month, Thursday, Friday and Saturday	Trip Required	Residency Required	28
University of Toledo	College of Business Administration	USA	Ohio	EMBA	1995	MBA	Sept	Friday evenings and Saturdays for two weekends followed by a weekend off	Trip Required	No Residency Required	15
University of Utah	David Eccles School of Business	USA	Utah	EMBA	1985	MBA EMBA	Aug	Once a week, alternating Fridays and Saturdays	Trip Required	No Residency Required	21

For the latest school information visit www.EMBAWorld.com

Distance Learning	Denomination	Application Fee	Deposit	Total Program Cost	Accreditation	Jointly Offered	Class Size	Undergrad Degree Req'd	Interview Req'd	Min Management Req'd	Min Work Experience Req'd
Distance Learning	US$		1000	62000	AACSB		35	Yes	Yes, except	3	5
Not Distance Learning	US$		500	57500	AACSB		55	Yes	Yes, except	3	5
Not Distance Learning	US$		1000	64000	AACSB		29	Yes	Yes, except	10	10
Not Distance Learning	US$		25	25000	AACSB		20	Yes	Yes, except	3	5
Distance Learning	US$	USD300	USD2,500	USD65,000	AACSB			Yes	Yes	3	5
Not Distance Learning	US$		125	0	AACSB	Tecnologico de Monterrey	48	Yes	Yes	5	5
no	US$	USD125	2000	USD75,000	AACSB	No	65	Yes	Yes	0	5
Not Distance Learning	US$		0	24000	AACSB	U. T Southwestern Medical Center at Dallas	30	Yes	Yes	7	7
Not Distance Learning	US$		250	50250	AACSB EQUIS		35	Yes	Yes	5	10
Not Distance Learning	US$		100	0	AACSB		16	Yes	Yes	3	7
Not Distance Learning	US$		USD1,100	USD31,900	AACSB		30	Yes	Yes	3	3
Not Distance Learning	US$		2000	38000	AACSB		60	Yes	Yes	0	6

For the latest school information visit www.EMBAWorld.com

University	School	Country	State	Type	First Year Created	Degree Offered	Start Dates	Class Times	Int'l Trip	Residency	Program Length
University of Washington	Graduate School of Business	USA	Washington	EMBA	1998	MBA	Sep	one monthly residential 3 to 4 days in length	Trip Optional	Residency Required	21
University of Washington	Graduate School of Business	USA	Washington	EMBA	1983	MBA	Sep	once a week, alternating Fridays and Saturdays, over two academic years	Trip Optional	Residency Required	21
University of Wisconsin-Madison	School of Business	USA	Wisconsin	EMBA	1993	EMBA	Aug	Friday and Saturday, alternating weeks	Trip Required	No Residency Required	18
University of Wisconsin-Milwaukee	School of Business Administration	USA	Wisconsin	EMBA	1974	MBA	Aug	once a week, alternating Fridays and Saturdays	Trip Required	No Residency Required	22
Vanderbilt University	Owen Graduate School of Management	USA	Tennessee	EMBA	1978	MBA	August	Alternating Saturdays over a 24-month period	One-Week Trip Required	One-Week Initial Residency Required	24
Villanova University	College of Commerce and Finance	USA	Pennsylvania	EMBA	2001	EMBA	Aug	Alternating Friday/Saturday	Trip Required	Residency Required	21
Wake Forest University	Babcock Graduate School of Management	USA	North Carolina	EMBA	1971	MBA	Aug	Friday and Saturday every other week (8:00 a.m. - 5:00 p.m.)		Residency Required	17
Washington University in St. Louis	John M. Olin Business School	USA	Missouri	EMBA	1983	MBA	April	Once a month (Thursday, Friday, and Saturday) with some Wednesday workshops	Trip Required	Residency Required	20
Washington University in St. Louis	John M. Olin Business School	USA	Missouri	EMBA	1983	MBA	September	Alternating weekends (Friday and Saturday) with some Thursday workshops	Trip Required	Residency Required	20
West Virginia University	College of Business and Economics	USA	West Virginia	EMBA	1995	MBA	Jan, Aug	evenings and weekends; Monday, Wednesday, Tuesday, Thursday or Friday, Saturday	Trip Optional	No Residency Required	24
West Virginia University	College of Business and Economics	USA	West Virginia	Online EMBA	2010	MBA	January, August	Online and Four 3-4 Day Residencies	Trip Optional	Four 3-4 Day Residencies (1 per semester)	24
Winthrop University	School of Business Administration	USA	South Carolina	EMBA	1987	MBA	Aug	once a week, alternating Fridays and Saturdays	Trip Optional	Residency Required	21
Wisconsin University	Wisconsin School of Business	USA	Wisconsin	EMBA	1993	EMBA	Aug	Friday and Saturday, alternating weeks	Trip Required	No Residency Required	18
Xavier University		USA	Ohio	EMBA	1977	MBA	September	Once a week, 8:00 am - 5:00 pm, Alternating Fridays/ Saturdays	Trip Required	No Residency Required	19
Yale University	School of Management	USA	Connecticut	EMBA	2005	MBA EMBA	Aug	Two residence weeks in August, followed by Friday and Saturday on alternating weekends.	No Trip	Residency Required	22
Youngstown State University	Williamson College of Business Administration	USA	Ohio	EMBA	1990	MBA	Jan, Sep	Once a week on Saturdays	Trip Required	Residency Required	18
	University of Minnesota	USA	Minnesota	EMBA	1981	EMBA	September	Friday and Saturday every other week for four semesters (summer off)	Trip Required	Residency Required	18
	University of Maine	USA	Maine	EMBA							

For the latest school information visit www.EMBAWorld.com

Distance Learning	Denomination	Application Fee	Deposit	Total Program Cost	Accreditation	Jointly Offered	Class Size	Undergrad Degree Req'd	Interview Req'd	Min Management Req'd	Min Work Experience Req'd
Distance Learning	US$		150	55000	AACSB EQUIS		45	Yes	Yes	4	7
Not Distance Learning	US$		150	55000	AACSB EQUIS		50	Yes	Yes	4	7
Not Distance Learning	US$		1500	73000	AACSB		40	Yes	Yes	5	10
Not Distance Learning	US$		1000	39000	AACSB		30	Yes	Yes, except	8	5
Not Distance Learning	US$	USD150	none	$89,500 (approx)	AACSB		51	Yes	Yes	5	8
Not Distance Learning	US$		75	80000	AACSB		36	Yes	Yes	0	8
Not Distance Learning	US$		75	59500	AACSB EQUIS		55	Yes	Yes		
Not Distance Learning	US$	100	2500	93600	AACSB		30-50	Yes	Yes	8	8
Not Distance Learning	US$	100	2500	93600	AACSB		30-50	Yes	Yes	8	8
Not Distance Learning	US$		50	0	AACSB		42	Yes	Yes, except	2	2
Yes	US$	USD50	None	In-state $30,452.00, Out-of-state $67,584.00	AACSB	No	35 per Cohort	Yes	No	2	2
Not Distance Learning	US$		750	20000	AACSB		20	Yes	Yes	5	8
Not Distance Learning	US$		1500	73000	AACSB		40	Yes	Yes	5	10
No Distance Learning	US$	USD0	USD1,000	USD58,750	AACSB	No	25	Yes, with exceptions	Yes	7	10
Not Distance Learning	US$		2000	158000	AACSB		0	Yes	Yes	5	7
Not Distance Learning	US$		30	26 000	AACSB		18	Yes	Yes	5	5
Distance Learning is not available			USD750	USD82,500	AACSB		60	Yes	Yes	5	8

University	School	Country	State	Type	First Year Created	Degree Offered	Start Dates	Class Times	Int'l Trip	Residency	Program Length
	Wesleyan College	USA	Georgia	EMBA	2001	MBA	Aug	alternating Fridays and Saturdays 4-10 Fridays 8-5 Saturdays	Trip Required	Residency Required	19
	University of New Haven	USA	Connecticut	EMBA	1976	MBA	Feb, Sept	one day per week 2:30 p.m. to 8:30 p.m. in Stamford and West Haven	Trip Optional	No Residency Required	21
	Benedictine College	USA	Kansas	EMBA	1996	MBA EMBA	May , Aug	Fridays (6:00 pm - 10:00 pm); Saturdays (8:00 am - 4:30 pm)	No Trip	No Residency Required	12
	Thunderbird, the Garvin School of International Management	USA	Arizona	EMBA	1991	MBA in International Managment	Aug	Friday/Saturday alternate weekends, 7:50 a.m. - 5:00 p.m. each day	Trip Required	Residency Required	21
	Thunderbird, the Garvin School of International Management	USA	Arizona	EMBA	2003	MBA in International Management	May	9am to 6pm, Monday through Saturday during most in-class sessions.	Trip Required	Residency Required	14
	Baldwin-Wallace College	USA	Ohio	EMBA	1978	MBA	Aug	Friday afternoon and all day Saturday on alternate weekends.	No Trip	No Residency Required	21
	Cleveland State University	USA	Ohio	EMBA	1979	MBA/EMBA	Aug	3 Saturday's/ One-Friday per month, 8 a.m. to 5 p.m. each class day	Trip Required	Residency Required	22
	Jacksonville University	USA	Florida	EMBA	1984	MBA	Jan	every other weekend, Friday and Saturday	Trip Required	Residency Required	16
	Lake Forest Graduate School of Management	USA	Illinois	EMBA	1979	MBA	Jan, Apr, Aug	Monday, Tuesday, Wednesday or Thursday evenings, or on Saturday	Trip Optional	Residency Required	22
	Ohio University	USA	Ohio	EMBA	1977	MBA	Sep	One Friday a month, remaining weeks meet on Saturday	Trip Optional	Residency Required	21
	Rensselaer Polytechnic Institute	USA	New York	EMBA	1987	EMBA	Sep	Fridays and Saturdays alternating weeks - 8:00 am - 4:00 pm	No Trip	Residency Required	18
	Rutgers - The State University of New Jersey	USA	New Jersey	EMBA	1980	MBA	Sep	alternating Fridays and Saturdays	Trip Required	Residency Required	20
	University of Nebraska at Omaha	USA	Nebraska	EMBA	1975	EMBA	Aug	Fridays (3:00 p.m. - 9:00 p.m.) and Saturdays (8:30 a.m. - 2:30 p.m.)	Trip Required	Residency Required	24
	Baylor University	USA	Texas	EMBA	1991	EMBA	Aug	Monday/ Thursday evenings and some Saturdays; classes begin in fall, every year	Trip Required	Residency Required	21
	Virginia Commonwealth University	USA	Virginia	EMBA	1994	MBA	Aug	Friday 12:30 to 6:15pm, Saturday 8:00am to 2:15pm alternating weekends	Trip Required	No Residency Required	21
	University of Oregon	USA	Oregon	EMBA	1985	MBA	Sep	Once a week, alternating Fridays and Saturdays	No Trip	No Residency Required	18

For the latest school information visit www.EMBAWorld.com

Distance Learning	Denomination	Application Fee	Deposit	Total Program Cost	Accreditation	Jointly Offered	Class Size	Undergrad Degree Req'd	Interview Req'd	Min Management Req'd	Min Work Experience Req'd
Not Distance Learning	US$		60	27000	SACS		15	Yes	Yes	5	5
Not Distance Learning	US$		950	44000			19	Yes	Yes	5	5
Not Distance Learning	US$		100	18000	North Central		31	Yes	Yes	5	5
Not Distance Learning	US$		3600	58000	AACSB EQUIS NCA		50	Yes	Yes	3	8
Not Distance Learning	US$		2500	34000	AACSB EQUIS NCA	Czech Management Center Graduate School of Business	23	Yes	Yes	3	8
Not Distance Learning	US$		15	0	North Central Association of Colleges and Secondary Schools		25	Yes	Yes	5	8
Not Distance Learning	US$		630	28000	AACSB		23	Yes	Yes	5	5
Not Distance Learning	US$		1000	32000	SACS		22	Yes, with exceptions	Yes	7	10
Not Distance Learning	US$		100	36400	The Higher Learning Commission and a member of the North Central Association		22	Yes	Yes	0	4
Not Distance Learning	US$		500	31000	AACSB		20	Yes	Yes	7	7
Not Distance Learning	US$		2000	29450	AACSB		17	Yes	Yes	6	8
Not Distance Learning	US$		1500	62000	AACSB		36	Yes	Yes	3	10
Not Distance Learning	US$		0	36500	AACSB		20	Yes	No	0	6
Not Distance Learning	US$		2000	47500	AACSB		38	Yes	Yes	5	5
Not Distance Learning	US$		800	37500	AACSB		38	Yes	Yes	0	6
Not Distance Learning	US$		1000	36000	AACSB	University of Oregon Oregon State University Portland State University	45	Yes	Yes	3	5

University	School	Country	State	Type	First Year Created	Degree Offered	Start Dates	Class Times	Int'l Trip	Residency	Program Length
	The Darden School of Business	USA	Virginia	EMBA	2006	MBA	June	Fri-Sat or Thurs-Sat, Approx every third weekend, four 7-day residencies	Trip Required	Yes: on grounds sessions only	22
	The University of Indianapolis	USA	Indiana	EMBA	1974	MBA	Fall, Spring	8 AM to 4:30PM Saturdays	Optional	Not required	20
Colorado State University	College of Business	United States of America	Colorado	EMBA	1988	MBA	Aug	4:30 - 8:30 p.m. Tuesdays & Thursdays	Integrated with International Business course		21
University of Chicago		United Kingdom	London	part-time EMBA	1943	MBA	June	16 weekly modules spaced every 5 weeks	13 weeks in London, 2 weeks in Chicago and 1 week in Singapore		21
	University of Sharjah	UNITED ARAB EMIRATES		EMBA	2000	EMBA	Jan, May, Sept	Evenings of Weekends	No Trip	No Residency Required	24
	London Business School	UK/USA	London/New York	Executive MBA - Global				Core courses taught in part one are monthly four or five day teaching blocks. In part two your timetable is dictated by your choices from a wide elective portfolio of both schools.			
	London Business School	UK/ USA/ HK	London/ New York/ Hong Kong	Executive MBA - Global	2009	MBA	May	Core courses taught in part one are monthly four or five day teaching blocks. In part two your timetable is dictated by your choices from the wide elective portfolio of all three schools.	Trip Required	No residency required	20
	London Business School	UK	London	EMBA		MBA		Core courses taught in part one are Fridays and Saturdays of alternative weeks. In part two your timetable is dictated by your choices from a wide elective portfolio.			20
	London Business School	UAE/ England	Dubai/ London	EMBA	2007	MBA	Jan Sep	Core courses taught in part one are monthly four or five-day teaching blocks. In part two your timetable is dictated by your choices from a wide elective portfolio.	Trip Required	No Residency Required	20
	Nycnrode Business Universiteit	The Netherlands	Utrecht	IMBA and Part-time MBA	1982	EMBA	October (full-time) and April (part-time)	The International MBA spans 13 months and the Part-time MBA spans 21 months in a modular format (2 modules are completed abroad)	Yes	Residency required	13

For the latest school information visit www.EMBAWorld.com

Distance Learning	Denomination	Application Fee	Deposit	Total Program Cost	Accreditation	Jointly Offered	Class Size	Undergrad Degree Req'd	Interview Req'd	Min Management Req'd	Min Work Experience Req'd
one-third distance learning	US$	140	2500	90,000 2006	AACSB	no	54	No	Yes		
Not Distance Learning	US$	USD50	USD200	$23 500	ACBSP, Member AACSB	University of Indianapolis Athens Greece	15	Yes	Option	0	5
as option if schedule / residency change necessitates program transfer	USD	$50	none	USD53,550	AACSB		24 maximum	not necessarily	yes		8
n/a	GBP	USD100	GBP2,500	GBP73,000	AACSB	no	90	yes	yes	n/a	10 to 15
Not Distance Learning	US$		55	29000	Local Government		25	Yes	No	3	5
	US$	200	4000	139974	AACSB, EQUIS, HEFCE, AMBA		76				
Not distance learning	US$	200	4000	125040	AACSB, EQUIS, HEFCE, AMBA	Hong Kong University, Columbia Business School		Yes	Yes	5	5
		120	2000	53000	AACSB, EQUIS, HEFCE, AMBA	No	78	Yes	Yes	4	4
Not distance learning	US$	120	4000	88200	AACSB, EQUIS, HEFCE, AMBA	No	78	Yes	Yes	4	4
No distance learning	Euro	80 euro		29500 (early birds: 27000) and 43800 for the Part-time	AMBA, EQUIS		25-30	Yes	Yes		3

University	School	Country	State	Type	First Year Created	Degree Offered	Start Dates	Class Times	Int'l Trip	Residency	Program Length
IMD University		Switzerland	Lausanne	Open enrollment program	1997	EMBA		Program structure: http://www.imd.ch/programs/emba/programstructure/content.cfm	Immerse yourself in three centers of action: Mumbai, Silicon Valley and Shanghai. These expeditions are real time lessons in how to investigate new trends and ideas, and how to evaluate their relevance for you and your company.		13
	IE Business School	Spain/USA		Blended (Online + Presential)			March			Presential Period at Brown University and IE Business School	15
	IESE Business School	Spain (Madrid)		Online or Part-time			Nov			Presential period in Shanghai	13
ESADE	ESADE Business School	Spain	Madrid Barcelona	EMBA	2001	MBA	Jan	Friday (13:30h - 20:30h) and Saturday (08:30h - 13:30h)	Trip Required	Residency Required	18
Escuela Superior Politecnica del Litoral - ESPOL	Escuela de Postgrado en Administracion de Empresas - ESPAE-ESPOL	Spain		EMBA	1998	MBA	Oct	Once a month from Thursday to Friday (32 contact hours)	Trip Optional	No Residency Required	22
IE University		Spain	Madrid	Blended (Online + Presential)			March			Presential Period at Brown University and IE Business School	15
IE University		Spain	Madrid	Online or Part-time			November			Presential period in Shanghai	13

For the latest school information visit www.EMBAWorld.com

Distance Learning	Denomination	Application Fee	Deposit	Total Program Cost	Accreditation	Jointly Offered	Class Size	Undergrad Degree Req'd	Interview Req'd	Min Management Req'd	Min Work Experience Req'd
			CHF 10,000	CHF 126,000 Details: http://www.imd.ch/programs/emba/admission/fees_and_expenses.cfm			55-65	Yes, with exceptions			
Blended	US$		19000	95000	AACSB, EQUIS	Brown University		Yes	Yes	4	7
Online version offered	Euro	120	10800	54000 + the contribution to the IE Business School Foundation (	AACSB, EQUIS, AMBA			Yes	Yes	4	
Not Distance Learning	Euro		65	41000	AACSB EQUIS AMBA		55	Yes	Yes	5	5
Not Distance Learning	US$		500	12000	CONESUP		28	Yes	Yes, except	0	4
Blended		€ 120		USD95,000	IE Business School is accredited by: AMBA - Association of MBAs EQUIS - European Quality Improvement System AACSB - Accrediting Agency to Advance Collegiate Schools of Business	Brown University		Yes	Yes		
Online version offered		€ 120		EUR54,000	IE Business School is accredited by: AMBA - Association of MBAs EQUIS - European Quality Improvement System AACSB - Accrediting Agency to Advance Collegiate Schools of Business			yes	yes	4	

University	School	Country	State	Type	First Year Created	Degree Offered	Start Dates	Class Times	Int'l Trip	Residency	Program Length
Universidad de Navarra	IESE Business School	Spain	Madrid and Barcelona	part-time. Executive.			September	Friday	Shanghay and N. York	No	19
	EADA	Spain	Barcelona	EMBA	1989	EMBA	Jan , Oct	MONDAYS- 18.00-22.00H FRIDAYS- 17.00-21.00H	Trip Required	No Residency Required	18
University of South Africa (UNISA)	Graduate School of Business Leadership (SBL)	South Africa		EMBA	1964	MBA	Jan	Study schools: February/March and August for one week.	No Trip	No Residency Required	36
	IEDC - Bled School of Management	Slovenia		EMBA	1991	EMBA	Jan	17 weeks in 4 modules (three 5-week and one 2-week); 8:30 - 17:30 Monday through Friday and 8:30 - 14:00 on Saturday	Trip Required	Residency Required	11
	IEDC, Bled School of Management	Slovenia		modular	1991	MBA	January (1-year program), June (2-year program), flexible intake on President's MBA (PMBA)	09.00 - 17.00 (plus individual and group preparation)	Yes	Yes, required during modules	Feb-04
University of Chicago		Singapore		Part-time		MBA	June every year	16 weeks stretch over 21 months	2 weeks in Chicago, 1 week in London and 13 weeks in Singapore		21
University of Chicago		Singapore		Part-time		MBA	June every year	16 weeks stretch over 21 months	2 weeks in Chicago, 1 week in London and 13 weeks in Singapore		21
University of Paisley	Ayrshire Management Center	Scotland		EMBA	1999	EMBA	Sep	Learning resources, student support and class discussion are offered online.	No Trip	No Residency Required	24
King Fahd University of Petroleum & Minerals	College of Industrial Management	Saudi Arabia				EMBA		8:00 am to 4:30 pm Wednesdays and Thursdays (every other week)	Considering	No	24
	IBS Moscow	Russia	Moscow	EMBA	2002	MBA	Feb, Oct	Three times a week and two Saturdays a month	Trip Required	No Residency Required	21
	Institute for Business and Public Administration from Bucharest-	Romania	Bucharest	EMBA	1993	EMBA	Sep	each week, alternating Fridays and Saturdays	Trip Required	Residency Required	21

For the latest school information visit www.EMBAWorld.com

Distance Learning	Denomination	Application Fee	Deposit	Total Program Cost	Accreditation	Jointly Offered	Class Size	Undergrad Degree Req'd	Interview Req'd	Min Management Req'd	Min Work Experience Req'd
No	Tuition fees include: academic fees and course materials. During the international week at CEIBS (China Europe International Business School) and the intensive week in NYork-USA, lunches, welcome and closing dinners and accommodation. No travel expenses are included.	EUR60,400.00	EUR6.40	EUR60,400.00	Equis, ACCBS, Ofcial MBA	No	60	Yes	Yes	0	5
Not Distance Learning	Euro		6050	24200	EQUIS AMBA		30	Yes	Yes	4	4
Distance Learning	US$		0	65000	South African Council for Higher Education & Distance Education Training Council		1723	Yes	No	3	3
Not Distance Learning	Euro		2300	23000	IQA		45	Yes	Yes	0	3
No		No	No	see above, costs for accomodation and other expenses depend on the individual participant, but range from	AMBA, IQA	No	up to 60	Yes, Bachelor's degree or equivalent; occasional exceptions made under special circumstances	Yes	0	7 to 8
N/A		USD100		USD127,925 or SGD180,000	AACSB	No	90-95	Bachelor degree onwards	Yes		7 to 10
N/A		USD100		USD127,925 or SGD180,000	AACSB	No	90-95	Bachelor degree onwards	Yes		7 to 10
Distance Learning	GBP		380	8000	Scottish Higher Education Funding Council		30	Yes	Yes	3	5
No	Yes	NA	NA	130 Saudi Riyals	AACSB	No	14	BS or BA	Yes	3	8
Not Distance Learning	US$		0	15300	Russian Ministry of Education		38	Yes	Yes	5	7
Not Distance Learning	US$		50	15000	AACSB Ministry of Education and Research	Kennesaw State University - Atlanta	90	Yes	Yes	3	5

University	School	Country	State	Type	First Year Created	Degree Offered	Start Dates	Class Times	Int'l Trip	Residency	Program Length
University of Minnesota	Curtis L. Carlson School of Management	Poland	Warsaw	EMBA	1995	EMBA	Oct	Saturday and Sunday, three weekends/month (summer off)	Trip Optional	No Residency Required	18
Massey University	Graduate School of Business	New Zealand	Palmerston North	EMBA	1988	MBA	May, Aug	Every third weekend for 25 months.	No Trip	Residency Required	25
Erasmus University - Rotterdam, The Netherlands	Rotterdam School of Management	Netherlands	Rotterdam	EMBA	2002	MBA	Sep	The OneMBA Program spans 21 months. It is offered in a modular format at the RSM. Participants attend six modules in Rotterdam and four global residencies.	Trip Required	Residency Required	22
Tilburg University	Tias Business School	Netherlands	Tilburg	EMBA	1999	MBA	Feb	Per year, 3 on campus residential sessions of 2 consecutive weeks	Trip Required	Residency Required	18
	Instituto Panamericano De Alta Direccion De Empresa (IPADE)	Mexico	Mexico City	EMBA	1991	EMBA	Sep	Monday and Friday from 2 p.m. to 8 p.m	Trip Optional	No Residency Required	24
Bocconi University	SDA Bocconi School of Management	Italy	Milan	EMBA	2003	MBA	Jan	6 modules per year, each module last one full time week + e-learning	Trip Required	Residency Required	24
Politecnico di Milano	MIP - Politecnico di Milano	Italy	Milan	EMBA	2001	EMBA	Mar, Nov	3-4 evenings every week (6.30 p.m.-8.30 p.m.) and alternating Saturdays (9.00 a.m.-1.00 p.m. or 9.00 a.m.-6.00 p.m.)	No Trip	No Residency Required	24
Tel Aviv University	Leon Recanati Graduate School of Business Administration	Israel		EMBA	1996	MBA	Sep	Thursday evenings and Friday mornings (plus intensive weeks)	Trip Required	Residency Required	21
Tel Aviv University	Leon Recanati Graduate School of Business Administration	Israel		EMBA	1992	MBA	Oct	Two days a week for 22 months	Trip Optional	Residency Required	22
City University of Hong Kong	Faculty of Business	Hong Kong	Hong Kong	EMBA	1997	MBA EMBA	Sep	Twice each week with classes normally on every Thursday evening and Saturday afternoon.	Trip Required	No Residency Required	22
Hong Kong University of Science and Technology	School of Business and Management	Hong Kong	Hong Kong	EMBA	1998	MBA	Jan	Two weekends per month from Friday afternoon to Sunday afternoon	Trip Required	No Residency Required	16
The University of Western Ontario	Richard Ivey School of Business	Hong Kong		EMBA							
WHU - Otto Beisheim	Graduate School of Management	Germany		EMBA	1997	MBA	Sep	Thursday to Sunday. 600 class hours (45 minutes per class session) are scheduled over a two-year period: 12 weekends and 6 live-in weeks.	Trip Required	Residency Required	24
Grenoble Ecole de Management	Graduate School of Business	France	Grenoble	EMBA	1999	MBA	Sep	Daily	No Trip	Residency Required	12

For the latest school information visit www.EMBAWorld.com

Distance Learning	Denomination	Application Fee	Deposit	Total Program Cost	Accreditation	Jointly Offered	Class Size	Undergrad Degree Req'd	Interview Req'd	Min Management Req'd	Min Work Experience Req'd
Not Distance Learning	US$		80	17580	AACSB NCA	Warsaw School of Economics	45	Yes	Yes	0	3
Not Distance Learning	US$		0	16000	AMBA		18	No	Yes	2	7
Not Distance Learning	Euro		5000	48000	AACSB EQUIS AMBA	Kenan Flagler Business School EGADE-ITESM Escola de Administracao de Empresas de Sao Paulo da Fundacao Getulio Vargas Chinese University of Hong Kong	78	Yes, except	Yes	4	6
Not Distance Learning	Euro		0	48000	AACSB	Purdue University (USA) Central European University (Hungary) ESCP-EAP (France)	62	Yes	Yes	5	10
Not Distance Learning	US$		44000	0	AACSB		65	Yes	Yes	3	7
Distance Learning	Euro		0	25000	EQUIS		45	Yes	Yes	2	4
Not Distance Learning	Euro		0	19400	ASFOR		40	Yes, except	Yes	0	2
Not Distance Learning	US$		75	0	AACSB	Kellogg school of Management Northwestern University	54	Yes	Yes	8	8
Not Distance Learning	US$		75	0	AACSB		46	Yes	Yes	8	8
Not Distance Learning	US$		6910	29180	self-accreditated and in the process of accreditation by AACSB		25	Yes	Yes	6	6
Not Distance Learning	US$		6450	80500	AACSB cfmd	The Hong Kong University of Science and Technology //// Kellogg School of Management, Northwestern University	50	Yes	Yes	0	10
Not Distance Learning	Euro		2	495	AACSB EQUIS FIBAA	Kellogg School of Management (main partner) Hong Kong University of Science and Technology Leon Recanati Graduate School of Business Administration, Tel Aviv Schulich School of Business, Toro	58	Yes	Yes	3	3
Not Distance Learning	Euro		1100	17000	AACSB EQUIS AMBA		53	Yes	Yes, except	3	3

For the latest school information visit www.EMBAWorld.com

University	School	Country	State	Type	First Year Created	Degree Offered	Start Dates	Class Times	Int'l Trip	Residency	Program Length
	INSEAD	France	"Fontainebleau"	EMBA	2003	INSEAD MBA for Executives	Nov	Modular Programme. One and two full week modules over a period of 14 months.	Trip Required	Residency Required	14
	Helsinki School of Economics	Finland	Helsinki	EMBA	1988	EMBA	Feb, Jun, Sep	Approximately once a month, usually a 3 day weekend. Class times vary at each delivery location.	Trip Optional	No Residency Required	20
	Henley Management College	Enlgand	Oxfordshire	EMBA	1988	MBA	Jan, July	4x4 week blocks over 12 months : face to face teaching for 16 weeks. Students expected to do 20 hours per week of study between the 4 modules	Trip Required	No Residency Required	12
Ashridge Business School	Qualifications Division	England	Hertfordshire	EMBA	1988	MBA	Jan	Beginning January and running through until December	Trip Required	No Residency Required	11
University of Warwick	Warwick Business School	England		EMBA	1985	MBA	Mar, Oct	Modular: Monday 10 a.m. - Friday 4 p.m. during 13, one-week (residential modules, plus occasional weekends)	Trip Optional	Residency Required	36
Aalborg University	Faculty of Engineering and Science	Denmark	Aalborg	EMBA	1997	EMBA	Sep	Monthly seminars are held from Thursday afternoon to Saturday afternoon. In-between seminars students work on their individual project and study the literature recommended.	No Trip	No Residency Required	22
Technical University of Denmark	Center for Technology, Economics and Management	Denmark		EMBA	1998	EMBA	Sep	Every second Fridays and Saturdays	Trip Required	No Residency Required	21
	Aarhus School of Business	Denmark	Aarhus	EMBA	1999	EMBA	Aug	Alternate Fridays and Saturdays, Friday 10 a.m. - Saturday 4 p.m.	Trip Required	No Residency Required	22
	Copenhagen Business School	Denmark	Frederiksberg	EMBA	1994	MBA EMBA MIB	Jan	Fridays/ Saturdays - 30 weeks a year	Trip Required	No Residency Required	21
University of Minnesota	Curtis L. Carlson School of Management	China	Guangzhou	EMBA	2001	EMBA	Oct	Saturday and Sunday	Trip Required	Residency Required	16
Washington University in St. Louis	John M. Olin Business School	China	Shanghai	EMBA	2002	MBA	May	Once a month (Friday, Saturday, Sunday, and Monday)	Trip Required	Residency Required	18
Washington University in St. Louis	John M. Olin Business School	China	Shanghai	EMBA	2002	MBA	May	Once a month (Friday, Saturday, Sunday, and Monday)	Trip Required	Residency Required	18
	Tsinghua University	China	Beijing	EMBA	2002	EMBA	Mar, Sept	Thursday through Sunday, once a month	Trip Optional	Residency Required	24
Cornell University		Canada and USA	New York and Montreal	EMBA		Queen's MBA and Cornell MBA	late june	All day Saturday, three consecutive Saturdays per month	2 International trips (One optional, One compulsory)	3 residential sessions	18
Queen's University	Queen's School of Business	Canada and USA	Montreal, Ottawa, Toronto, Mississauga,	MBA		Queen's MBA and Cornell MBA	late June	All day Saturday, three consecutive Saturdays per month	2 International trips (One optional, One compulsory)	3 residential sessions	18
Concordia University	The John Molson School of Business	Canada	Quebec	EMBA	1985	MBA	Sep	once a week, alternating Fridays and Saturdays	Trip Required	Residency Required	20

For the latest school information visit www.EMBAWorld.com

Distance Learning	Denomination	Application Fee	Deposit	Total Program Cost	Accreditation	Jointly Offered	Class Size	Undergrad Degree Req'd	Interview Req'd	Min Management Req'd	Min Work Experience Req'd
Not Distance Learning	Euro		13500 euros	90000 euros	AACSB EQUIS		74	Yes	Yes	4	7
Not Distance Learning	Euro		5000	50000	EQUIS AMBA		38	Yes	Yes	5	8
Not Distance Learning	GBP		1000	31000	AACSB EQUIS AMBA		22	Yes	Yes	5	8
Not Distance Learning	GBP		1000	29500	AACSB EQUIS AMBA		17	Yes	Yes	5	5
Not Distance Learning	GBP	0	0	23400	AACSB EQUIS Assn of MBAs	No	50	Usually	Yes	4	4
Not Distance Learning	Euro		6000	24000	Danish Ministry of Education		20	Yes, with exceptions	Yes, except	5	5
Not Distance Learning	Euro		0	35	AACSB		50	Yes	Yes	5	5
Not Distance Learning	US$		0	36696	EQUIS	University of Southern Denmark	25	Yes	Yes	5	5
Not Distance Learning	Euro		0	58000	EQUIS		50	Yes	Yes	5	4
Not Distance Learning	US$		300	30300	AACSB	Lingnan College, Sun Yat Sen University	40	Yes	Yes	0	5
Not Distance Learning	US$		2500	42500	AACSB	Fudan University, Shanghai, China	47	Yes	Yes	5	5
Not Distance Learning	RMB		2500	478000	AACSB	Fudan University, Shanghai, China	47	Yes	Yes	5	5
Not Distance Learning	US$		0	50000	Chinese Central Government		60	Yes	Yes	5	8
Yes	Canadian	none	USD22,000	USD98,000	Association of MBA's, AACSB, EQUIS	Cornell University (The Johnson Graduate School of Management)		Yes	Yes	5	8
Yes	CAN$	0	2000	98000	Association of MBA's, AACSB, EQUIS	Cornell University (The Johnson Graduate School of Management)		Yes	Yes	5	8
Not Distance Learning	CAN$		2000	45000	AACSB		21	Yes	Yes	0	5

University	School	Country	State	Type	First Year Created	Degree Offered	Start Dates	Class Times	Int'l Trip	Residency	Program Length
McGill University	Faculty of Management	Canada	Quebec	EMBA	1996	MIM	Mar	Five 2 week modules	Trip Required	Residency Required	16
Queen's University	Queen's School of Business	Canada	Ontario	EMBA	1992	MBA	mid-August	All day Friday and Saturday morning of every other week	2 International trips (One optional, One compulsory)	3 residential sessions	15
Queen's University	Queen's School of Business	Canada	Ontario	EMBA	1994	MBA	mid-Aug	All day Friday and Saturday mornings every other week	2 International trips (One optional, One compulsory)	3 residential sessions	15
Queens University		Canada	Montreal, Toronto, Calgary, Ottawa, Edmo	EMBA		Queen's MBA	January	All day Sunday and Monday mornings every other week	None	3 residential sessions	12
Queens University		Canada	Everywhere in Canada	EMBA		MBA	mid August	All day Friday and Saturday mornings every other week	2 International trips (One optional, One compulsory)	3 residential sessions	15
Saint Mary's University	Sobey School of Business	Canada	Nova Scotia	EMBA	1990	EMBA	Aug	Friday and Saturday alternating weeks	Trip Required	No Residency Required	20
Simon Fraser University	Faculty of Business Administration/ Harbour Centre Campus	Canada	British Columbia	EMBA	1968	MBA	Sep	Friday and Saturday every other weekend.	Trip Optional	Residency Required	24
University of Calgary	Faculty of Management	Canada	Alberta	EMBA	1995	MBA	Aug	Term begins with 1-week intensive course. Continues for 8 sessions (8:00 a.m. - 5:00 p.m.) Friday and Saturday every second week.	Trip Required	Residency Required	20
University of Ottawa	Executive MBA Program	Canada	Ontario	EMBA	1992	MBA EMBA MHA	Aug	One day per week: Alternate Fridays and Saturdays or alternate Sundays and Mondays, 8 a.m. - 6:30 p.m.	Trip Required	Residency Required	21
University of Toronto	Joseph L. Rotman School of Management	Canada	Ontario	EMBA	1998	MBA	Jul	Pre-program orientation in Toronto followed by four residential modules (Europe, South America, Asia and North America).	Trip Required	Residency Required	16
University of Toronto	Joseph L. Rotman School of Management	Canada	Ontario	EMBA	1983	MBA	Apr, Sep	Fridays and Saturdays every two weeks, with four residential modules.	No Trip	Residency Required	12
University of Western Ontario	Richard Ivey School of Business	Canada	Ontario	EMBA	2004	MBA	Jan	Four-day residence modules each month over a 16-month time period	Trip Required	Residency Required	16
University of Western Ontario	Richard Ivey School of Business	Canada	Ontario	EMBA	1998	MBA	Aug	Saturdays and Sundays with two residence periods (2 and 1 week) in Hong Kong and Canada	Trip Required	Residency Required	22
University of Western Ontario	Richard Ivey School of Business	Canada	Ontario	EMBA	1991	MBA	Sep	Two Fridays and two Saturdays per month over a 16-month time period	Trip Required	Residency Required	16

For the latest school information visit www.EMBAWorld.com

Distance Learning	Denomination	Application Fee	Deposit	Total Program Cost	Accreditation	Jointly Offered	Class Size	Undergrad Degree Req'd	Interview Req'd	Min Management Req'd	Min Work Experience Req'd
Not Distance Learning	US$		0	75000		Lancaster University MicGill University IIMB Bangalore Japanese Universities INSEAD	35	Yes	Yes, except	7	10
Yes	CAN$	0	2000	84000	AACSB, Association of MBA's, EQUIS		35	Usually	Yes	5	8
Yes	CAN$	0	2000	84000	AACSB, Association of MBA's, EQUIS		180	Usually	Yes	5	8
Yes	Canadian	no	USD2,000	USD67,000	Association of MBA's, AACSB, EQUIS	No		Yes	Yes	1	3
Yes	Canadian	none	USD2,000	USD84,000	Association of MBA's, AACSB, EQUIS			Usually	Yes	5	8
Not Distance Learning	CAN$		1000	38000	AACSB		20	Yes	Yes	5	5
Not Distance Learning	CAN$		1000	45000	No Accreditation		46	Yes	Yes, except	5	8
Not Distance Learning	CAN$		60	55000	AACSB	University of Alberta	41	Yes	Yes	7	15
Not Distance Learning	CAN$		150	58000	AACSB OCGS		41	Yes	Yes	5	5
Not Distance Learning	CAN$		8000	75000	AACSB	St. Gallen University	25	Yes, with exceptions	Yes	8	3
Not Distance Learning	CAN$		8000	75000	AACSB		30	Yes, with exceptions	Yes	8	3
Not Distance Learning	CAN$		0	75000	EQUIS		52	Yes, with exceptions	Yes, except	3	6
Not Distance Learning	CAN$		7273	87273	EQUIS		48	Yes, with exceptions	Yes, except	3	5
Not Distance Learning	CAN$		0	75000	EQUIS		39	Yes, with exceptions	Yes, except	3	6

University	School	Country	State	Type	First Year Created	Degree Offered	Start Dates	Class Times	Int'l Trip	Residency	Program Length
York University	Schulich School of Business	Canada	Ontario	EMBA	2002	MBA	Jan	Alternate Weekends: Fridays: 12 noon - 6:00 pm; Saturdays 9:00 am - 6:00 pm & Sundays: 9:00 am - 2:00 pm	Trip Required	Residency Required	18
	Sobey School of Business	Canada	Halifax, Nova Scotia	EMBA			August	Friday and Saturdays	Yes	No	20
Faculdades Integradas de São Paulo	Escola de Dirc	Brazil	Sao Paulo	EMBA	2000	EMBA	Feb , Jun , Oct	All Fridays and Saturdays, plus one intensive week (Monday to Saturday) per semester.	Trip Optional	No Residency Required	24
Instituto Veris - IBMEC São Paulo	IBMEC S	Brazil	Sao Paulo	EMBA	1987	EMBA	Feb, Apr, Jul, Oct	Evenings, twice a week (7:30pm - 10:30pm)	Trip Optional	No Residency Required	22
University of S	Fundacao Instituto De Administracao - Faculdade de Economia, Adm	Brazil	Sao Paulo	EMBA	1993	EMBA	Feb, Aug	Fridays and Saturdays every 15 days	Trip Required	Residency Required	18
	Business School S	Brazil	Sao Paulo	EMBA	1995	EMBA	Mar, May , Aug, Oct	meet on various dates and times	Trip Required	Residency Required	16
	Brazilian Business School	Brazil	Sao Paulo	EMBA	2000	EMBA	Mar, Apr , May , Jun	T and Th: 7pm to 10pm or Saturday: 9a to 4pm	Trip Optional	No Residency Required	24
	Fundacao Dom Cabral	Brazil	Novo Lima	EMBA	1997	EMBA	Mar, Aug	6 presential modules of 7 days, plus 460 hours of distance education	Trip Optional	Residency Required	16
	Fundacao Dom Cabral	Brazil	Novo Lima	EMBA	2002	EMBA	Mar, Sep	2 presential modules of 6 days, plus one presential module of two weeks in Vancouver Canada, plus 12 presential modules of 2 days (Friday and Saturday). Plus 460 hours of distance education	Trip Required	Residency Required	18
Vlerick Leuven Gent Management School	VLG Management School	Belgium		EMBA	1972	MBA	Sep	two evenings and one afternoon per week	Trip Required	No Residency Required	20
University of Minnesota	Curtis L. Carlson School of Management	Austria	Vienna	EMBA	2000	EMBA	Mar	Thursday - Sunday Monthly plus Distance Learning component	Trip Required	Residency Required	14
	Danube-University Krems	Austria		EMBA	1991	MBA	Sep	2 years part-time program: 10 modules, each of them lasting 9 full	Trip Required	No Residency Required	24
Queensland University of Technology	Brisbane Graduate School of Business	Australia		EMBA	2001	MBA EMBA	Nov	Three days per month (Friday-Sunday) every month and for two-week sessions in January each year, over a 20-month period	Trip Required	No Residency Required	20

For the latest school information visit www.EMBAWorld.com

Distance Learning	Denomination	Application Fee	Deposit	Total Program Cost	Accreditation	Jointly Offered	Class Size	Undergrad Degree Req'd	Interview Req'd	Min Management Req'd	Min Work Experience Req'd
Not Distance Learning	CAN$		125	85000	AACSB	Schulich School of Business Kellogg School of Management	45	Yes	Yes	4	7
No		None	USD1,000	$40 K			35	Yes	Yes		
Not Distance Learning	Real		2500	25000	Brazilian National MBA Association		20	Yes	Yes	4	8
Not Distance Learning	Real		0	33200	Brazilian Ministry of Education		40	Yes	Yes	1	3
Not Distance Learning	Real		0	45000	AMBA	Owen Graduate School of Management - Vanderbilt University Judge Institute of Management Studies - Cambridge University E.M.Lyon	35	Yes	Yes	5	10
Not Distance Learning	US$		1404	10800	AACSB		144	Yes	Yes	3	8
Not Distance Learning	US$		0	6500	AACSB		18	Yes	Yes	2	3
Not Distance Learning	Real		0	32000	None		52	Yes	Yes	3	5
Not Distance Learning	Real		0	28000	None		33	Yes	Yes	2	3
Not Distance Learning	Euro		0	27500	AACSB EQUIS AMBA		65	Yes	Yes	3	3
Not Distance Learning	US$		60	0	AACSB	Wirtschaftsuniversität Wien	21	Yes	Yes	0	5
Not Distance Learning	Euro		0	22200	FIBAA		28	Yes, with exceptions	Yes	5	7
Not Distance Learning	US$		3930	26450	AMBA		14	Yes, with exceptions	Yes	5	5

University	School	Country	State	Type	First Year Created	Degree Offered	Start Dates	Class Times	Int'l Trip	Residency	Program Length
	Melbourne Business School	Australia	VICTORIA	EMBA	2002	"EMBA - students graduate with a full MBA from the University of Melbourne.	One intake per year which usually commences in late September or early October.	Up to 40 hours per week faculty contact with at least a further 30 hours of private study, preparation and group work..	Module 2 is conducted in USA (Kellogg School of Management), Germany (WHU) and China (MBS).	Fully residential for the duration of each of the four modules.	14
	Queensland University of Technology	Australia	Queensland	EMBA	2001	Grad Cert in Bus Admin, MBA, IMBA, EMBA	February	One weekend per month (Friday-Sunday) for 22 months and an intensive session and international trip in April	13-15 day study tour to China is optional	No residency required	22
IAE	Escuela de Direcci	Argentina	Buenos Aires	EMBA	1981	MBA EMBA	Apr, Aug	Three different groups: 1) Mondays full day; 2) Friday afternoon and Saturday mornings; 3) Thursdays, Fridays and Saturdays every three weeks	Trip Optional	No Residency Required	21
Ivey Business School		Hong Kong	Ivey Business School offers Executive MBA and non-degree Executive Development programs to executives from Hong Kong and across the region. All programs in HK are taught by Ivey Business School"	MBA			July/August	HK <-> Canada	2 Residence periods	18 months	

For the latest school information visit www.EMBAWorld.com

Distance Learning	Denomination	Application Fee	Deposit	Total Program Cost	Accreditation	Jointly Offered	Class Size	Undergrad Degree Req'd	Interview Req'd	Min Management Req'd	Min Work Experience Req'd
No	AUD$	No	$2,000.00 (non-refundable) payable upon offer acceptance.	*$96,000 This EMBA program fee includes tuition, text books and study notes, accommodation and most meals on class days for the four modules, along with Melbourne University, Kellogg School of Management and WHU fees.	EQUIS	No	Maximum of 40 students.	Not essential, but a Graduate Management Admissions Test (GMAT) is required for those without an undergraduate degree.	Yes	0	10
No	AUD$	None	None	USD46,560	AACSB, EQUIS and AMBA	No	20 to 40	No	Yes	5	5
Not Distance Learning	US$		50	17	AMBA		70	Yes	Yes	4	5
	HK$1500		HK$620,000 for 2008 intake	EQUIS	N/A			Yes	Yes		

INDEX